dreams are letters from the soul

dreams
are
letters
from
the
soul

DISCOVER THE CONNECTIONS BETWEEN
YOUR DREAMS AND YOUR SPIRITUAL LIFE

CONNIE KAPLAN

harmony books / new york

Published by Harmony Books, New York, New York.
Member of the Crown Publishing Group,
a division of Random House, Inc.

www.randomhouse.com

HARMONY BOOKS is a registered trademark and
the Harmony Books colophon is a trademark of Random House, Inc.

Printed in the United States of America

Design by Karen Minster

Library of Congress Cataloging-in-Publication Data

Kaplan, Connie Cockrell, 1948–
Dreams are letters from the soul : discover the connections between
your dreams and your spiritual life / by Connie Kaplan.
1. Dreams. 2. Dream interpretation. 3. Spiritual life.   I. Title.
BF1091 .K17 2002
135'.3—dc21   2001039889

ISBN 0-609-60791-X

10   9   8   7   6   5   4   3   2   1

First Edition

This book is lovingly dedicated to my children:

Lauren Kaplan
Sara Kaplan
Ben Kaplan

You are my best teachers and my best friends.
You know how to love in ways I never dreamed.
You know how to live with abandon I never knew.
Thank you.

my deepest thanks

To my mother Nila Cockrell, for passing the gift of dreaming to me.

To my sister Marsha Hartos, for generously sharing her dreams and literary expertise.

To my sister Nancy Jackson, for years of friendship, support, and "being there."

To Andrew Harvey, for personal words of encouragement that inspired me immeasurably.

To Matthew Fox, Brian Swimme, and Stuart Cowan, for words of encouragement that they never even knew they shared.

To Russell Salamon, for invoking brilliance in anyone who reads his poetry.

To Heather Valencia, for her never-ending out-flowing of visionary genius.

To Jamie Sams, for her never-ending out-flowing of beneficence.

To Bonnie Solow, for her heartful life path and her heartfelt support.

To Patty Gift, for being such a gift.

To Robert Gerard, for his wise counsel and ancient wisdom.

To Freya Bame, for continuing to dream with me, advise me, and chastise me from the other side.

To the team at Harmony Books, for sticking with this project and creating a beautiful result.

To my circle of dreamers who have been with me forever and for always: Jeanne Dancs Arthur, Peggy Braswell, Sara Cooper, Ellie Farbstein, Tamar Frankiel, Judy Greenfeld, Elaine Levi, Barbara Meyer, Melissa Mullin, Lynn Mitchell, Peggy Oram, and Wayne Wolf.

To the other dreamers who contributed so generously to this book:
Lynette Bowen, Cammie Doty, Cristina Gonzalez, Lorrie Hill, Lindy Hokins,
Jennifer Houle, Annette Hulefeld, Annette McMurrey, Thea Soroyan,
Christine Thompson, and Judith Yost.

To the many other dreamers around the planet who have connected with each
other in order to dream a new dream.

And most important . . .

To Vic Kaplan, my dream come true.

· CONTENTS ·

dreams are letters from the soul

PART ONE

a love story

I hope you will read this book as if it were a series of letters to you from a lover who is on a voyage. Each section in the book describes how our dreams guide us through the different legs of the great spiritual journey of life—the journey to understanding ourselves and the journey to love. We are all on this voyage, whether we know it or not. It's not an option; it's a deep and undeniable reality. The love letters in this book are designed to help you make this life pilgrimage with more clarity, more understanding, more grace.

Those of us who take this spiritual journey seriously devote time and energy to deepen and evolve our knowledge of it. We meditate, we study how the masters and mystics have taken the journey, and we strive to be conscious of our own spiritual unfolding. Others are more casual about this part of life, occasionally attending church or simply following the traditions of our parents' religion. And, unfortunately, large numbers of us have chosen to live in denial of the spiritual element of our lives.

> There is no one in this world
> Who is not looking for God.
>
> —Hafiz[1]

Yet it doesn't matter what we think or do. We may have abandoned our spiritual self altogether. Philosophy and religious thought may never have entered our waking consciousness. That doesn't essentially change anything. Our spiritual self doesn't abandon us. We still dream. Sleep still regenerates us, and dreams still guide us unwittingly on our path.

Sleep is our excursion into the unseen realms of the Creator's many dimensions. In sleep, we dissolve into the wholeness of Creation; when we awaken, we return renewed to perceptual reality. Sometimes, when we awaken, we remember the stories of our dreams.

These stories are like messages—letters, if you will—from the level of the soul. Like letters, these dream stories must be opened, read, and understood or else the communication is incomplete and ineffective.

WHAT IS THE SOUL?

> *The soul, as it were, was created at that point which divides time from eternity; it touches both of these points.*
>
> —Meister Eckhart[2]

In order to fully appreciate the dream teachings, it's important for us to work with the same definition of the term *soul*. I titled this book *Dreams Are Letters from THE Soul*—as opposed to *Dreams Are Letters from YOUR Soul*—for a very specific reason. My journeys into soul consciousness have taught me something very important: *Soul* is collective, not personal. When I use the term *soul* I refer to a vast level of consciousness—one that exists before, beyond, and throughout the separation and isolation that we experience as individuals in human form. *Soul* is impersonal because it is universal. It is a unifying term, not a separating one. We are not individual souls. We are instead individuations of a collective level of soul consciousness.

Picture a meadow on a partly cloudy day. Think of the sun hiding behind a cloud. You can see beams of light shooting out. They look like spotlights, searchlights if you will, radiating from behind the cloud. In your imagination, follow one of those beams and allow it to illuminate a tree some distance from you. In this analogy, the sun is the source of life, or the Creator's light, veiled by the cloud. The cloud veil consists of the thoughts and beliefs (yours and the collective's) that both prevent you from experiencing the Creator directly and protect you from receiving too much cosmic energy too quickly. In a sense, this veil prevents the "spiritual sunburn" that might occur to your nervous system if you are infused with energy for which you are not physically prepared. The tree is you, rooted in the ground of your motherlike Earth, stretching toward the light of your fatherlike sun. The sunbeam is the soul.

The soul is the avenue through which the realm of the cosmos (the Creator or God) communicates with the realm of form. It is not a personal sunbeam. It is a transpersonal source of Love. It is the tree's connection to The Source. The sunbeam is the vehicle through which the tree and the sun relate.

The level of soul from which our dream letters come is a unified level. When we sleep, we melt into universal consciousness, and the soul imprints messages into our minds. Those messages are designed to inspire us to remember our essential natures. Our dream stories are what we recall of that imprint, and they guide our spiritual journey.

WHAT DOES THIS BOOK TELL ME ABOUT DREAMS AND THE SOUL?

Each section of this book speaks about the different kinds of messages we receive and the different levels of Love we experience through dreaming. As we develop deeper alignments and clearer lines of communication with the level of the soul, we also develop more sophisticated types of dreaming.

Part One recounts some of my adventures in the dreamtime. In it, I tell you a little of my personal biography, using my story to bring out some important teachings about the true nature of humanity's most common spiritual practice—dreaming. I hope my story will evoke your story.

Part Two describes a level of dreaming that I call the personal dream. In these dreams we learn more about ourselves—our own psychology, our own journey, and the unique gifts that we have to offer.

Part Three describes collective dreaming. These dreams take us outside ourselves so that we access information not local to us. In this type of dreaming we telepathically and clairvoyantly receive data from a collective information source.

Part Four discusses the transformative dreams we can access once we've developed our spiritual skills. These dreams heal us, teach us, advise us, and show us how to heal and teach others in dreamtime.

In Part Five, I discuss the most subtle types of dreaming that humans encounter. In these dreams we meet up with other dreamers and work together in the dreamscapes. Through these dreams we literally effect changes on our planet. Sometimes we even work outside our planetary consciousness to help design the flow of cosmic energy.

In Part Six, I give you, to the best of my ability, some guidelines on how a dreamer lives and interfaces with a world that is seemingly in chaos and at war with itself.

Finally, I encourage you to pay special attention to the wording and phrasing of the dreams I share with you in this book. How a dreamer reports her dreams gives the listener or reader important clues as to the mood of the dream experience and the unspoken feelings surrounding the dream story. Whenever possible I've presented the dreams exactly as they were written in the dreamer's journal to preserve the precise frame of mind of the dreamer as she remembered the story.

DREAMING AND THE MOON

In a previous book, *The Woman's Book of Dreams: Dreaming as a Spiritual Practice*, I introduced some fairly radical—although I believe ancient—ideas about dreaming and its connection to the moon. Since the moon is our night-light, she has a great deal of influence over what we experience as we sleep. She is the light, the cosmic energy, that guides us through our nightly journeys. Her phase, her location in the heavens, and how her energies might be interfacing with the personality of the dreamer all impact enormously on our dreaming patterns.

As a part of their regular dreaming practice, I encourage my students to look up the phase and location of the moon on the night they have a dream, and to chart their dreams according to the moon's monthly movement through the zodiac. This type of familiarity with the moon and its effect on dreaming gives you a sense of the cyclical nature of dreams and of your personal dream patterns. For example, you will most likely find that you have similar dream themes on the full moon every month. In *Dreams Are Letters from the Soul*, I refer occasionally to the astrology of the moon as I discuss the various types of dreaming in each section.

Also in this book I speak of "dream circles." This is an ancient prayer form, and it is the way I encourage people to work with their dreams. It involves meeting with a group of trusted dreamers on a regular basis, creating a sacred space, and through ceremony moving into dreamtime (while awake) together to explore the spiritual energies that inform and inspire dreaming. If you are interested in dream circles but don't know of a circle in your area, go to our website: www.turtledreamers.com. We have an online circle there, and you may find ways to connect with other dreamers in your area.

The popularity of my first book surprised me. I discovered that many people long to discuss their dreams with someone who recognizes their spiritual source—someone who moves beyond the psychological and personal messages of the dream into the collective arena. *Dreams Are Letters from the Soul* resulted from the many requests I've received to go further with the discussion of dreaming as a spiritual practice.

THE MYSTICAL PATH

You will discover as you read Part One of this book that my education into dreaming and its power came in a most unusual and sacred way. I consider my introduction to the real work of the dreamer to be a mystical experience.

In an attempt to more thoroughly understand my own dreaming journey, I've become a student of many mystical traditions. Reading books, sermons, poetry, and personal journals of the mystics, I have been astonished to find profound similarities among the various traditions: Jewish and Christian, Sufi and Buddhist, modern and ancient. The messages are similar, and the experiences are almost identical. They are simply described in different words. And, in fact, many of the mystics speak eloquently of dreaming as an integral and vital part of their tradition. I've sprinkled this book with boxed love notes from mystics and poets (like the ones from Hafiz and Meister Eckhart earlier in this introduction). These messages, like the dream messages, are designed to awaken us to a more fundamental awareness of life's truth.

The personal story that I share with you in this book may strike you as dramatic. It is. My own spiritual process dramatically altered my life. And yet, in some ways, it is quite ordinary. That's what I love about sharing the message of the spiritual journey—it's an ordinary, natural, inevitable part of life. Only through the eyes of spiritual awareness can we see the normality of the miracles we experience when we surrender to the unfolding of a life of service.

In the Sufi tradition, the spiritual seeker is often called a Lover, and the spiritual journey is considered to be the Lover's wanderings in search of the Beloved (God). In that sense, I am a Lover, and this is a love story.

ONE

teachers of the dream

*The more conscious you become, the more you will
be able to have dreams worth having.*

~Sri Aurobindo[1]

THE MORE I TELL THE STORY OF MY OWN PLUNGE INTO DEEPER
levels of consciousness, the more people I meet who have had stun-
ningly similar experiences. The fact that you are reading this book
means you are a dreamer and reflects that you are aware of the spiritual nature of your life's journey. Indeed, we could go so far as to say
that you know you are on a mystical trek. Every authentic mystical
journey resonates with every other. I share my story in the hope that
it will encourage you to tell yours.

Actually, I'm starting my story in the middle. The first parts of it
are probably very similar to your own: I heard the call to examine my
spiritual self, and I set out on a path. I didn't have the inspiration or
motivation to go to exotic lands in search of a guru. Instead, I read
books, attended seminars, and found a few teachers. That's where the
story starts.

By the mid-1980s I was living the American Dream. I had a good
career in television production, a wonderful husband, a house in a
great neighborhood, a perfect (in my eyes, at least) three-year-old
daughter, a red Saab four-speed convertible, and a live-in house-
keeper. I had a spiritual practice that included yoga, meditation, and
Native American teachings, and I was participating in various charitable drives to raise money for worthy causes. It was a good life.

One day I woke up feeling a little achy. I went to work anyway, because that's what one did in my line of work. (There's an unwritten law that you never call in sick during film or television production: You worry either that "The show must go on and it can't go on without me," or "If they find out that the show *can* go on without me, I'll lose my job.") Despite the pain, I went to work that Monday morning. By noon I felt really ill and asked my producer to get someone to fill in for me. By the end of the week I was worse. The primary symptoms were extreme fatigue and complete loss of mental agility. Within about two weeks I could no longer retain detail, prioritize activities, or recognize many familiar sounds and faces. I had lost my mind—or at least the mind that had served me so well thus far. I had no energy. I felt that I was "used up" and that I no longer had the strength to stay alive.

My husband and I, along with our insurance company, spent thousands of dollars looking for a cause. No one ever reached a medical diagnosis. After exhausting all the Western medical models of what might be wrong—testing for everything from a brain tumor to multiple sclerosis—I spent another small fortune on alternative healers. I did things available *only* in Los Angeles. I swallowed disgusting herbs until I admitted I'd rather die than go through another day with that taste in my mouth. I even let someone inject mega doses of vitamins into my arm intravenously, which nearly killed me because I discovered I was allergic to the B complex they used. I let someone else stick thousands of needles in me—acupuncture. Oh, and there was the guy who had a hot tub filled with purple water and healing microbes! I was Reikied, Rolfed, wrapped, massaged, crystalled, and aromatherapied. I went to an oxygen bar before it was chic. I had my aura read and used colored lights to do an aura makeover. Nothing worked. When I told my doctor, a family friend, all I'd tried and how horrible I still felt, he gave me the name of a very reputable Beverly Hills psychiatrist. That was as close as I ever came to a medical opinion of what was "wrong."

I don't intend to critique either the Western medical model or alternative therapies. Under appropriate circumstances they can be beneficial and lifesaving. It's just that in my case, the "problem" was not physiological, psychological, or auric. I had the "mystic's disease." This was a spiritual unfolding, not an illness at all.

Through this whole process, no one ever told me that it was a perfectly normal and natural part of the mystic's journey to have an annihilation phase. Since I'd never considered the possibility that my life was mystical, I never considered that I was being birthed into something more—that my authentic self was emerging. In fact, it certainly felt as if I were being diminished to nothing. It was at least ten years before teachers such as Matthew Fox and Andrew Harvey came into my life and told me the truth about the mystic's journey. But I'm getting ahead of myself.

I didn't go to the psychiatrist. Instead, my husband and I took the money that we might have spent on the couch, so to speak, and rented a cottage at the beach. This was a one-room cottage with no phone, no doorbell, no radio, no television, no dishwasher, no washing machine, no gardeners with blowing machines, no boom box—I could not tolerate noise. I unplugged the refrigerator during the day so I wouldn't have to listen to the motor sound. Sometimes I even used earplugs because the ocean waves were too loud. Each morning I went there after I sent my daughter off to preschool. I slept all day, punctuated with occasional short walks on the beach. Late in the afternoon I returned home, had dinner with my family, and went back to sleep. This schedule of sleeping sixteen to twenty hours a day lasted the better part of eighteen months.

At one point I asked my husband if he wanted me to go away. "Aren't you disappointed that you got such a dud for a wife?" His patience was amazing. He said, "If all we get to do is have dinner for the rest of our lives, that's enough."

During those long naps at the beach, teachers came in the dreamscapes and "awakened me" to the spiritual power of dreaming. Ironically, during this mystically imposed sleep I was more active than ever. It's just that I was active while asleep. It was like being in a doctoral program in a dream university, and it was impossible to take a day off and sleep through class.

> In the howling storm of love
> What is the intellect but a gnat?
>
> —Rumi[2]

Unfortunately, I didn't have the "connect the dot" skills to understand what was happening to me. But I had been in Jungian analysis about ten years earlier, and had developed the habit of writing down my dreams in a journal. Even though I spent a good portion of my day asleep, I did take the time while awake to scribble my dreams in a book. Because I had virtually hundreds of dreams, it was hard to see the patterns. However, even in my mentally dull condition, some patterns came leaping off those pages. Primarily, I noticed that the same teachers were showing up repeatedly. Even though each dream was slightly different, the quality and essence of the dreams with each teacher were startlingly similar. Let me introduce you to my dream teachers.

STAR WOMAN

> *She closed her eyes*
> *and the universe ceased to exist*
> *While others built worlds*
> *from unknowing, she rested.*
>
> —Russell Salamon[3]

Star Woman had no form. I sensed her. Every time she came, the dreams were mostly darkness. I dissolved into her. I lost the sense of self, ego, body—like we do when we first float into the dream state. But this was different; I stayed in that darkness for long periods. It was more like a coma or an anesthesia-induced sleep than a dream. Then, when it was time to wake up, a great silent brilliant explosion of light would awaken me. During the entire eighteen-month period, I had very little energy, but after these dreams I awakened energized and ecstatic. I always wondered whether I'd just seen (prophesied?) a bomb or a cataclysmic explosion. Should I be afraid of the apocalypse? Should I be ashamed of myself for daring to think I could prophesy? Yet the ecstatic feeling in my body was not fear, nor shame. My journal entries recording those dreams were beautiful.

> I saw myself leave my physical body and leap into the Darkness. I lost direction and just floated. Then I leaped into the Light and awoke startled.

> I was released from my body and ran joyously to a Teacher who stood in the Darkness. As I reached her arms I heard a host of voices chanting "Connie has come home!" I felt so happy. I melted into nothingness. Finally, I returned to my body. There was enormous energy running up and down my spine.

I went into the Darkness. I sensed a Guide. I said, "We're at the source of truth, aren't we?" She affirmed, although I don't know how. I couldn't see her, nor could I hear anything. I remember nothing else until the baby woke me up. I was highly energized and the light in the room was magnified.

At the time, I didn't realize that the same teacher was coming, nor did she have the name yet. The name and understandings came years later.

GRANDMOTHER TEACUP

This teacher was so sweet. She reminded me in personality of Grannie, an adopted grandmother who had been dead about fifteen years. I call her Grandmother Teacup, because every time she came in the dream she took me to a peculiar, bizarre, outrageously eccentric tea party.

One of the most interesting aspects of these dreams was that I never remembered having seen Grandmother Teacup before. In other words, every time she came, it was as if for the first time. Each time she would invite me to a tea party, and I'd joyfully accept. We'd go to some house or building or garden, and she'd ask me to set the table. In each case there was a very specific spot for the teacup. Her fierce eyes watched to see if I would know where to place the cup. We didn't get to have tea until I found the right placement. Each time we went to such a party I knew that the protocol at that party was unique, and that I must observe carefully in order not to make a tragic error.

I remember one dream in particular, I found the place for the teacup fairly easily, so we sat down for tea. I commented that the china pattern was the same as mine. Grandmother Teacup told me the name of the pattern, which wasn't the name of mine, and I looked back down. Lo, the pattern had changed. I looked back up, astonished. She said, "No, I mean _____," and named another pattern. I looked back down, and the pattern had changed again. This shifting of patterns continued throughout the dream.

It was only when I wrote these dreams down and eventually reread them that I realized that she was coming often. Who was she? Was I having an *Alice in Wonderland* fantasy? A flashback? Was she simply teaching me dream etiquette? Like the Star Woman dreams, it would be years before I could begin to answer these questions with any clarity.

OUTWARD BOUND MAN

There was a teacher who looked like a body builder. He took me on amazing jungle-gym journeys. Sometimes the jungle gyms resembled strong rope webs like the ones army cadets or firefighter trainees have to climb. Sometimes they resembled delicate spider webs. Sometimes they looked formidable, like giant galactic-sized metal playground jungle gyms.

I didn't like these dreams. Never having been much of an athlete, "working out" was not my favorite activity. I had no clue why I needed to take P.E. in dream school. It seemed that I was being trained in survival techniques—just like an outward bound program. And worse, I wasn't alone. There were a number of us climbing around on those knotted webs. My clumsiness had an audience.

I will admit that these dreams kept my physical body in marvelous shape. I have never been stronger, leaner, or more muscular than I was during this time when I did nothing but sleep. My husband was astonished by the physical changes. A friend from high school who had since become a surgeon came to visit during that period. We went to take a long walk on the beach, and when he saw me in my bathing suit his mouth dropped open. He assured me I had never looked so good.

In one outward bound dream I slipped and nearly fell to my death. I whined quite loudly to my teacher, resulting in one of the few times he spoke to me.

> Your own belief that you are a separated human keeps you out of balance. You believe that you must separate and polarize in order to balance. Actually, you must merge. Merge with me. Merge with humanity. Open your heart.

Eventually, after enough of these trips, I began to see something metaphoric and powerful in them. I found the following journal entry from 1987:

We climbed again.
Consciousness is carried
We are always evolving
We meet on the cross.
I move vertically
You, horizontally
And where we meet—in the center
There is a moment/movement
There is the unexpected
There is opportunity
To love
Then we move on
We cross with others.
And all the crosses
We call the grid.

GRANDFATHER JACK

The next teacher was an old man who looked Native American. I called him Grandfather Jack. He wore a red bandanna around his head, and his deeply wrinkled face convinced me that he must be over one hundred years old. I named him Grandfather Jack because he always took me to the desert to chase jackrabbits in the dark. He showed me how to throw my vision slightly out of focus so that I could see the light emanating from the rocks, the plants, and the animals—each being had a unique sort of light. As I learned to discern plant light from sand and rock light, I navigated more and more quickly through the desert to try to catch up with the rabbit light. I wasn't much fonder of chasing rabbits than I was of climbing cosmic jungle gyms, but I found the work with the light fascinating, so I didn't complain as much to Grandfather. It was many years before I noticed that these dreams usually came on the new moon—the darkest night of the month.

Once, in a rapid run (in the dream), I came to a cliff. I saw no light in the abyss below. I stopped and froze with fear. Grandfather whispered in my ear, "If you had any balls, you'd jump." This impropriety, this crude sexual innuendo, and this blatant disregard for endangering my life angered me. I let him know my feelings in no uncertain terms. He rolled on the ground laughing. He said that's what was wrong with women.

> You have no sense of humor. A woman takes everything seriously. Within the void, there's no contrast. All humor is lost. The ability to shift energy through laughter is man's giveaway to woman.

Properly scolded, I did laugh at myself. He was right. Through these past few months, I'd completely forgotten how to belly laugh. That night I rolled on the ground with him guffawing at my own "commitment to the darkness," as he called it. Finally, when I regained my composure, he said,

> Everything is perfectly designed and executed. If you'll make that leap more often, you'll carry more potential.

Here's a mystery about Grandfather Jack. A few months into my illness my husband and I went for a long weekend to Two Bunch Palms, a resort in the desert near Palm Springs, California. To my enormous surprise, above the fireplace in the dining room was a portrait of Grandfather Jack. Al Capone originally built Two Bunch Palms as his desert hideout. The best information I could obtain from the present owners is that Grandfather was a friend of Capone's.

THE MERMAID

There was a mermaid woman. She wasn't quite a mermaid, because she didn't have fins—she had legs and a human body. She wasn't quite a woman either, because she could breathe underwater. When she came for me, the dreams were underwater. Sometimes we just sat in the bottom of a swimming pool chatting. Sometimes there were beautiful diving adventures in an ocean of color and texture. Always, our ability to breathe underwater amazed me. Here's a sample dream.

> I was on the swim team. I had a partner, another woman. I didn't know her well. We did a swimming diving routine that especially thrilled the audi-

once because we could stay underwater so long. We would dive down deep—I did a side corkscrew dive, where I leaped up and over my partner's more conventional dive. We would meet at the bottom of the pool and talk about the transformative nature of Love. We'd come back up, wave at the crowd, and dive deeply again, pledging ourselves to an eternity of Love. Eventually, we surfaced, walked away from each other, and acted as if we were strangers.

One day, sitting on the deck of my beach cottage, I was feeling very depressed over my illness and my general uselessness, specifically to my husband and daughter. By this time I'd been "asleep" for almost a year. I don't know whether I drifted into a dream or whether this was a waking vision, but the Mermaid came up out of the Pacific Ocean and sat with me. She told me that I could die if I wanted. She assured me that I had done a lifetime of spiritual work already, and that no karmic penalty would result from my "accidental" death. But if I lived, the mystery and beauty of my life would be unfathomable. She got up and walked slowly back into the ocean. Obviously, I chose life. She didn't lie. The mystery and beauty is unfathomable.

CRYSTAL CAVE WOMAN

Another teacher always took me into caves. I named her Crystal Cave Woman because the caves were crystalline. Sometimes the floors were covered with crystals. Sometimes the walls seemed to be mirrors, or facets of gigantic crystals. I vaguely remembered, through my muddled mind, that Merlin's cave was crystalline—the one in which he taught Arthur the highest of the wizard's magical wisdom. I wondered if Crystal Cave Woman was a she-wizard, reminding me of the most important, most ancient dreaming teachings.

The cave walls were covered with ancient drawings, and she had me sit and contemplate them. The drawings always had at least one representation of the crescent moon—a moon above the figures, a crescent in the horns of the animals, a moon in the arms of a person, a tool that looked like a scythe. In each dream she gave me paper and chalk and asked me to duplicate the drawings. Sometimes I drew them on my leg or arm. When my rendition of the drawings met her approval, she let me take a nap. Taking a nap in a dream is absolutely exquisite! She always had a big bear or buffalo robe for me to wrap myself in, and then, just as I dozed off, she put her right hand on my abdomen and pointed to the moon visible through the cave opening. I slipped into the darkness of sleep within sleep as she traced in the air a triangle between the moon, my belly, and the drawings on the cave walls. She was never there when I awoke, but then I never awoke in the cave.

I was not able to accurately remember any of those cave drawings in my waking consciousness. There is an occasional sketch or a partial design in my journal, but nothing significant. There was something so deep about the sleep within sleep that the drawings were imprinted in a level of consciousness I could not reach in waking reality. However, just a year or so later, someone gave me a copy of Joseph Campbell's *Mythologies of the Primitive Hunters and Gatherers,* and there on a page with the subtitle "The Temple Caves" I saw the drawings. They were from the caves of Lascaux in southern France. Campbell writes of them: "In these temple caves the mystery [of the universe] is made known. . . . These forms of the paintings are magical: midway between the living species of the hunting plains and the universal ground of night. . . ." According to Crystal Cave Woman, these were the images of the night, the dreaming images of our ancestors.

Like Outward Bound Man, Crystal Cave Woman didn't teach just me. There were many of us in those caves. We were like a sisterhood . . . cousins . . . a sorority.

We were in the Cave of Reflection. The walls looked like broken mirror chips—like the collage I had made in college. In the Cave of Reflection everyone mirrors little fragments of everyone else. Likewise, everyone sees little fragments of themselves in everyone else. It seems as if we're being asked to remove our mirror chips and put them back together as a whole mirror. As the chips come off and reassemble into wholeness, we begin to live in a holy way. Our essence—our core self—our authentic being is at last revealed. Now we're no longer unconsciously wearing shattered shards. Instead, we're consciously holding a mirror of the healed self, and anyone who so desires can look deeply. This is a very humbling process.

More than any other dream teacher, Crystal Cave Woman gave me a glimpse of what was really happening. Mermaid Woman had offered me a way to die. But Crystal Cave Woman was offering me a way to live. The crystals, the drawings, the moon, the sleep within sleep— they were all part of a puzzle she was showing me. Through Crystal Cave Woman's dreams, I had a vague, very dim sense that I was in a transformation rather than simply suffering from an undiagnosable disease.

Also, more than any other teacher, Crystal Cave Woman talked to me in the dreamtime. As we entered the cave one time she said:

This is the Temple of Grace. Through healing, you inherit the key.

In another dream the cave itself spoke. Hearing the cave's voice deeply moved every person present. (I wish I knew who the other people in that cave were. Was it you?)

I am sentience itself. I am the form that consciousness takes before you. You are the vehicle consciousness takes to reach me. You are among the Chosen, because you have chosen to listen to me. Walk my continents with the intent of restoring Love to my Heart. The crystals are my brain cells. Do you know my Heart cells?

DAVID

There was one other teacher, and this one I recognized. It was David, my first love. At the time, I didn't see these dreams as part of the unfolding process. In fact, because of these dreams, I worried that I was in a psychological degeneration. I felt guilty about them. One of my journal entries reflected my concern:

It seems that almost every night I dream of David. Usually it is a dream in which we've decided to marry and spend the rest of our lives together. It's ecstatic. We're unbelievably happy. How can I be having these dreams? Isn't this a betrayal of my husband? Can one be guilty of an affair in the dreamtime?

For many years after I met him David was the most important relationship in my life. We initiated each other into loving and being
loved, in ways only high schoolers can. Our love was sweet and tender
and young and idealistic and virginal.

We had kept in touch, loosely, all of our adult lives. We had discussed the whys of our breakup many times, and while there was
genuine affection for each other, there was no unfinished business that
would keep me psychologically tied to him in an unhealthy way. Yet
each one of these David dreams contained an intensity and an ecstasy
that was unparalleled in my waking consciousness. In fact, if they
hadn't been so ecstatic, if they hadn't felt so good, if they hadn't been
so divinely sweet, I would have been more deeply troubled. Instead, I
savored them. Like all the rest of these dreams, I didn't fully understand them for many years. Eventually, however, I came to understand
them as among the most pivotal and important dreams of my life.
More about that later.

So, that's an introduction to my dream teachers and a sampling of
the kinds of experiences I had while asleep. What caused all this? I
think Crystal Cave Woman's cave said it. Because I chose to listen, I
was chosen to hear. That's the part of the mystic's journey of which
few people in our culture speak. When you choose to listen, you will
be told. When you get to a certain level of development, you have to
physically die, as Mermaid Woman offered, or you metaphorically die
in order to wake up to the unfathomable mystery. I chose to wake up.

I hope my story has stirred something in you. Perhaps some bone-
deep memory. In the next chapter I explain my gradual understanding
of all these dreams.

TWO

the dreamer's creation story

The whole universe originated in the dream of Vishnu.
~BUDDHIST TRADITIONAL THOUGHT[1]

I'VE NEVER KNOWN WHAT TO CALL THAT PERIOD OF MY LIFE. "ILLNESS" seems inappropriate and inaccurate. I've considered other possibilities, like: the time when I dreamed myself awake, or my great awakening, or the annihilation of my former ego. All those seemed both insufficient and grandiose. I could call it my year of two thousand dreams—Y2D. Whatever I label it, this period profoundly shattered my former beliefs and obliterated the way I lived my life.

> *Reason can never understand the love of Love, can never dance in the incandescent madness of vision, can never become lucid through the drunkenness of ecstasy. Yet reason can never completely give up the desire to understand. . . .*
>
> —Rumi[2]

When I first began to come out of it, I was desperate to find someone who could tell me what all this had meant. I searched for teachers who would listen to my dreams and explain their purpose. In retrospect, I recall feeling panicked that ultimately there was no meaning and no greater purpose. What if I'd just been sick and delusional?

There's not much help in the Western tradition for understanding that kind of dreaming experience. There are plenty of therapists and dream teachers who will analyze and interpret dreams, but that wasn't really what I needed. I wanted comprehension of the totality of the experience. I wanted to know why the dream teachers kept coming, who they were, what they wanted from me. I knew these dreams were not about my personal psychology. Most of them weren't even about me. But I still wanted to know what they meant. I ran from teacher to teacher, shaman to shaman, author to author — Anglo, Hispanic, Native American, African, Tibetan, Sufi.

Little by little I was able to piece some things together. Of course, I'd hoped to find my own female version of Carlos Castaneda's teacher, Don Juan, who would just take me under her wing and tell me everything I needed to know. But she was not to come. Instead, an understanding of this time had to unfold for me through living my everyday life.

Ten years after my involuntary crash course in the dream, I enrolled in a waking-life doctorate program at the University of Creation Spirituality in Oakland, California. Ironically, it was in a physics class called "The New Cosmology" that I experienced a profound and unparalleled level of clarity and discovery about my dreaming days.

Mathematical cosmologist Brian Swimme and physicist Stuart Cowan taught this course. Although neither of them ever mentioned dreaming in the class, and although to this day I've never had a private conversation with either of them, that class and their insights surrounding the genesis of the universe opened some of the doors to my understanding. Let me demonstrate with another story.

THE DREAMER'S CREATION STORY

In *The Universe Story*, a book coauthored with Thomas Berry, Dr. Swimme described the Void as the cosmic soup of all potential. This soup is the great blackness out of which the physical universe enters the realm of perception. Within that blackness, that Formlessness, that Noplace, that Nothingness (pronounced "No thing-ness"), everything that ever happened, ever could have happened, ever will happen, and ever might happen rests in complete repose. Out of that blackness, one moment in time about 15 billion years ago, a great silent blast of pure energy burst forth and expressed itself as light.

STAR WOMAN—DREAMING THE VOID

As Dr. Swimme articulated the magical and mystical Void—the invisible source of perceptual reality—I found myself slipping back into the dreams of Star Woman. She had no form. She was that Formlessness of which he spoke. She took me into the blackness—the Nothingness. Nothing happened in those dreams, and then I was awakened with, exactly as he described it, a great silent blast of pure energy bursting forth and expressing itself as light. I'd always awakened from those dreams highly energized.

Star Woman, when she came, took me into the genesis of the cosmos. Those dreams reminded me that when we dissolve into sleep, we actually return to the Nothingness that is before and beyond any concepts of time and space. A journal entry from that time states it clearly.

> It's a profound silence. It's a stillness that I've never experienced. I hear something like, "Think no thing of yourself. Simply experience the radiance of Who You Are. To embody this silence you must *be* it. Don't think about being it. Give that all away—there is no system, no set of rules, no philosophy."

Dreamtime is a return to the cosmic soup of all potential, the embodiment of silence, so that we can regenerate, heal, and bring forth in our magnificent, ecstatic awakening a new expression of the light energy we call life.

"All the energy that would ever exist in the entire course of time erupted as a single quantum—a singular gift—existence."[3] This quotation from *The Universe Story* is an outrageous and riveting statement. *All the energy* that has been used to run all the galaxies, to birth all the babies, to fire up all the stars, to lick all the ice cream cones of a lifetime—*all the energy* burst forth in the first few moments of that originating primordial silent flare.

This idea is crucial to the dreamer's creation story. We must know, first and foremost, that we participate in a universe that is inextricably bound to its origin. Every time we brush our teeth we're recycling energy that's been around for 15 billion years. How hilarious and arrogant that I would have thought that I didn't "have" the energy to stay alive. Am I not as linked to the original burst as any ant, any planet, any lizard, any star? The energy is there for the taking. One doesn't own energy; one borrows it to use and then gives it back. I could see, only then in that physics class ten years later, that Star Woman's ecstatic way of awakening me from those dreams was a reminder that every being is sourced in the light, and that the energy of life force is limitless because it is never "used up."

GRANDMOTHER TEACUP— DREAMING NEW BEGINNINGS

One of the most unimaginable aspects of the new cosmology, as we understand it now, is that the original blast, the original primordial flaring forth, occurred in a very small space. In fact, Stuart Cowan said that initially all the energy that runs the universe could have been contained in a common teacup. Of course, when he said that, I almost jumped out of my chair.

Suddenly, Grandmother's tea parties became more than galactic etiquette lessons. From the context of the new cosmology, every quantum of energy is the center of the universe. This is an omnicentric universe—every quantum was born simultaneously and is simultaneously re-creating and regenerating itself in every nanosecond. Every location that we might define as space is the center of the known universe, for every shred of energy existed in that original cosmic teacup.

The dreams of the tea parties taught me to allow every context, every circumstance, every setting to be original, primal, primordial. They challenged me to read the cosmology of the scene rather than to define it from my own belief systems. Grandmother Teacup's eye ruthlessly oversaw my table setting to show me that where one places the cup (where one places one's attention or one's beliefs about the nature of being) determines everything about his or her experience of being.

Grandmother taught me the basic law of mysticism—to let each moment, no matter how seemingly familiar, unfold its own expression of life force. How else can we experience the wonders of the universe?

How else can we be so dazzled by the beauty of life that we fall in love with it? And if we aren't in love with life, how can we live it fully?

If one's belief system and life context are too small or too concrete to encompass the vastness, one cannot experience the mystery. Whether you know it or not, you limit yourself, and others around you, if you in any way diminish your capacity for wonder. How do we diminish the capacity for wonder? Through familiarity, cynicism, judgment, anger, and fear, and unfortunately, through institutionalized education. As my teenage daughter says, "Mother, what is less awesome in life than a high school math class?" Isn't it true that by the time we've finished high school, our capacity for awe is greatly diminished, and by the time we've acquired another diploma or two, it's all but eliminated. Unfortunately, the more we think we know, the less we allow ourselves to authentically experience raw wonder. Our expertise becomes our enemy.

That's the lesson and paradox of the tea party dreams. Your understanding of the beginning of the beginnings depends entirely on where you place the teacup—where you put the original primordial eruption in your own cosmology. Your perspective, your ethic, your cosmic rules create your own genesis.

OUTWARD BOUND MAN— DREAMING THE COSMIC ORDER

That rich cosmic soup of all potential holds within it an unseen, unknowable structure of the cosmo-genetic principles and laws. These are the rules through which the cosmos creates order. According to cosmologists like Swimme, these rules were born as a part of the initial flaring forth. Each time we dissolve our consciousness into that blackness, we directly perceive, not through the intellect but through physiology, the cosmic order.

What is that structure? Physics tells us that every form has a crystalline pattern held within the cells of that form. Physics, metaphysics, Kabbalah, mystical Christianity, Sufism, the occult, and all the Mystery Schools agree on one thing: There is an unseen realm out of which the seen is formed. It is the matrix of creation. Dreamers call this unseen field of energy the Dream Weave.

Scientists have recently begun to realize the basic flaw in the old model of reductionism and dissection for the sake of observation. Einstein spent his last years looking for the unified field theory, or "a theory of everything." He was convinced that, indeed, the universe is One diversified Whole. The universe is a way of Being. It is the unified principle. Perhaps it can't be stated, because it simply *is*.

Historically, humans have interfaced with the great mystery of life through dreaming, visioning, shamanic journeying, and mystical experience. The past two hundred years, however, evolved as a mechanical and technological era, which disconnected many of us from that kind of deep experience, from the root of our own roots, as the poet Rumi calls it. The thread that has kept us connected, albeit unconsciously, is the dreaming thread. We still dream, no matter what kind of technology we play with in waking time. Now we're waking up again to the power of the mystical journey, and we're telling our stories in order to stir those ancient memories in each other.

The jungle-gym dreams, which I had interpreted to be about survival training, reminded me how to travel on the Dream Weave—that is, how to negotiate the unseen realms—with grace and confidence. This restored a memory that dreaming is absorbed and understood through the physical body. Through our dream work, we can experience a direct physical, energetic relationship with the order of the cosmos. If we are skilled in our dreaming practice we can investigate the unseen structures of the universe simply by taking a nap. I like that.

GRANDFATHER JACK—DREAMING THE LIGHT

Not much happened in our universe for the first few hundred thousand years after the teacup explosion, except some massive expanding, cooling, and stabilizing. Eventually, though, the cosmic principle of organization bubbled up out of the Void, and an atom formed. Swimme and Berry describe it: "The creation of atoms is as stunning as the creation of the universe. Nothing in the previous several hundred thousand years presaged their emergence. These dynamic twists of being leapt out of the originating mystery and immediately organized the universe in a fresh way."[4]

The first atoms, hydrogen and helium, changed everything. They organized themselves into giant swirling clouds, simultaneously changing all that had been and reorganizing the structure of all future existence. They swallowed all that had come before them and regenerated the cosmos as completely new. The universe was no longer a giant fireball expanding and cooling. Suddenly it was an organizational flow of primeval energy.

Within those brewing galactic-sized hydrogen clouds, vortices of energy formed that eventually developed density and heat and birthed themselves as stars. Some of those stars became so hot and so dense that they engulfed the other star systems around them. These gluttonous devouring balls of primal fire reached such unfathomable temperatures that they burned themselves to death. In the last two weeks of a star's life, it burns so hot that it literally melts hydrogen and helium together in all kinds of unique and astonishing ways, thus creating all the other elements of the physical cosmos.

This paradox, this creation through destruction, this violence that gives birth to everything else, is the crux of the mystery of all existence. Through the death of a star, all the elements that make up the planets spew into being. Each of these elements contains a unique crystalline pattern and is fused with intrinsic qualities that inform and perpetuate life itself. It's such an amazing concept: All the elements that make up our planet didn't originate here. They are stardust, flung into the galaxy as ash, and attracted to each other through some unknown cosmic bonding principle. We are the phoenix rising out of a dying star. Indeed, all the elements that make up our bodies are stardust. We are walking stardust that recycles 15 billion-year-old energy. This is, quite simply, an amazing concept.

According to modern physics, one of the fundamental guiding and organizing principles of the universe is memory. Memory gives the universe the ability to re-create itself. On earth, cellular memory empowers and drives all life-forms. Every cell remembers its origin through its physiology, its DNA. All procreation occurs through memory embedded in that DNA, which is then shared with its progeny. Indeed, in some wise abyss of our consciousness, each of us remembers our star origins.

Grandfather Jack may not have been teaching me about chasing rabbits at all. Perhaps he was reminding me that every form is just light. Every aspect of perceptual reality is stardust, and within an understanding of that, one can use and see the light of every being. Every element on this planet has unique inherent beingness. Every combination of elements, therefore, speaks its own language, sings its own tune. Shamans know that. Shamans speak of our star ancestors. Shamans learn the song of the stones, the music of the spheres. Shamans use the tone of the drum made from a specific animal skin to achieve the special vibrations needed for their communities or clients to heal. They learn to see the inner driving force—the light—of every form. Grandfather Jack was a shaman of the dream. He taught me to read the light of each species, indeed of each individuation of each species, in order to see my own path clearly and to negotiate and navigate it gracefully.

THE MERMAID—DREAMING LIFE'S SOURCE

On this planet, all kinds of unique circumstances allowed for a marriage between the two elements hydrogen and oxygen. When they bond in the correct proportions, water results. There's no hint in either of them alone that the potential for water is present. But when they combine, the very stuff of life breaks through. The great cosmic soup of all potential is metaphorically represented in our planet's vast oceans.

Indeed, it was about 3.8 billion years ago in the primitive oceans that one of the laws of order expressed itself in a completely new way. The law we call synergy (a mutually enhancing relationship between two entities) burst forth when some atoms decided to synergistically wed. Some atoms got together and agreed to carry out certain responsibilities to the whole. Some ate. Some remembered. Some transformed the food into useful energy. Some (the wild, naughty atoms) reproduced. Some sat on the boundary and held everything together, stabilizing the system. The single-cell organism that resulted was the beginning of life as we know it on this planet. Through the principle of memory, that first organism, that first cell, is literally *in* your body, for it was in that first cell that DNA began its complex journey into the exploration of the many ways life could be expressed in physical form. Prior to the creation of this organism, the universe was unfolding as a set of highly complex chemical reactions. Now, suddenly, there was a synthesized being with a metabolism that could reproduce itself without paracitizing something else: Life.

Soon those organisms ate and procreated enough that a new law of cosmic order emerged. We call it symbiosis, a system of cooperation for mutual benefit. Life could participate with itself in order to differentiate. It could create new levels of being, unique complexities of internal and external form, and many varied archetypes that were previously nonexistent. Life on this planet is literally predicated on a specific set of ground rules that demand coexistence. All life—every frog, every fungus, every tree, every human being—shapes all other life through mutual cooperation. And it all started in the water with one cell.

The original cell procreated (thanks to those wild ones) so many millions of times that it eventually developed a food crisis. It ate all the food, at least all the food it knew how to eat. Life on the planet was literally in jeopardy of extinction. But Life didn't want to die. It took thousands of years, but eventually, after millions of genetic mutations, a group of cells aligned with some atoms

> Dreaming like rivers
> we meet in the sea.
> Then the waters all know us
> and we know where the sea
> does not end.
>
> —Russell Salamon[5]

that could metabolize light (photosynthesis), and plants were born. Stuart Cowan suggests that rather than use the word *kingdom*, which has gender-dominant implications, we simply drop the *g* and use the word *kindom*, which is a more accurate representation anyway. I like that. So the plant kindom, which could metabolize light, emerged, and since light was in seemingly limitless supply, plants were the salvation of Life.

Ironically, the plant kindom was so prolific and fruitful in its diversity that it eventually created an air-pollution crisis. The plants' exhaust fumes (oxygen) became a big cloud around the planet that started choking it to death. Another cry for help and another few thousand mutations resulted in a strange-looking creature crawling up out of the water and taking a breath. The evolution of lungs that breathe and transform oxygen was the turning point that saved all life on the planet, and the animal kindom was born. These creatures transformed the oxygen fumes into something the plants could use—carbon dioxide. They ate the plants, thus preventing them from over-proliferating. Even more interestingly, they ate each other for the same reason.

My mermaid dreams didn't seem so strange when put in the context of the universe story. Of course, we can remember how to breathe underwater. Every cell in our bodies carries the DNA of that original organism—the water being. If we are to remember and acknowledge all of ourselves, we must certainly remember and honor our water selves.

That's part of who we are: beings who came up out of our natural home—the water—to give ourselves to life through Love. No wonder breathing underwater felt so natural in those dreams.

CRYSTAL CAVE WOMAN— DREAMING THE WORLD INTO BEING

Humans don't know exactly who we are or how we happen to be here. There are, however, some things we do know. We know that the original hominids, our earliest ancestors, carried DNA staggeringly similar to the chimpanzee. We were (still are) 98.4 percent identical to primates. That's close. That's first-cousin close. But it's not close enough. We are so different that without another discovery—finding the missing link—we can't actually say that we evolved from the primates. We can only say that the similarities are interesting, but the differences are even *more* interesting.

What is the main biological difference between us and the other primates? *Our rate of development.* Chimpanzees develop almost ten times faster than we do. A literalist might say that we are *slow* chimps. Is that in itself not an amazingly humbling piece of news?

What does that mean about us as a species? It means that we have long childhoods. It means that human babies experience years and years devoted to play. It means that in our formative time we develop creative use of the imagination. It means that in our developmental years, it is our job to *dream up* realities and make them come true. And then, we never stop. Our imagination never stops dreaming a new way, and we never stop playing. Dreaming, playing, and thereby manifesting our dreams are our significant contributions to life, and our significant difference from all other kindoms.

If you look back through time to those early hominid days, you see that a very clear spiritual pattern developed, unique to the human species. Because of this singular attention given to the development of imagination, the cycles of birth and death, of hunting and resting, of planting and harvest, of day and night became important aspects of life. Like no other species, the human family saw the connections, the cycles, the patterns of life. Anthropological studies of Neanderthal clans, for example, clearly show that they were highly ritualistic in the way they buried their dead. This indicates a society with a cosmology founded on a deep respect for life, a cosmology with a big "heart."

We can imagine that the menstrual cycle was also a profound experience for early humans. They probably knew its connection to the cycles of the moon. They eventually knew its connection to procreation. They respected their blood, for they knew it to be life's fluid. Women bled cyclically but had no wound and didn't die. Women took time away from their normal duties in the community, and went to the sacred caves to honor the bleeding, and to dream. They dreamed together, they shared their dreams, they drew images of them on the walls of their caves, carved them into their sacred stones, and modeled them in their clay pots and icons. These were the first dream circles!

Those were the crystalline caves to which Crystal Cave Woman took me. Crystal caves are sacred—crystals have long been considered power stones, and there is anthropological evidence that even the earliest hominids revered them. Crystals are Earth's skeletal structure. Crystals hold Earth's memory, and stirring memory was the point, I believe, of my whole dreaming experience. Crystal Cave Woman was evoking in my memory an energetic relationship with the crystalline structure of cosmic order. It was through the crystals that the mirroring aspect of the dreams was shown to me. The cave drawings were representations of our ancestor's dreamtime. Those were the dreams that first alerted our species to our cocreative power—the power of dreaming.

Those cave times were very special for our early dream sisters. For one thing, they were rare. In those days, from the time a woman had her first moontime until she died fifteen or so years later, she was usually either pregnant or lactating. Bleeding times were few and far between. After they went to the caves for their bleeding time, they would go back into society and have another baby. Indeed, for them, the birth of each baby marked the birth of a new dream. When they did eventually return to the cave months later, our early dreaming sisters could look at the images on the walls and see that the dream had manifested. They could see that it was time to dream a new dream.

Crystal Cave Woman demanded that I reproduce those cave drawings as exactly as possible. She rewarded me for "manifesting" the dream images by letting me take a nap. She literally reinstated humanity's most ancient dreaming practices into my own dreamtime. As I look back into my dream journals from that time, I can see the tracks of those dreams. I can see that they have manifested. I can see that I gave birth during that era—that time people would call illness—to a new dream.

TIME TO DREAM A NEW DREAM

One night, recently, I was up particularly late watching the news. In my city it's always full of the latest rape, murder, and violence count. I realized that the mass media is our collective cave wall. For too many of us, daily life is a violent and frightening dream that has manifested.

Our species has created a food crisis similar to that of the original cellular beings. We have created an air-pollution crisis similar to that of the plant kindom. But most important, we have created a crisis in imagination. Because we manifest our dreams, we're forcing every being, every species, and every aspect of the ecosystem to live within our dream. We have forgotten our responsibility and accountability to the Sacred Dream.

It wouldn't be that hard for us to dream a new dream. Ever since the first astronauts turned the camera around and showed us this beautiful blue-green jewel of a planet, we've begun to remember our starness and our uniqueness. We now see that we are one living organism. We must shift our way of thinking and living so that the whole organism can thrive. We must take a deep look at our cave walls.

It's time to dream a new dream.

redefining dreaming

I think dreams come from the universe.
~MATTHEW FOX[1]

ALTHOUGH IT'S CERTAINLY NOT THE CASE IN ALL TRADITIONS AND ALL cultures, in the West we most often define "dream" as the story we remember when we wake up from sleep. The *Living Webster Encyclopedic Dictionary* defines "dream" as "a succession of images or ideas present in the mind during sleep," indicating that it is primarily a brain activity. Depending on our religious beliefs and psychological biases, we either regard this story as "just a dream"—something to be quickly discarded—or we regard it as something to interpret so that we'll know more about ourselves. My dreaming experiences taught me that neither of these is accurate, adequate, or particularly beneficial.

In my experience, it is absolutely essential that we completely redefine "dream" in order to become aware of its full implication. We can no longer relegate sleep and dreaming to a corner of life that is considered personal and private. For every three and a half years of your life, you are in the dreamtime one year. That's too much of life to ignore, and it's too myopic to think that it is all about you.

REDEFINING THE DREAM

I have come to feel that "dreaming" is an encounter with Truth in the great creative Void. Let me explain.

When we lay down to sleep, we put our body into a position that changes our relationship to ordinary consciousness, to gravity, and to our normal physical operating procedures. In waking reality, we're vaguely aware of the power of certain body positions and the overt messages (body language) that certain postures send. Native American shamans and Tibetan dream yoga, however, teach the value of specific positions during sleep. Because most of us are unschooled in the language of physique, few realize that the horizontal position—the sleeping position—liberates our minds and bodies from the limitations we experience in the vertical, waking reality.

> In the waking state you are conscious only of a certain limited field and action of your nature. In sleep you can become vividly aware of things beyond this field. . . . To be conscious, reject all but the divine Truth; the more you get that Truth, and the more you cling to it in the waking state, rejecting all else, the more the inferior dream-stuff will get clear.
>
> —Sri Aurobindo[2]

As we go to sleep, we drift into the blackness. We literally leave behind any conscious awareness of the body, the bed, the room, and the covers; instead, we feel the familiar, warm, inviting, delicious darkness. If you've ever been able to maintain a shred of personal awareness in that blackness, even for a split second, you remember how awesome it is to be engulfed by its rich and velvety presence. Especially if you're really tired or extraordinarily stressed, this experience is unparalleled. Is there a more welcomed or more desired state of being than those early moments of sleep?

In that blackness the body relaxes completely. In my dreams, when Crystal Cave Woman let me take a nap, as I drifted to sleep she pointed to my belly, to the moon outside the cave opening, and to the drawings on the walls of the cave. In some of those dreams I saw that, as our bodies fully and completely relax, as we drift toward sleep, we unwind these amazing energetic filaments (invisible fibers that come out of our bellies). Through them we connect to the cosmic order, which is represented most clearly to us by our nearest heavenly neighbor, our magnificent moon.

> When seen from the moon, our sky looks pure and clear and without blemish. The teachers call the moon, that heavenly body closest to the earth, the midwife of the heavens.
>
> —Meister Eckhart[3]

In other words, when it's time to go to sleep, we physically change our relationship to the Earth, we connect with the moontime (the night/the darkness), and our consciousness adjusts to a new way of perceiving.

That's when the dreaming occurs. Then, in the Nothingness, through those fibers, an energetic unity transpires. That is the direct experience of divine energy. That is the dream.

DO NOT TAKE THIS PERSONALLY!

It is important for the dreamer to recognize the nonpersonal nature of this dreamspace. That blackness, that Void, that nothingness, is not about you. That place is holy and whole. It is the Godhead, as Meister Eckhart would call it. It is the Ein Sof to which Kabbalists refer. It is beyond the reach of the individuated being's comprehension.

The nonlinear, nonrational nature of dreaming is paradoxical. The source of the dreaming is impersonal—it is not about you. And yet that source gives you a personal experience.

In her book *Being in Dreaming*, Florinda Donner relates her understanding of dreaming as a physiological event. Her teacher, also named Florinda, spoke to her about her own dreaming: "Obviously you're plugging into the source itself. Everybody does that—plugs into source itself."[4] Master dreamers know that and do it consciously. The elder Florinda also explained to Donner how the dreaming is taught in the sorcerer's tradition. "With women . . . dreaming instructions begin by making them draw a map of their bodies—a painstaking job that reveals where the visions of dreams are stored in their bodies."[5] When I read this, I saw that Crystal Cave Woman had made me carefully draw the images of the dream, and then she put her hand on my belly to show me where the dream images are stored and where the dream fibers that "plug into source" are rooted.

When we dissolve into the darkness, "plug into source," we first restore and regenerate physically. But in addition, we also have energetic and physiological experiences. We go places, see things, have encounters with other beings! During these experiences, we perceive the messages of the soul. These experiences, in fact, are magnetized to us *as* messages from the soul.

THE DREAM STORY

Eventually, the part of the human brain that likes to make sense out of things realizes that these experiences need to be integrated into waking life. The personal mind, then, writes a story, which to the best of its ability describes the energetic event.

This is the hardest part of redefining dreaming. Most people want the story to be the dream. It's difficult to make the shift into seeing the

> *No image aims at or points to itself.*
> *It rather aims at and points to the*
> *object of which it is the image.*
>
> —Meister Eckhart[6]

story as simply a metaphor for what happened in sleep. Just as I did when I "woke up" from my long dreaming experience, most people want the story to mean something, and most people want it to mean something about them.

Well, of course, the story does mean something and it does tell us something about ourselves. It is, after all, the dreamer's mind that writes the story. So, if nothing else, the dream story tells us something about our minds, and our personal set of symbols and images. It also tells us something about our own ability to see the unseen—our specific gifts and skills in the Void.

For example, if I have a violent image in the dream story, it doesn't necessarily mean I am a violent person. It does mean, however, that I carry a configuration of energy that resonates with violence. Provided I have learned to work with these tendencies in my character, it means that I can be of service to humanity by helping to transform violent energies before they become violent actions.

In waking life we often say that if you recognize a quality in someone it's because you have it in yourself. This is the same idea. If an image shows up in a dream story, it's because you encountered an energy that reminded you of that image. You carry some degree of the energy of that image in yourself. The dream image mirrors your potential for *compassion.*

Compassion is the ability to extend nonjudgmental loving kindness into a situation. The wider your range of experiential understanding of the human condition, the more compassion you can hold. If you are a prostitute in the dream, it doesn't mean that you are a prostitute; it means that you can extend compassionate, loving understanding to the prostitute mentality that exists in the waking world.

While the dream story tells us something about the dreamer, in order to fully appreciate dreaming we must move beyond a superficial and personal interpretation of the symbols. We must penetrate the energy that evoked the images. This is why it wasn't enough for me to find a good dream interpreter. I needed to grasp and comprehend the totality of the experience. The dream always appears to be personal if we see only the story. However, the energetic experience that evoked the story was highly impersonal.

This new definition of dreaming is complex because it's multi-dimensional. It says that dreaming occurs completely outside the parameters of the human mind. According to this definition, dreaming is nonrational, nonlinear, and nonverbal. Like the unified field theory for which Einstein searched, dreaming can't be fully defined because it just *is*.

SPIRITUAL PRACTICE AND DREAMING

It is extremely important to develop a practice around going to sleep that helps the dreamer clear the mind, body, and psyche. If you go to sleep ensnared in emotions or stress, the dreaming will be skewed. Many traditions have prayers, mantras, or specific movements that help the dreamer eliminate all nonbenevolent thoughts and emotions before going to bed. In my first book, *The Woman's Book of Dreams: Dreaming as a Spiritual Practice,* I outlined some very useful and dynamic techniques that enable dreamers to receive the clearest possible transmission of energy during dreamtime. Another excellent resource is *Entering the Temple of Dreams: Jewish Prayers, Movements, and Meditations for the End of the Day* by Tamar Frankiel and Judy Greenfeld, two of my colleagues and dream sisters. They do a brilliant job of describing the ancient teachings of Jewish traditional evening prayers and practices.

My dream teachers taught me to develop a specific spiritual practice around preparing for sleep. I later learned that this idea is very

old. One can find references to it in most ancient spiritual literature.
An example is in *The Essene Gospel of Peace*, an Aramaic manuscript
dated from the third century.
The Essenes were a group of
Jewish fundamental spiritualists.
They translated much of the He-
brew Bible into Aramaic, using
their own vernacular, so that the
ancient teachings were more easily understood and accessible to them.
In addition, they incorporated other teachings, presumably from their
own spiritual practices, into a group of documents that were discovered in the mid-twentieth century. The *Gospel of Peace* is apparently
one of these. Based on what this Gospel says of dreaming, I think the
Essenes must have been master dreamers. For example:

> But when the sun is set, and your Heavenly Father sends you his most pre-
> cious angel, sleep, then take your rest, and be all the night with the angel
> of sleep.[8]

This passage appears in the midst of an explanation of the difference between the Earthly Mother's angels of day and the Heavenly
Father's angels of sleep. The Essenes believed that one must be fully
ready and present to receive teachings from these angels in every moment of life. Unfortunately, most of us have forgotten how to receive
the teachings of the dreamtime angels.

THE STAGES AND LEVELS OF DREAMING

During the first few years after I "woke up," I discovered some very
important cycles and patterns that had existed within the dreaming
experience. Through the timing of the Crystal Cave Woman dreams,
I saw especially that certain types of dreams come in cycles, and that
these cycles are directly connected to the cycles of the moon. The
moon's phase and zodiacal position have enormous influence on the
dreaming of a given night.

More important, I saw that dreaming itself comes in different
stages and levels. Let me explain. At the beginning of Chapter One, I

---

*Enlighten my eyes . . . for You
are the illuminator in sleep of the
pupil of the eye.*

—Hamapil, Jewish bedtime prayer[7]

mentioned that I had a spiritual practice that consisted of meditation, attending Native American ceremonies, and participating in charitable fund-raising. That's not totally accurate. I came to this dreaming period after a lifetime of spiritual practice. My father was a Methodist minister, so spirituality was an important part of my upbringing. Even though I left organized religion shortly after I graduated from college, I never left the pursuit of spiritual truth. Studying dreaming had been a part of that pursuit, for I had noticed even as a young girl that my dreams were reliable sources of factual, otherwise inaccessible, information. And a few years prior to my illness, I made a powerful oath to do whatever was necessary to achieve inner peace.

I give you that new piece of my story because it helps me explain that there are *stages of dreaming* that become available to the dreamer as he or she reaches new levels of spiritual development. I like the word *stage* because it refers not only to a step or a degree of progress but to a platform of performance. A dreaming stage evolves from the dreamer's progress in his or her spiritual understanding of life, and that progress literally creates a platform on which the dreamer can stand.

Early in one's spiritual development, the dream stories are personal and instructive. They give the dreamer direct information about himself or herself, and they offer guidance and nurturance. These dreams come, whether we ask for them or not, whether we are on a disciplined path or not.

Eventually, if the dreamer vows to achieve a spiritual understanding of life, and develops a more sophisticated awareness of the true nature of life, the dream stories become progressively more universal, communal, collective, and ecumenical. Then, finally, if the dreamer persists and reaches advanced stages of spiritual growth within his or her lifetime, the dream stories stop altogether, because the dreamer and the dreamed become one unified whole. An evolved master dreamer is the embodiment of Einstein's unified field theory.

THE FIRST STAGE OF DREAMING:
PERSONAL DREAMING

First, let's talk about the way we usually experience the dream: personal dreaming. Most Westerners spend their entire lives in this stage. It is a stage that remains constant until the dreamer makes his or her first moves toward developing a spiritual consciousness. If the dreamer cannot move beyond a self-centered, narcissistic, childish view of life, first-stage dreams will be his or her only dreams.

Personal dreaming is a stage in which we are asked to broaden our personal belief systems and to mature spiritually. In this stage, we must transform our consensus-based, unconscious systems of thought. It sounds like a tall order, but how else can we be fully available for the transmissions awaiting us from the angels of sleep? Angels can't override the personal will of the human.

We can, through use of personal will, cleverly disguise, even to ourselves, our limited thinking as uniqueness and rightness. We can use our narrow-mindedness to block the messages of the dream angels. We can willfully refuse to open the letters from the soul. First-stage dreams ask us to grow, to open our minds, to open those letters!

THE SECOND STAGE OF DREAMING:
COLLECTIVE DREAMING

The definition of dreaming changes organically as we reach different stages in our spiritual development. In the first stage, the dreaming message is about learning to expand one's personal belief systems so that deeper truths can be accessed. In the next stage, after we set a spiritual intention and accomplish certain personal expansions of consciousness, we are able to experience dreams in a broader way.

In this stage of dreaming, the brain that writes the story has been freed of some of its neuroses. These new types of dreams are not local to the dreamer. The dreamer may discover information to which he or she could not possibly have access through any other means. They are dreams in which the dreamer perceives the yet undiagnosed illness of a pet, the state of mind of a distant friend, or the trouble that may be brewing in the inner city. How many times have I congratulated someone on a new job before they got the job? How many times have you heard from a long-lost friend the morning after you dreamed about him or her? How many women have dreamed the gender and facial features of their babies while they were still pregnant? These kinds of dream experiences happen frequently. All too often, though, we push them aside as "just dreams" and ignore the gift they bring us.

As a result of a broadened consciousness reached through spiritual practice, the dreamer develops the ability to attract and manifest previously untapped levels of truth. These kinds of dreams are shocking, because we actually wake up knowing something we're not "supposed" to know.

Second-stage dreaming, however, is the level of dreaming in which we must develop self-trust. The second stage of dreaming instructs the dreamer to trust his or her psychic and telepathic abilities.

THE THIRD STAGE OF DREAMING:
TRANSFORMATIVE DREAMING

[The] unknown angels will teach you many things concerning the kingdom of God, even as the angels that you know of the Earthly Mother instruct you in the things of her kingdom
—The Essene Gospel of Peace[9]

The next stage of dreaming occurs only when the dreamer has reached a level of comfort with the second stage. Then, the dreamer can move to an even deeper relationship with dreaming, because he or she is living in deeper relationship with Truth.

At this level the dream definition changes yet again. Now the dream is not just about gathering information, nor is it just about personal expansion. Now the dreaming is about practicing the experience of truth in every state of consciousness. The teachers of the dreamtime are able to directly transmit information to us, for we are in a state of receptivity that is unparalleled in any other level of consciousness. If we are able to receive deep truth in the dreamtime, we can practice acting on that truth in waking reality.

Here we see in this ancient version of the dream teachings a description of the spiritual nature of the partnership between sleeping and waking. Both sleeping and waking are learning states, and each state mirrors the other.

As my personal experience demonstrated, the third stage comes in dramatic ways. To receive transmissions of truth, one must be fully available. One must experience third-stage dreams from a nonpersonal, profoundly detached, totally receptive perspective. There's no "my" in this stage—the ego is not allowed to choreograph this one. For this reason, these dreams often initially reveal themselves under the most bizarre conditions. This stage cannot be faked.

One of my (waking life) teachers experienced such a transmission while under anesthesia during life-saving emergency surgery. Another friend received a most profound dream transmission during an extremely stressful period when assassins were actually stalking him. Mine came only after I "lost my mind." Other members of my dream circle have had such dreams in the first few days after the death of a friend or loved one. The dream angels will use any *authentic* opening as an opportunity to communicate truth to a dreamer!

THE FOURTH STAGE OF DREAMING:
PHILANTHROPIC DREAMING

When the dreamer no longer needs the dream to be about himself or herself at all, the fourth stage of dreaming has arrived. At this point, the definition of dreaming rewrites itself one more time, including but also going beyond all previous definitions. By now, the energetic experience in the great holy darkness is absolutely pure. The dreamer has learned to go into sleep with no personal history, no baggage, no needs. He or she can dissolve into the Void with no attachment to life, death, dream, truth, meaning, or consequence.

The dreamer can only reach this stage of dreaming from a totally selfless place—the space of a dream bodhisattva, so to speak. One simply uses the energy of dreamtime to serve, with no need for validation, feedback, or even dream memory.

Something interesting happens to the imagery in this stage. One is no longer limited to one's own lexicon of images. In this stage the dreamer's consciousness is so thoroughly liberated that it can access all systems of imagery and literally create new forms. The shape-

shifting dreams, in which the dreamer becomes another kind of creature or being, for example, most typically occur in the fourth stage. If
assistance is required from the animal kindom, the plant kindom, the
galactic realm, or the angelic kindom, the dreamer actually becomes
the appropriate form in order to retrieve the needed information.
Sometimes we remember those dreams—we were an eagle, a wolf, a
tree. Sometimes we simply awaken with an undeniable sense of having
been "elsewhere."

There is one level of fourth-stage dreaming that almost stands
alone. This one is very difficult to discuss or describe. I call it soul
dreaming. Some people reach a level of spiritual development that
puts their dreaming on a dimension that cannot be reproduced in a
story. These dreaming experiences simply cannot be told, and so no
attempt is made to do so. In this stage, even the personal mind of the
dreamer dissolves into the One Mind, the Mind of Unity. One of my
friends describes it as being in the eye of God. There is no description, nothing to be said.

At this level, the dreamer is not separate in any sense from what is
dreamed. The dreamer is the dream; the dream is the dreamer. And
both are totally merged with form and formlessness, visible and invisible, lover and Beloved. The dreamer has found his or her core self,
his or her essential being, and all experience—waking or dreaming —
radiates from that!

THE DREAMER'S IMPERATIVE

Heather Valencia, one of my waking life teachers and a dear friend,
says that in dreaming we offer ourselves and give hospitality to
the Great Mystery. As a well-trained southern woman, I love that
analogy. It makes my job as a dreamer quite clear: I am a dream hostess! What, then, is the hostess's protocol?

First, it is to expand my understanding of the definition of dreaming so that I can give it a large enough space in my life.

Second, it is to search out every nano particle of belief that keeps
me separated from all potential, all wholeness—from the source. Each
whisper of separatist belief must be pierced with the truth of unity
consciousness.

Third, it is to be very cautious about interpreting the symbols of the dream. I can certainly look for meaning, as long as I realize that the experience that evoked the image is the *real* dream.

Finally, it is to be disciplined in my spiritual practice so that I can develop the mental stability, the emotional clarity, and the physical strength to give hospitality to the Great Mystery. Any mental neurosis, emotional weakness, or spiritual flabbiness diminishes the welcome the angel of sleep, God's most blessed angel, deserves!

PART TWO

personal dreaming

the first stage

I hope you enjoyed both my story and the Dreamer's Creation Story. The next section, the next love letter, is about you. I want to go more deeply into the kinds of dreams that encourage you to wake up.

Everyone experiences first-stage dreaming throughout their lives. Only the rarest of beings totally outgrows it. Most of us continue to need wake-up calls and psychological tune-ups throughout our lives. However, first-stage dreaming usually becomes slightly less common as we reach other stages of spiritual development.

I call first-stage dreaming "personal" dreaming because the dream stories of this stage are about the dreamer's personality. They point to issues the dreamer has in his or her life. They orbit around the habits and tendencies of the dreamer's waking reality.

Perhaps I could have called this stage "dreaming the human condition." In the first chapters of this book we discussed how the dreamer's spiritual growth is reflected in, informed by, and evoked by his or her dreaming. We could also say that the evolutionary journey of each person is tracked and mapped by the dreaming. In the beginning of our awakening we are plagued with concerns, confusions, internal and external splits of consciousness, and genuine puzzlement as to what "life" is all about. As soon as we begin to truly hear the wake-up call that first-stage dreaming creates, the dreams show us the work we need to do!

Shame, guilt, emotional numbness, and self-directed hatred usually appear in one form or another in the adult human's psyche. They are the result of life's many confusing experiences, given to us by parents, relatives, siblings, schoolteachers, religious teachers, and childhood peers. Our first spiritual task is to investigate those feelings, bring them to awareness, and clear them from our unconscious system. They are the web of the misunderstandings and untruths we've been told about ourselves and our society, and they literally hinder our movement in spiritual consciousness. We simply cannot hold our heads high and move toward true compassion and deep service to life if we are wearing the mantle of personal shame, guilt, or hatred.

First-stage personal dreaming is a most reliable source of deep insight into the emotional shackles we bear. Dream stories about our own participation in the cruelty and depravity of the collective human condition force us to look at the dark mirrors of the parts of us that are denied and disenfranchised, the parts of us that are cruel and depraved. Some of our dream stories are ruthless and relentless in pointing these things out. These aspects of ourselves will not stop acting out until we embrace them, love them, become them, and then become the compassionate potential within them.

Now, don't misunderstand what I am saying. There's nothing wrong with being human, nothing *inherently* wrong, at least. In fact, incorporating the unity consciousness we experience in the dreaming with the dualistic, paradoxical nature of the everyday world *is* our blessing and our "work." I do not want to suggest that we need to become anything other than our most actualized human selves. And that actualization is the goal of the spiritual journey.

In the everyday human world, we experience what I call duality consciousness, and what some theologians call "I and thou" consciousness. We see ourselves as separate entities who interact with other separate entities. In dreaming, however, we transcend that separation and encounter a unity consciousness in which we realize that we are interconnected with everything and everyone. Our minds may write the dream stories from the dualistic perspective, especially if we are in first-stage dreaming, but the experience in the Void is an experience of unity. Eventually, as we walk the path of the spiritual practitioner with more regularity and familiarity, duality consciousness fades and unity consciousness becomes our dominant state of mind. Beginning that shift is the goal of first-stage dreaming.

THE PITFALL

The danger of first-stage dreaming is that as you begin to see yourself more clearly, you become even more depressed or self-hating. Because so many first-stage dreams persist in pointing out what needs to be changed or what needs to be transformed, you may begin to feel discouraged, as if the job is too overwhelming. It may feel too hard to be an awakened human. Indeed, depression is our greatest enemy. If the false self keeps the personality operating at a diminished capacity, spiritual growth is virtually impossible. Being human becomes an experience of being broken, sinful, and hopeless. These are the lies of the false self.

THE SAFETY NET

Every level of dreaming and spiritual growth has pitfalls; every level has a safety net. The safety net on every level is spiritual practice. Dreaming is a spiritual practice in and of itself. However, if you do not also augment that practice with a waking practice, you will not be able to resist the temptations to fail, temptations that come in different forms and in every level and every stage of dreaming. You must adopt a practice that constantly and consistently clears your mind, emotions, and physical body of nonbeneficial energies. It is part of the human's life to be tempted to fail, and it is important to see those temptations for what they are and to transcend them.

I don't in any way encourage you to turn from your humanness, to deny it, to even transform it into anything else. I do encourage you to *be* it so fully and completely that it delivers to you all the richness and glory and fullness and beauty that the divine Creator intended you to experience. Ridding yourself of the shoulden and lies, the neuroses and pathologies, the narcissism and grandiosity of the human condition in no way negates the fact that you are human. Correcting your errors amplifies and augments the truth that has been diminished and belittled through your narrow misunderstandings.

If you fully appreciate the stories of the dreamtime, personal dreaming becomes your "Friend." I experience this Friend as the cosmic being who shows me all my potential, and all the potential of the universe, through my dreams. Rumi's experience of the Friend is that he or she will not stop pestering and chasing you until you are completely swallowed by your own divine nature. Your personal dreaming will also not stop until you are ensnared, enveloped, ensnarled, and inspired to move toward your most authentic expression of self.

mundane dreams

Sometimes a cigar is just a cigar.

~Sigmund Freud[1]

THE FIRST LEVEL OF PERSONAL DREAMING, WHICH I CALL MUNDANE dreaming, is unfortunately predominant in Western societies. If you don't remember your dreams, if you have dreams that simply replay or rearrange the events of the day, if you have dreams that anticipate the events of the day to come, or if you have dreams that solve problems in your life that you haven't had time to solve while awake, you're most likely dreaming on the level of your most mundane self.

The phrase *mundane dreaming* may sound so boring that one doesn't want to examine the dreams at all. Women often will come to dream circle and say, "I have nothing to share tonight. All my dreams have been mundane lately." While it is true that these are not the most exciting and profound dreams, they do have value on several levels, and they are an undeniably important part of the dreamer's path.

WHY DON'T I REMEMBER MY DREAMS?

As I've traveled around the country holding dream circles, teaching about dreaming, and talking with people about their dreams, the one question I hear most often is "Why don't I remember my dreams?" There are several possible answers, but the one that draws the most "ahas" is "You're too tired." Almost every time I say that to someone, their countenance changes from one of sincere and open questioning sprinkled with genuine concern about themselves, to one of realizing a very deep truth about their lives.

Mundane dreaming occurs when the dreamer is too tired. Recent studies show that approximately 95 percent of all adult Americans are sleep-deprived. Our fast-paced, high-stress work ethic has resulted in a whole society of people who desperately need rest but don't take the time to get it.

In addition, the spiritual systems of the West augment the problem by not teaching the importance of spiritual practices like meditation and retreat. As a result, sleeping and dreaming time is often spent desperately trying to regenerate the body and solve the problems of waking reality. The journey of the dreamtime gets hijacked by a fatigued body and an overly stressed mind. This sad circumstance creates a society in which almost everyone is sleepwalking. The events on the front page of the paper and on the eleven o'clock news mirror the chaotic state of our exhaustion.

When we drift into the cosmic soup of all potential at the onset of sleep, our physical condition certainly makes itself known. After all, one of the main purposes of sleep is physical regeneration. Dreaming in the Void involves direct perception of the energy of the unseen realm. That perception isn't mental, it's physical. We absorb dreams through the physical body, most specifically through the fibers of our womb chakra.

> *Matter is never at rest, and reason never rests until it is filled with everything that is within its potential.*
> —Meister Eckhart[2]

As I mentioned earlier, shamans tell us (and I have seen this in my own meditations) that when we go to sleep, we literally connect to the Void through these energetic filaments in our lower abdomen. If the physical body is under enormous stress and is being pushed to its outer limits, the need to rest during sleep rather than learn or grow takes primary importance.

I've often said that I may be the only person in America who is not sleep-deprived. Indeed, since I first "went down" with my bizarre mystical dreaming experiences in 1986, I've continued to require ten to twelve hours of sleep each day. If I don't get them at night, my body demands an afternoon nap. The rest of me gladly obliges, since I've convinced myself that sleeping is my work!

The human physical system is complex, beautiful, and enigmatic. And yet it is predictable and readable if one learns the vocabulary. It monitors itself in most precise ways. When the human body is too stressed, it sends out every alarm, every warning, every plea possible. One of those signals of crisis is that it cuts off dream memory. If you can't remember your dreams, make an attempt to get more rest. Take a vacation. Radically rearrange your lifestyle. If you can't remember your dreams, your body may be pleading for help.

The second possibility for why you're not remembering your dreams is that you're running from the Friend who is trying to awaken you. You know, it's far more frightening to self-actualize than it is to die! We pretend that death is our enemy, that dying is our primary fear, but in fact, realizing our potential terrifies us far more.

> You think you are earthly beings, but you have been kneaded from the Light of Certainty. You are the guardians of God's Light, so come, return to the root of the root of your own self.
>
> —Rumi[3]

If the Friend is after you in your dreaming spaces, it's because it's your time to wake up spiritually. The battle between your waking ego and your dreaming self may create such a schism that you simply cannot put words or images to it. If you are without a compassionate partner or teacher who legitimately understands the demands of a true spiritual awakening, you may simply be caught in a maze of unfathomable dreaming experiences.

Of course, there's another possibility. It's possible that there is no need for you to remember the dream because you *have become* the dream. It's possible that you are working on the fourth stage of dreaming, not the first. Which is it, my friend? Are you tired? Are you enlightened? You know the answer. If it's the latter, skip immediately to Chapter Sixteen.

DREAMING YESTERDAY AND TOMORROW

African shaman Malidoma Some once told me that the initiations in his village, and in most indigenous cultures, are designed to take the initiate to the very edges of his or her consciousness in order to shatter the limitations that person places on perceptual reality. Those rituals usually involve life-threatening situations, because only under extreme circumstances will most of us release our belief systems and operate from a deeper, more primordial connection with life. During such an experience, all kinds of hormonal and chemical juices are produced that place the body in an extreme state of alert and awaken the physical self to a mindfulness that extends beyond the mind. The purpose of such a ritual is to give the initiate an opportunity to learn and memorize the feeling of being outside typical human consciousness, or consensus reality. If the experience successfully shatters the initiate's comfortable boundaries, the elders of the community then gently assist him or her in processing and integrating the experience back into the ordinariness of daily life. Listening to the dreams of their student and watching their daily activities, the elders can determine the initiate's new perspective and help him or her reconstruct a healthy ego. Through this experience, the initiate is forever changed. He or she senses a physical, mental, and emotional expansion yet is able to operate in a healthy way within the community. The purpose of these initiations is to put each person in direct relationship with his or her soul's contract with life.

In those cultures that still practice tribal initiation, one may experience only one or two initiations in a lifetime. It may require years to completely understand and embody an experience like that. These initiations often reach the level we would call a mystical opening, for they change the initiate's perception and perspective altogether, and create a bridge between the ordinary world and the spirit world. One or two of these deeply authentic experiences in a lifetime is considered a lifetime's worth of work.

During our conversation, Malidoma expressed that one of the almost insurmountable problems of modernity, especially in Western culture, is that we are faced with life-threatening situations all day every day, and we have no communal and spiritual context to support us. We don't realize that getting on a freeway or walking across a busy intersection or boarding an airplane is an initiation-level experience, because we're literally dulled to the physical attentiveness required to navigate in our cities and in our world. We're asleep! We're unconscious of the truth of our state of being. We've overridden our instinctual responses to the extent that we don't realize the extreme, life-challenging nature of our daily activities.

In addition, we have no elders welcoming us back home from the freeway trip to the supermarket to help us to integrate the experience. Many times a day, we intentionally hurl ourselves into an arena of potential death, often with the people we love most (our children, spouses, friends) in tow, and call it normal. We ignore the hormones and chemicals that are coursing though our veins crying out for heightened awareness, and we override any instincts we may have for special mindfulness. We talk on the cell phone through all this! We're mad. We're out of our minds. We're absolutely insane. We have diminished what should and could be opportunities for mystical openings and made them mundane events to which we pay no special attention.

And yet we dream about them. In spite of the fact that most of us don't honor our dreaming, the dreaming doesn't betray us. It continues to keep us in touch with our deepest truths. Look through your dream journals and see what proportion of the dreams involve driving a car, walking across a busy city street, traveling on an airplane, or doing some other ordinary task in which your life is threatened. What are these dream symbols? More important, what is the energy that evoked these images?

Most of these dreams are mundane dreams in the sense that they are simply reflecting the most normal and routine activities of the previous or following day. However, the fact that you have them and remember them over and over and over is a profound event—a cry for attention. You're trying to remind yourself to treat your life more sacredly. In a sense, mundanity becomes your spiritual teacher through these dreams.

DREAMING UNDER STRESS AND FATIGUE

My teenage daughter, Sara, was enrolled in a high school in Los Angeles during the year that so many school shootings occurred. I was on a book tour and staying in a hotel in Boulder, Colorado, just a week after the Columbine shootings when I had the following dream:

Sara and I needed to make a quick escape from a school. There was shooting in the background. We hopped onto a motorcycle. I drove. We navigated the halls of the school. The front door was locked. We backtracked
and found a classroom with an external door. Lots of people were running
out of the school. There was extreme danger.

This is clearly a mundane dream. The images and ideas were drawn
directly from the experiences of the past few days. They were not particularly veiled or highly symbolic images—a cigar is just a cigar in
this case! I was worn out from traveling, and I was concerned for my
daughter's safety. I felt tight, drawn, restricted, diminished before bed
that night. There's nothing spectacular about this dream.

However, rather than discount the dream story as a mere extension
of the energy I took to bed with me (which it clearly was), I tried to remember and embody the energetic experience in the Void that invoked it. My physical condition during that night (one of stress and
fatigue) had certainly influenced the dream story profoundly. The
story warned me that it is indeed dangerous to be that tired. The message from myself to myself was that fatigue attracts danger. Yet the
deeper energy of the dream provided an escape—clarity to get out
of that belief system (as represented by the school) must be found.
In other words, it was the belief system of the consensus reality that
was tiring me out as much as anything else. The consensus reality
at the time was one of fear, victimization, and grief. My story instructed me to escape from those restrictive halls into the light, into
the fresh air, into the open spaces, into a different way of thinking. Mundane dreams, like all personal dreams, will ask you to expand your belief systems if you listen deeply to the energy behind the
story.

Later that same year I was in Portland, Oregon. I had encountered
some very powerful dreamers on this trip, and had been deeply moved
by the support they gave me in my work. However, I was exhausted by
the stress of travel. My body does not tolerate flying well. The next
day I was scheduled for an early flight on a small plane, to be followed
by a two-hour drive in a van to reach my destination. My sleep was
restless. I saw the following dream:

> I was driving in a car in the Pacific Northwest with three other people. I felt tired and anxious. As we drove along I was deeply moved by the beauty of the landscape. Suddenly we drove over a small hill and began to descend into a valley. The beauty of the valley and its crystal clear lake were overwhelming. I said, "This is the whole journey! This is all the beauty I'll ever need." We drove across the lake on a hidden floating bridge. It was amazing to be driving on water.

Again, this is clearly a mundane dream, reflecting the stresses of the day before and the journey of the day to come, for indeed the drive revealed many beautiful spots, and the last bridge I crossed (to my great surprise) floated on the lake's surface. However, the dream story is not to be discounted, because the energy behind the dream is a truth-speaking energy. Dream-driving on water can only be an image that is evoked by a powerfully supportive energetic field that heals, restores, and moves us forward. The beauty of the awareness and consciousness of the dreamers I'd encountered on this journey was all I needed. My work, my travels, my horizontal dream movement was supported by this unseen bridge through the ocean of awareness—the crystal clear lake.

Now, in this case, it was not a consensus reality that was fatiguing and stressing me. It was, instead, my own lack of consciousness. I was in an initiation. I was hopping on and off planes, in and out of cars, into and out of life-threatening situations. When one is on an extended journey, it is no less an initiation than when one is in the tundra of Africa facing lions. However, I'd failed to hear and integrate the messages my body was giving me on this trip. I'd made it into a superficial experience by narrowing my perspective of it, and it was fatiguing me. I was dulled to the flow of my adrenaline, and I was unaware of the true depth of the support and energy I was receiving from the dreamers I'd met. The mundane dreaming will awaken you to the need to open and expand.

SOLVING PROBLEMS IN THE DREAM

There are so many stories of people solving problems in their dreams that it is almost too ordinary to talk about it. However, I will share a few amazing stories with you.

Mundane dreaming can provide answers to the questions of daily life. Most often, however, these kinds of answers don't occur in the dreams until you've exhausted yourself looking for them in the ordinary way. It's as if the dream realm finally realizes that you are going to totally deplete yourself if you don't find the answer, so it gives it to you. The late Willis Harman, one of the founders of the Institute of Noetic Sciences, researched many such dreaming serendipities—in these cases, dreams that changed not only the course of the dreamer's life but of all human life—and reported them in his book *Higher Creativity: Liberating the Unconscious for Breakthrough Insights*.

Niels Bohr, a world-renowned physicist, the undisputed grandfather of quantum physics, had spent years trying to create a model for studying the atom. After exhausting himself and jeopardizing his health in his search for the answer, he had a dream of a beautiful solar system with celestial bodies orbiting a central sun. This dream led to what's now called the Bohr model of atomic structure, with the electrons circling the nucleus. This discovery resulted in his winning a Nobel Prize.

Sir Fredrick Grant Banting had been struggling for years with the problem of treating diabetes. Years of laboratory research had eliminated many ideas, but no successful models emerged. He had almost given up when he had the dream that showed him a laboratory procedure for the mass creation of insulin. Many people have been saved and the quality of many lives has been changed as a result of this dream.

On the night before Easter Sunday in 1920, Otto Loewi, a physiologist, awoke from a dream with the answer to a question he'd been pondering on and off for seventeen years. He tells about this experience in great detail in his autobiography, *Perspectives in Biology and Medicine*. He had been trying to find a way to prove that the nervous system in the human body had a chemical component as well as an electrical one. He saw the answer in a dream. He woke up then and quickly jotted it down, feeling elated that he had finally discovered the answer to this long-deliberated question. However, when he tried to decipher his own handwriting the next morning, he could not read the note, and in fact he couldn't even remember what the dream had been about. He just remembered that it was important. The next night he had the same dream, and this time, rather than writing it down, he arose from his bed—at 3:00 A.M.—and went into his laboratory and performed the experiment on a frog. This dream led to the theory of the chemical transmission of nerves and resulted in his winning a Nobel Prize in 1936.

Elias Howe had worked for years trying to create a machine that could sew. The problem with such a machine was passing the needle through the material, thus pulling the thread through it. His answer actually came in a nightmare in which he was being tortured by some dark-skinned painted warriors who were apparently planning to kill him. In his terror, he noticed that the spear heads coming toward him had eye-shaped holes near their tips. He woke himself up from the hideous dream with the answer to his long-sought-after question. It is reported that he, like Loewi, got out of bed immediately and carved a rough prototype for the sewing machine needle with the hole at the "wrong" end. It's a little humorous that the story of this dream was so frightening—as if to say, wake up and get this or else! Maybe his dream enemies were tired of this problem and wanted to move on!

VERIFYING AND VALIDATING THE DREAM

Of course, the challenge with these types of dreams comes in trying to fully understand them. One could easily have discounted Howe's spear nightmare as "just a dream." It was necessary for him to recognize the value of the image of the spear with the hole in the end, and then apply the image to his problem. He had to open this letter from the soul, read it, decipher its meaning, and follow its instruction. I'm sure there are many such letters that remain unopened, or that are misinterpreted and discounted.

Because dreaming occurs outside the typical band of consciousness, but the memory of the dream story occurs within that band, it takes a certain skill to recognize the messages of dreams that are relatively mundane. That is one of the other values of mundane dreaming. In addition to asking you to expand your consciousness and broaden your parameters, mundane dreams give you practice in perceiving value, practice in creative thinking, and they are tools for understanding the realm of the imagination.

I could have, for example, simply ignored the dream I had in Boulder as an obvious result of the stress of the community blending with the fatigue of my own body. However, the side door in a classroom alerted me to the fact that the dream had an odd twist, something of value. Similarly, Howe could have ignored his nightmare. But since he had spent years looking for the place to put the hole in the needle, the hole in the spear alerted him to an important message in the dream. Loewi could have ignored the dream the second night, or just scrawled it down again, but having the same dream on two consecutive nights told him that there was something there that needed to be tested.

As dreamers, it is important for us to recognize the creative potential within our dreams—even within the most mundane and ordinary of them. Indeed, a part of the dreamer's path is to learn and grow within each stage of dreaming.

WARNING! DEMANDING A DREAM DOESN'T WORK

The issue around mundane dreams is, of course, that they don't all "mean" something or provide answers. When I was initially in my deep dreaming years and I considered myself ill, I was often given dreams of elaborate ceremonies or healing rituals. Some of them I tried to duplicate in my waking life, convinced that the dream story contained some magical pill that was going to cure me and send me back to work. I was wrong. The dreamer's mental state evokes certain aspects of the dreaming. In my desperation to get well I willfully demanded that the dreams heal me.

That, too, was a deep learning. One doesn't program, demand certain information from, or willfully use the dream. Some teachers and scientists do teach dream control, but those are systems that, ultimately, don't work for the spiritual benefit of the dreamer. If you demand a certain kind of dream, set the stage, ask for answers, do a specific dream ceremony or spell, you'll be given the dream you've asked for because it is your mind that writes the story. But the information will not necessarily be accurate, because your personal will has overridden the journey into the dimension of universal Truth.

Each circumstance I've described in which people received specific answers to questions came through the dream spontaneously. Each of these men had pondered and investigated the question for a long time. Men's dreaming is quite often goal-oriented. When a man (or the masculine energy of a woman) contemplates a question, the answer may come in a dream. However, the dreaming doesn't obey the laws of waking consciousness. It is an energetic experience, not a mental one. It's very important to understand this fundamental aspect of the dreaming because it's important not to treat dreaming like waking reality.

If you try to control the dreaming, you'll receive a mundane dream that points out your errors, flawed belief systems, erroneous thinking, and willful relationship to the Great Mystery. Now, as consciousness expands and you move into the other stages of dreaming, there are ways of incubating specific types of dreams. I will speak more about this in later chapters. In the first stage, however, it is literally impossible to "control" the dream and get accurate information or truthful images.

> The physical mind almost always interferes in the dream and gives its own version. It is only when there is a clear experience that it does not try to interfere.
>
> —Sri Aurobindo[4]

In addition to abstaining from attempts to control dreams, I always recommend that a dreamer try not to interpret his or her own dreaming. It's better to let the meaning of the dream unfold. Just as willfulness may skew the message of the dream, willfulness may also make you completely miss the information of the dream. I share my dreams with my circle, with my family, with my sisters. I listen carefully to the wisdom of those I trust, and I wait for the dream to reveal itself to me in waking reality. Especially in this first stage of dreaming, the personal ego is still highly involved and invested in being in charge. The safeguard for that is forming a circle of trusted dreamers with whom you share your dreams. Form your circle, create your sacred cave, and listen deeply to each other.

YOU DON'T OUTGROW MUNDANE DREAMING

Mundane dreaming is the first level of first-stage dreaming, and it comes to anyone at any time. Even dreamers who are capable of achieving fourth-stage (and beyond) dreaming will, from time to time, create a mundane dream story because of ordinary daily circumstances. Fatigue and stress affect us whether we're living a relatively low-key life or in the fast lane, whether we all but ignore our spiritual aspects or we're well disciplined in our spiritual practice. One doesn't "outgrow" mundane dreaming just because one has moved to the higher stages. The mundane dreaming is incorporated into the other stages. It comes less frequently, and the more sophisticated dreamer usually sees its intended message almost immediately, but it still may come!

FIVE

psychological dreams

*. . . during the night, when the conscious mind is
asleep, the heart is able to tell its story.*

~LLEWELLYN VAUGHAN-LEE[1]

I WANT TO START THIS CHAPTER BY MORE THOROUGHLY DISCUSSING
the unfolding levels of each stage of dreaming. The stages unfold
slowly, so that the dreamer has time to build the physical, emotional,
mental, and energetic bodies that he or she can fully contain the spiritual energies of each stage. These stages are deliberate, sequential,
and linear. A person can't stand on a stage that hasn't been built. Even
though, in the most esoteric
perspective, time doesn't exist
and everything "happens" simultaneously, from our ordinary
perspective, we must take one
step at a time, build one stage at
a time, and finish one part of our journey before we move to the next.

> The wine of divine grace is limitless:
> All limits come only from the faults of
> the cup.
>
> —Rumi[2]

If we don't proceed step by step, it would be like pouring wine into
a clay chalice that has been shaped but not fired. The raw, dry clay
would simply absorb the wine and crumble. In fact, if the clay had
been fired once, but not in a kiln hot enough to turn it to stone, the
vessel would still not hold the wine. This is often the case—clay gets
fired more than once to gradually take it to its strongest configuration. A partially fired vessel will absorb the wine, be stained by it, and
eventually crack. The chalice must be fired to its fullest potential, in
the right timing, if it is going to maintain its integrity when filled with

the wine. Clay's chemistry changes as it reaches different levels of dryness, as it goes through different firings, and as it is shaped and strengthened into a finished vessel.

Similarly, spiritual voyagers must build and fine-tune their personal vessels, making them strong enough to hold the light of Truth, making them courageous enough to look at the mirrors of illusion, and making them wise enough to stand on the solid, ethical ground of love. Each level of dreaming opens another opportunity for the dreamer to mature his or her vessel. Just as with the clay vessel, each stage of the work must come in its own timing, and must reach its most stable alchemical state before the next stage can be introduced.

This clay analogy of the process of spiritual unfolding is not mine. It's ancient. It's in the Bible, it's in all sorts of esoteric literature, it's in the oral traditions of many indigenous peoples. In her book *Centering in Pottery, Poetry, and in the Person*, the late M. C. Richards—potter, poet, and renowned author—shares her own process of spiritual unfolding by making use of this analogy. She speaks of the firing—the ordeal by fire—as a crisis of conscience. She states it this way:

> I think it is structural, this necessity of ordeal by fire. The physics of transformation require it. For structural changes in the moral form of a person are alchemical changes, producing alterations in pulse, breathing, and circulation. They are bodily changes. . . .[3]

As your mind expands through the purification of the fire, your physical body also changes. These changes allow you to vibrate to more and more subtle and sublime energies. Your dreams will reflect this new physiological state.

Human beings have been infused by fire and formed by fire.

—Hildegard of Bingen[4]

When your mind creates a dream story, it uses the images available to it based on your expansion of consciousness at the moment. If you haven't forged a spiritual vessel that can hold the fine wine of your own divinity, you'll create mundane dream stories that encourage you to "wake up" to the more subtle levels of the energy you're encountering in the blackness.

When you thoroughly appreciate and integrate one level of dreaming, your vessel stabilizes and solidifies in a way that allows an opening to the next level.

In this book we're walking through each of the levels *as if* each follows the one before in linear fashion. However, the work is more a spiral than a line—more like spheres within spheres than like a ladder.

PSYCHOLOGICAL DREAMING— DREAMING PURGATION

The second level of first-stage dreaming, psychological dreaming, is a far cry from the final firing of the dreamer's vessel. Instead, it is an early and very important step toward creating the container the dreamer needs. At this level the dreamer has heard the call to awaken, and has decided to answer that call by beginning a process of self-investigation. This leg of the journey usually requires the help of a mentor trained in psychology, therapy, or psychiatry. The human ego is rarely strong enough or courageous enough to authentically investigate itself without a trusted guide. I recommend finding a great therapist.

"Purgation," as used in Christian terminology, represents the phase of religious development in which one rids oneself of all unclean thoughts, emotions, and actions. Psychological dreams are purgation dreams. By the time we have reached adulthood most of us have unknowingly adopted so many flawed patterns, unclear thoughts, and out and out lies that we are spiritually toxic. We must be purified if we are to move forward on a spiritual journey. Psychological dreams help us do this.

Often, if we hear the call to awaken, we experience a period of ela-

> In a dream the Sheikh asked me, "Can you get up and give your place to someone else?" I thought . . . the dream meant that I should give my place to someone else who could benefit more from the Sheikh's presence. . . . That evening . . . the Sheikh said to me, "The real interpretation of your dream is this: you must forget yourself and 'give up your place' to the Supreme Reality." These words . . . marked the beginning of my spiritual evolution.
>
> —Lahiji[5]

tion. It feels so good to realize some of the wider and wilder possibilities of ourselves, and it feels so right to play in a broader arena. The crisis of conscience to which M. C. Richards refers has brought us to the kiln, ready to be fired and liberated. We feel energized by the first tastes of that psychological freedom, but not for long.

Soon we crash into our old patterns of behavior. We love to be comfortable, and we will go to great lengths to sustain it, even in the most hideous situations. Many times long-term prisoners and lifelong caged animals will remain inside the walls that are familiar to them, even if the door is open and the invitation to emerge is made. Deep psychological investigation is not comfortable. The only way one takes it on is if one's "comfortableness" becomes too painful to bear.

> *there is some shit I will not eat*
>
> ⁀E. E. CUMMINGS[6]

Sometimes we have to be blasted out of our familiar ways for this next level of stage one to "take." This funny quote from e. e. cummings is also tragic, in that so many people spend major portions of their lives in harmful situations. We unconsciously poison ourselves. I've spent many hours counseling clients who are afraid *not* to be victims. They simply cannot imagine what life would be if they weren't tossed around and beaten down by it. Their ego, formed in childhood, demands that they be "wrong" or "at fault" or "the peacemaker" or "the black sheep."

It's difficult to see the patterns of one's own ego, because one lives inside them. They're transparent from the inside. Often some sort of catastrophic event—a divorce, a death, an illness—is needed to make us realize that we have to draw that e. e. cummings line—to stop "eating" what's not good for us, and to look at and transform our damaging patterns.

Psychological dreams, then, become dreams of purgation to those ready to receive help. The dreams will mirror your waking behavioral and emotional patterns, and under the tutelage of a good counselor or therapist, you'll slowly make internal and external changes. You'll look at each lie you've woven into your system, unravel it, get to the truth, and move beyond the self-created cage.

THE SPLIT

The lies we live with create an internal split too severe to allow any expansion of consciousness or spiritual movement. What is that split? In one part of yourself, no matter how far you stray from it, and no matter how unconscious it becomes, you *know* that you are good, that you are divine, that you are a holy being, and that you are a participant in the creation of the world. Remember in the Dreamer's Creation Story we talked about how memory is part of the DNA that makes up every cell? Through that memory you have access to every level of being: from the initial bursting forth of consciousness 15 billion years ago, through the creation of the stars, the solar systems, the oceans, life on this planet, and your entire genetic lineage all the way back to early hominid. On that level of cellular memory you know your innate goodness—you know that you were born in blessing.

> *The more unencumbered you keep yourself, the more light and clarity of vision you will discover.*
>
> —Meister Eckhart[7]

On the psychological level of this lifetime, you've been presented with other possibilities—that you're broken, not divine, a victim, a sinner, a split personality, a betrayer. Because the psychological messages are more immediate, louder, and seem more "real," and because society reinforces them, you believe them. That creates a split between your conscious choices and your deep truth.

When I was in the throes of my profound dreaming time, I had a classic psychological dream. It's so emblematic of myself at the time that it is still painful to write about it:

> I was two people. One of me was leaning across a table or a couch, the other of me was shoving a double-edged sword up my anus through my torso.

Is that painful to read or what? How divided was I? How separated? This dream was clearly designed to wake me up and get me thinking about the dualistic aspects of my life. I woke up from that dream sweating. Mercifully, I immediately fell back to sleep and had the following dream:

I was practicing a martial art. As if my eyes were a special energy-sensitive camera outside my body, I could see the movements of my hands and feet leave a bluish neon pattern of light. It was the color of the Virgin Mary's garments. The movements were creating a definite gridwork. It seemed like a map of my energy field. It was incredibly beautiful.

These two dreams together seemed to be a picture for me of the choice I had to make. Would I live the split, or would I live within the divine virginal (unharmed) energy field that I knew to be mine? The split is too painful! The split cannot exist concurrently with a spiritual deepening. It has to be seen, recognized, embraced, loved, bridged, transformed, acknowledged, integrated, and owned. We have to wake up from the duality and live the Oneness. The second level of dreaming totally commits itself to that process.

WARNING: DO NOT STOP HERE!

In the last half of the twentieth century, most of the writing about dreams and dream work was limited to the psychological aspect of dreaming. For that reason I'll not attempt to make an exhaustive statement about how to work with psychological dreams. It's been covered. I do encourage you to find a good dream-oriented therapist, preferably one who also has a strong personal spiritual practice, and go for it! Discover yourself, look at your splits, experience your archetypal connections to the collective. Become all of yourself.

I also encourage you to find (or start) a dream circle so you can share some of your dreams with others. This dream circle needs to be a group of dreamers who meet regularly and are thoroughly dedicated to looking at dreams as if they were encouraging letters from the soul telling each member how "right" life is. The group is not to ignore the dark aspects of the dreams, but they must go beyond the typical psychological perspective. It's important to have this kind of balancing agent when you're doing every level of dream work, but especially when you are working on first-level dreaming. If you do not have a circle of skilled friends with whom to discuss your dreams, your mind will totally indulge itself in misinterpreting them!

There's a tendency to get stuck in this phase and at this level of dreaming. The ego loves to study itself, and as long as it can keep your mind (which writes the dream stories) ego-obsessed, it can continue for a lifetime creating dreams that you can interpret to be about your neuroses and pathologies. The tragic piece of this is that if you stay here—if you continue for years and years to see only the psychological aspect of your dreaming, and if you continue to allow your false self to be the designer of your spiritual growth—you will not advance. This is no joke.

If you go to a dream circle while you are in the therapeutic process, you may find that many of the dreams you and your therapist see as totally about you could be about someone else, or could be a dream you shared with many other people. This kind of experience urges you to move beyond yourself into a more collective understanding of life!

For example, in one dream circle a woman presented a dream about her first boyfriend. She was embarrassed, humiliated, and concerned by her seeming psychological connection to this old relationship. She and her therapist had discussed the many possibilities about why she was addicted to her first love. However, as the various women in dream circle commented, we learned that almost everyone there, myself included, had seen their first important love interest in their dreams *on that same night*. This could not have been strictly about the psychology of the dreamers. From that circle, we knew that although the characters were different in each woman's dream, the energetic experience for all of them must have been very similar, it must have reminded them of first love. That experience showed us that we must not be too me-oriented when looking at our dreams. We need the balance of the circle's experience to check ourselves and our navel-gazing tendencies.

One woman who had been in therapy for several years called and quizzed me ruthlessly about the dream circle. She had heard about it from a friend. She was brilliant, had a Ph.D. in comparative religion with several published books and a résumé packed with teaching positions at impressive universities. After I "passed the test," she decided to come once to experience the dream circle firsthand. She came back a second time. She came back consistently for three months. She quit her therapist and has missed very few dream circles in four years.

Why not stop here? There's an unfortunate trend in the West to confuse psychology and spirituality. In fact, deep psychological clean-up work is necessary before the mystical, spiritual path can authentically unfold for you. But the two are not to be confused with each other. Psychological investigation and psychological dreaming are a step, an early step, toward a true mystical, understanding of life's potentials.

EMOTION AND DREAMING—
A CRACK IN THE CLAY

Almost every dream has an emotional component. That's why it is so easy to get stuck in the psychological dream phase. It seems that there is a never-ending flow of the emotional river within each dreamer, and each emerging feeling appears to be worthy of deep investigation.

> *True compassion requires ridding one's self of self-importance, detaching from afflictive emotions, and achieving purity of heart.*
> —The Dalai Lama[8]

The emotional system of the human being is unique and complex. Every emotional response is multilayered. When we experience emotion, we are not only responding to what is in front of us in the present, we are also bringing up our entire personal history. Often any feeling is fraught with memories—subtle or gross imprints from the past.

When clay is drying, preparing itself for the ordeal of fire, it sometimes develops very subtle hairline cracks. The potter must ruthlessly search for every crack, because if he or she puts a cracked piece in the kiln, it is sure to shatter, possibly breaking nearby pieces. An unhealthy, unattended human emotional body is like a crack in our spiritual vessel. It creates an internal split that is deadly, both for us and for those near to us. If we "shatter" while journeying on the spiritual path, it's usually because there was an undetected flaw in the emotional system that was not addressed in the early stages.

When emotions appear in dreams, and they do in every stage and every level of dreaming, it is always important for the dreamer to examine the feeling with unbendable objectivity, as if he or she were the potter looking for a crack in the clay. However, it is a mistake to think that the emotion of the dream is the "meaning" of the dream.

Emotions in dreams are almost always our false ego self responding to the spiritual progress of our journey. For example, fear in the dream often indicates that when your mind wrote the story reflecting your leap into the darkness that night, it scared itself! The leap was so free that the ego felt a deathblow. Similarly, joy in the dream indicates that the ego is pleased with the journey's progress. Sometimes that's because the progress is going slowly enough to make the ego feel safe, but usually it's because there has been an integration of spirit and mind. When a dreamer views emotion in the dream as a communication between the false self and the soul, the attraction to staying stuck in psychological dreaming lessens.

To move beyond first-stage dreaming, the dreamer must mature his or her emotional body through purification. You must be courageous enough to eliminate attachment to your personal history. This is a formidable task. It requires almost superhuman strength and discipline. However, it is a *must do*. The motivation is clear: If you are attached to your personal history, you cannot possibly see yourself clearly. If you view the world through eyes that are clouded with emotional sludge, you cannot possibly see the world clearly.

Start with therapy (which helps identify the issues), but eventually the work is finished through spiritual practice. Whatever form of practice you choose, if you're devoted and determined, you will accomplish your task. Buddhism and other mystical schools offer some marvelous practices for clearing emotions. I use a technique similar to one taught in Carlos Castaneda's books called recapitulation. Recapitulation requires a daily cleansing of the emotional body by pulling my emotional attachment to the outer world back into myself. In this way I have all my emotional energy available to me, ready to be authentically responsive rather than historically reactive to every moment.

As a dreamer, I must develop compassion: compassion toward myself, compassion toward the other beings in my life, compassion toward the world. True compassion can only exist in the emotionally mature being. Immature "compassion" is sentimentalism and attachment. Real compassion requires nonattachment; nonattachment requires a mature emotional system. As the Dalai Lama says, compassion requires freedom from afflictive emotions!

JUDGMENT DREAMS—
THE LESSON OF COMPASSION

Some of the types of dreams that come up in dream circle ask the dreamer to investigate his or her personal internal splits. I am especially interested in dreams where the dreamer projects judgment into the story.

Here's an example from Carlene, a woman in my dream circle who takes her spiritual work very seriously:

> I was sitting on the floor in a circle at an ashram attending some sort of spiritual ceremony. One woman spoke of how she had left her husband for J. (the guru of this ashram). He seemed very proud of himself for "healing" this woman and bringing her to true love. I was astonished and wanted to scream out that he was unethical and not a teacher but a horny old man.
>
> Another woman then began to speak of how she had also changed her whole life for J.: quit her job, moved closer to the ashram, etc. Again, he was so pleased with what she had done. She announced that she would marry him.
>
> Then an announcement was made that J. would marry four women that afternoon in a large ceremony. I was absolutely enraged that this kind of unethical behavior was happening and no one was stopping it. Everyone else seemed happy.

In waking reality, the problem of spiritual teachers who act inappropriately toward their students, particularly sexually, is rampant.

The dream story, however, is quite a different matter. Just as biological rules are different in dreamspaces, just as gravitational laws are relaxed in dreamscapes, just as movement in time and space take on unusual relativity in dreamland, so do moral and ethical rules change when one creates a dream story.

In the waking reality, Carlene knew this guru, and he had indeed been accused of sexual improprieties with some of his female students. Carlene's (possibly justified) anger at him spilled into a dream story, blurring the deeper message. The women in dream circle spoke to her of the possible information coming through this dream: the power of marrying or merging oneself with the four directions or the four dimensions; the beauty of love's power to transform people; the cooperative and joyous nature of a true spiritual community; the profound joy a teacher has when his students find happiness and peace within themselves.

While Carlene is usually compassionate and has a pure heart, her disappointment in this guru's behavior had smothered her ability to move forward. The dream told her to lift her judgments and carry on. It wasn't telling her to condone inappropriate behavior. In fact, it was telling her to nip her own inappropriate attitudes in the bud.

Judgment dreams can come in reverse form, too. For example, Lauren was ashamed of herself when she woke up.

I dreamed I was marrying a doctor. I was quite happy with the whole plan, dancing around and singing. I was busily making romantic wedding arrangements.

Lauren is happily married with two lovely children in her waking reality. When she awakened from this dream, she felt guilty. She felt as if she had been cheating on her husband. In fact, no thought or memory of her husband and children had been present in her dream. She wondered whether she had some unconscious desire to abandon them. Dream circle helped her realize that this dream wasn't about betrayal or cheating. This dream was about union and healing. It was about the joy of experiencing the sacred marriage between the divine feminine and the healer. It wasn't about having an affair. It was about the energy and vibration involved in preparation for creating a healing ceremony. The postdream guilt was the problem, not the dream story itself.

In both of these cases, it would be important for the dreamer to be either in a circle of compassionate and well-schooled dreamers, or to be with a therapist who had a strong spiritual understanding of dreaming potential. If left to their own devices, the dreamers would have stayed mired in their judgments: Carlene in her judgment projected outwards, Lauren in her judgment directed toward herself. In neither case did the dreamer (alone) remember to search for the energy behind the story to find the dynamic in Truth that evoked it.

DREAMING BEHIND THE DENSEST VEILS

Many of us inherit psychological wounds that create internal splits. The sins of the father visited on the children, so to speak, often hamper us, and we don't even know it. However, if we become skilled at reading the psychology of first-stage dreams, we may be able to identify these issues.

Sara, a forty-three-year-old writer and long-time dream circle member, shared the following dream:

> I noticed I had a zipper in my stomach. It went from my sternum to my navel. I asked my mother, "Why do I have this zipper?" She said, "Oh, we're all born with zippers, dear." I said, "You don't have one." She showed me her scar saying, "I had mine removed by a cosmetic surgeon."
>
> My dad came out of the bathroom wearing his boxers. I asked him why I had this f— zipper. He laughed because I'd used the "f" word. He didn't have a zipper. He just walked off laughing.
>
> Then I remembered Scott (my lover) doesn't have a zipper either. Maybe, since he's younger, the cosmetic surgery techniques were better and so I just couldn't see his scar.
>
> I felt violated and repulsed. I felt they'd done something horrible to me and that I was never going to be able to have children as a result.
>
> I looked closely. The skin was flapped over the metal part of the zipper, just like it would be on a dress, so externally the line looked like a dolphin's slit.

This dream provides a profound image. The opening in Sara's torso repulsed and scared her. She truly felt that if she unzipped, her guts would fall out. She didn't consciously know the exact nature of this wound, but it felt dirty, sexual, resulting, possibly, in infertility.

Dream circle pointed out to Sara that an opening of this sort provides direct access to the innermost core, the solar plexus, and enables the carrier to bare her guts.

Indeed, when we carry unnamed and unnameable psychological wounds, we do feel horribly vulnerable. We do feel that to look into them would be life threatening, that our guts could spill out resulting in literal death. The psychological process is not comfortable. Most of us would rather just zip up our mouths or our brains.

However, when we discover the zipper, it's darn near impossible to forget about it. When our dreaming Friend presents us with the image that simultaneously opens a potentially painful story, and offers a healing of magnificent proportions, we're hooked. We now must choose whether to allow this injury to be an opening to the heart, to the healing not only for ourselves but also for our genetic lineage both past and future. Our other choice, of course, is to take Sara's mother's route and have the thing "cosmetically" removed. We can use good old-fashioned denial, we can use New Age "see only the light" super-ficiality, we can have a stiff upper lip.

Sara, of course, is choosing to open the zipper. How do we know that? Because the last image of the dream takes her outside her family and her personal history. She sees herself as a dolphin. Dolphins leap and play and give birth and dance and give joy to those fortunate enough to see them. Sara had been swimming with the dolphins just a few months before she was given this dream image. During that trip, she had (as do most people who swim with dolphins) a profound emotional purification. The energy of the dolphins will heal Sara's zipper, will put love there rather than scar tissue, and will help her open up and spill out her guts, only to find the valuable pearl of her innermost core.

PAST LIFE DREAMS?

There's another category of dreams that, for lack of a better term, I call past life dreams. I don't know, of course, if they are actually recall from past lives, but these dream stories are staged in eras different from our own. They are like little plays. In the dream story, the dreamer is either witnessing an event seemingly from a distant past, or is playing a character from a different historical time. After studying

hundreds of these types of dreams and discussing them with my circles, I talk about them as if they were past life memories. They speak
to an inner split that may be just on the verge of our understanding—
not veiled, as the genetic scars like Sara's, but also not quite reachable
by normal thinking processes.

These dream stories tend to come in one of two forms. First, they
may be a gift to the dreamer, out of the otherwise inaccessible realm
of deep memory, explaining something about a relationship that exists
in the present. In other words, let's say in the Void, the dreamer encountered a vibration that "felt like" a specific person he or she knows.
However, because the feeling was vague, or can't be well represented
by modern images, which stem from the dreamer's present relationship with this person, the dreamer's mind couches the story in a past
era. This may be an actual event that happened in another lifetime between the dreamer and the dreamed, or it may just be that it was better framed in another time. Here's one of my dreams of this type:

> I was a gentlewoman in the Old South. A man with a whip came to take
> my most beloved slave. She had belonged to my late grandfather. The man
> with the whip was taking her as last payment of my grandfather's debt.
> She was going willingly and graciously. I used all my southern belle charm,
> taking the man's arm as we ambled toward the buggy. I assured him that
> there would be no need to use the whip. He agreed that she seemed intel-
> ligent and agreeable. As I hugged her good-bye, I whispered in her ear that
> if it took forever, I would buy her freedom.

The woman in this dream reminded me vaguely of a friend in this
lifetime. The man reminded me of her brother-in-law, her husband's
brother. In fact, I had played an important role in her "freedom" (if
you count spiritual freedom) in this lifetime. And, indeed, there was a
dynamic between her and her brother-in-law that required some
working out and some boundaries. This dream gave me a peek either
into a past life relationship between the three of us, or at least into
an old-fashioned dynamic or attitude that may exist within and between us.

The women in my circle also pointed out that this may be a dream
story showing me something about my work. I have felt an undeniable

call toward working primarily with women. And of course, the first step of that work was freeing myself from my own slave mentality, a mentality that many women carry unconsciously. We've been in servitude for thousands of years. From a psychological perspective, this dream reminded me of my commitment, one that is older than just this lifetime, to my freedom, to my friend's freedom, to the freedom of all men and women. The man in this dream was not bad. He was simply mistaken. He believed in and perpetuated slavery. In the Void that night, I clearly encountered the very subtle energies of the enslaved mind, the mind that believes it is right, no matter how outrageously wrong its thinking. That's the limited mind about which Outward Bound Man warned me!

The second possibility for these past life and historical dream stories is that they give the dreamer the opportunity to simply take a walk in history, bearing witness, remembering. It is during this first stage of dreaming that we learn to simply witness, an important spiritual lesson. The witness doesn't change anything. When a clear witness is present in our dreaming, it indicates that we have reached an ability to understand—to stand under—what we know. We typically discount the value of the witness, both in our waking and our sleeping realities, when in fact, the ability to simply see something, and to see it in the dimension of Truth, liberates us from our flawed and opinionated minds.

In our egotistical desire to make every dream a psychological statement about ourselves, we've completely trampled the "dream witness" program. Some dream interpretation systems teach us to view every object in the dream as aspects of ourselves. I've met people who have practiced this kind of gestalt work and have ended up being even more self-indulgent and narcissistic. I suggest that at the first level of dreaming, these witness dreams ideally serve the opposite purpose. They come to remind us that every dream is *not* about us and our psychological process. They remind us that it may be time to expand our vision beyond our own navel. Some dreams are purely witness dreams. Sometimes we simply go into the darkness and practice beholding. Sometimes it's that simple, that delightful. These dreams address an inner split that forms as a result of our being too narcissistic. These dreams say to the ego, "Take a break." They are given to the dreamer to remind him or her to practice seeing things clearly. Often these witness dreams are staged in ancient times to call attention to their nonpersonal nature.

Now, pay attention to this next dream. I'm going to present it in three different places in the book to demonstrate how a dreamer of third- and fourth-level dreams can experience multiple-level dreaming.

This dream came on the full moon in February 2000. The moon was void of course that night.

> I am in a Roman city thousands of years ago and simultaneously at this time. Robert is with me, along with other friends in the dream. The stone streets, buildings, public baths are all sepia brown, and the images I see are as well.
>
> I move back and forth in this dream, between being in and among the images of the scene, and being outside of it, seeing it on a sepia-colored blueprint of the city.

Jeanne, the dreamer, simply witnessed this scene. There was nothing in this scene that called her to do anything other than to *see*. This dream demonstrated to Jeanne that she has accomplished the task of stilling the ego. She is a purposeful and conscious dream witness. Jeanne's partner, Robert, and several friends are with her in this dream story as support, as fellow voyagers. When Jeanne was in the blackness, the experience that evoked this story, she must have felt supported, safe, accompanied on a journey in consciousness. This journey didn't need to "mean" anything. It was an exercise in *seeing*. We'll come back to this journey in a later chapter.

THIS WORK IS REAL

In the last decades of the twentieth century, psychological work gained a respected and honored position. There are, however, still remnants of an old school of thought that banishes psychology to the realms of the not real, the shameful. Some people still think that the need for psychological work shows mental weakness and moral defects.

Psychological work is real, it is beneficial, and it is necessary for the development of our potential.

> *The processes of psychological integration and purification create an uncontaminated inner space within which the wayfarer can come to know ... the deep mysteries of the heart.*
>
> —Llewellyn Vaughan-Lee[9]

The result of deep psychological work—indeed, the result of the psychological level of first-stage dreaming—is that the vessel begins to forge itself! It becomes strong without the inner splits that make it crack, without the lies that tear at the fiber of being, without the crises of conscience that paralyze the journey. Psychological dreams, gifts from the Friend, letters from the level of soul, escort you through this level of dreaming.

SIX

lucid dreams

*. . . waking up in dreams and sleep is a metaphor for waking up
to the equally illusory nature of everyday reality. In fact . . .
in sleep, in dreams, one comes closer to understanding the
nature of reality than in waking consciousness.*

~SERINITY YOUNG[1]

AT THIS POINT, DESCRIBING THE LEVELS OF DREAMING BECOMES EVEN
more challenging. A dreamer can become lucid (can wake up yet stay
in the dream) in any stage and on any level of dreaming. In fact, the
more sophisticated one becomes as a dreamer, the more often he or
she will be aware of the dreaming process as it occurs. However, lucid dreams are a part of first-stage dreaming, because it is at this point in the spiritual

> *Our truest life is when we are in
> dreams awake.*
>
> —Henry David Thoreau[2]

process that the psychological structure of the dreamer begins to
ripen, and the dreamer's "skill" starts to be tested.

The word *lucid* is rooted in the same Latin word as light—*lucere*.
The word *lucidity* typically refers to transparent or clear perception.
The term *lucid dreaming* means that the dreamer becomes aware (clear)
that he or she is dreaming. Prior to this we've talked about how the
dreamer experiences the energy in the blackness, and then later the
mind creates the dream story that the dreamer remembers when he or
she awakens. During a lucid dream the dreamer's ordinary awareness
"wakes up" while the mind is writing the dream story. Because the
dreamer stays in the dream (the physical body is still asleep), he or she
can actively and consciously participate in writing the story.

83

In the beginning, lucidity comes without warning and without the dreamer's overt participation. It just comes. You suddenly realize you are dreaming! It's liberating, interesting, energizing. In later stages of the dreamer's path you may learn to awaken yourself. And in the latest stages, you will simply be lucid (clearly perceiving the true nature of reality) all the time, in the dreams as well as in waking. For now, though, let's discuss what happens when one suddenly and involuntarily becomes lucid while asleep.

When the dreamer wakes up within the dream, he or she has literally unlimited possibility of movement. We already know that we have the ability to do all kinds of "impossible" things in our dreams. When we can do those "impossible" things while being fully aware of that doing, then the potential for spiritual growth is amplified. However, with that nearly unlimited potential comes potential for extreme danger.

BEWARE! CONTROL FREAK AWAKE!

First, let's look at the possible danger, then we'll look at some of the positive potentials that lucid dreaming brings. The danger involves the personal ego of the dreamer, which is why lucid dreaming is considered a part of personal dreaming. When you wake up in the dream, there is a strong temptation to "take control" of the dream story. In other words, not only does your awareness awaken, but your ego also awakens. The danger is that lucidity will simply become another tool of the false self, another opportunity for the ego to flex its muscles. Why is that dangerous? Because it can prevent any and all further spiritual development.

Many teachers and sleep researchers coach dreamers to use lucidity as an opportunity to take control. This is dangerous for people who are relatively inexperienced on the spiritual path. It leads to a false sense of power, and it allows the ego to control any further development. In other words, if the limited self, the small-minded self, can keep the attention of the dreamer focused on exciting things like flying or having outrageous dream sex, the attention to spiritual growth will be diffused.

The *false self* is a term that is interchangeable with the word *ego*, and is for me a preferable term because it is self-defining. The false self is afraid at this stage of spiritual expansion. It feels out of control. It feels a little like it's dying. It has been "exposed" during the psychological work as being false and not fully representing the authentic wholeness of the dreamer. It develops a psychology of its own at this point, and begins fighting for its very existence. The false self has no way of knowing the magnificence of the true self, nor can it know the possibilities of real power (power that is not harnessed by fear), so, afraid of change, it puts all its energy behind maintaining the status quo. Unless you are an advanced spiritual practitioner, I can't stress strongly enough how important it is *not* to try to grasp control of the dreaming at this stage.

Instead, I encourage you to use lucid dreaming as part of your practice. This phase is a test! It's a test of the dreamer's ability to surrender personal will. It's a test of the dreamer's sincere desire for spiritual growth. It's a test of the dreamer's ability to relinquish control to a design greater than he or she can create.

PRACTICE BEING AWAKE

Indeed, lucid dreaming is part of your spiritual practice. It is practice at being awake at all times. It gives the dreamer the opportunity to truly imprint and remember that all of perceptual reality has dream qualities. How we perceive and what we perceive are determined by our minds. While that fact is easy to forget in normal awareness, we know it to be true in the deepest levels of our consciousness. In typical waking circumstances, it appears that we objectively witness whatever happens in life. We believe that we have no real input into what happens, but that we do have some level of control over how we respond to what happens. However, when we wake up in the dream, we know that we're participating in creating what we perceive and how we perceive it. We can make shifts in perception, slight or great, and see the effects of our shifts. It's much easier to actually comprehend the illusionary nature of all reality when we're dreaming. As Serenity Young said in *Dreaming in the Lotus*, "in dreams, one comes closer to understanding the nature of reality than in waking consciousness."

Lynette, my friend and dreaming sister, is wise enough to let a lucid dream take its own course. She shared this one with me.

In the dream I saw a door that caught my attention. I became lucid. It was incredible because the physical sensations were so extreme and acute. I knew I had to open the door because I knew that a lucid dream held such fascinating potential.

I remember consciously moving my arm and hand. I was struck by the sharp awareness of physically and mentally opening a door. It's hard to describe.

On the other side of the door the room was moving. It was variegated shades of pulsating blue, and I saw visions of people and events unfold out of the color and then enfold back into the pulsations of color. This wasn't happening sequentially, but like waves. I was simply fascinated.

By allowing the dream to unfold and enfold in its own timing, Lynette simply practiced being awake. A less evolved person might have leapt into one of those scenes and become the central character. Lynette, instead, allowed herself to witness the illusory nature of perception. This dream experience sticks with her in her waking reality now. She sees the unfolding and enfolding of the ordinary world and is secure enough not to grasp control of events.

PRACTICE CHANGING YOUR PATTERNS

In the last chapter we spoke of how psychological work with a good therapist can help the dreamer look at his or her patterns and change the ones that are not beneficial. Lucid dreaming offers that possibility, too. In fact, changing the patterns through lucid dreaming is even more efficient and more powerful than changing them through the tedious work of psychotherapy.

In *The Tibetan Yogas of Dream and Sleep*, author Tenzin Wangyal Rinpoche discusses the Buddhist belief about lucid dreams. The Buddhist practice known as "dream yoga" is primarily focused on lucidity. He states: "Dream yoga . . . is used to train the mind to react differently to experience, resulting in new karmic traces. . . . It is not about force, about the consciousness acting imperially to oppress the unconscious. Dream yoga relies upon increased awareness and insight to allow us to make positive choices in life."[3] In other words, dream yoga uses lucidity to broaden the awareness and change the programming of the dreamer's waking actions!

This idea offers us as dreamers an amazing technique of spiritual practice through dreaming. Often, during my intense dreaming days of the late 1980s, I knew I was dreaming. In fact, when one of the teachers showed up in the dream, I'd say to myself, "Okay, here we go to the cave again!" I was well schooled in the power of the practice of allowing the dream to unweave my patterns.

It is the mind, usually the unconscious mind, that writes the dream story. That's partially why the images are so often obscure and unclear. The goal of lucid dreaming is to wake up during the writing of the dream story, to observe our "typical" reactions (patterns) to situations in the dream stories, and then to change them slightly or let them unfold differently as we use our conscious mind to edit the story. Then it follows that we will also learn to do that in waking reality. It is also out of the unconscious mind that our waking emotional patterns and behaviors emerge. Lucid dreaming is practice in communication between the mature, clearly perceiving self, and the immature, less clear, or falsely perceiving self.

> The sleep consciousness can be effectively dealt with only when the waking mind has made a certain amount of progress.
>
> —Sri Aurobindo[4]

Judy came to me through a recommendation. In our first meeting she asked me to help her stop dreaming. Most of her dreams were nightmares, and more often than not she awakened in the middle of the night almost paralyzed with fear. We also discovered that the same fear often comes in her waking reality. When she first started coming to dream circle, she believed that something very dark inside herself was the source of this fear. Through the circle she learned some techniques for redreaming fear (this occurs when one goes on an imaginary journey into a dream while awake and changes the dream slightly). Eventually, she began to experience lucidity in dreaming, and the circle taught her how to let the dream unfold differently. This dream marked a turning for Judy.

I'm rock climbing with Pam and a bunch of others. It keeps getting harder and harder as we climb steep rocks. We get to this one that is literally a wall, straight up and down. Everyone else is too scared to approach it. I go little by little, eyes closed because I want to get up it without seeing the far fall downward.

Finally I reach the edge. My arm hooks firmly onto the ledge and I am secure. I wedge myself in so I can lift the others up easily. Then I become afraid to move again or to climb further. I tell Pam.

Suddenly, I become lucid and realize I'm in the same familiar fear pattern again. Pam and I somehow shift into a hotel room. I know that recognizing the fear pattern shifted us, although I'm still holding on to the rocks in the room. I've popped into another dimension. I finally release the rocks. Pam and I are amazed because we don't have to go back down the mountain or back to the rocks. I enjoy the safety of the room.

I ask her if she will come for Shabbat.

Judy didn't "take control" of this dream and will herself to fly off the rock to safety. She simply recognized the pattern, and that authentic seeing transformed the dream. She allowed it to unfold in a new way—popping into a new dimension.

Then she did the most magical and transformational thing one can do in a dream. She honored it by asking Pam, her climbing/transforming partner, to come to a holy meal. She honored the shift by bringing it to the altar of thanksgiving.

This was not the beginning of Judy's spiritual transformation. Indeed, this dream came several years after she had made her deep commitment to the spiritual path. It also doesn't mark the end of her spiritual journey. But it did imprint and distinguish a decided change in her dreaming and in her waking relationship to fear. She accomplished, in this one dream, a profound shift in a lifelong pattern.

I'VE NEVER HAD A DREAM THAT WASN'T A NIGHTMARE

After the first class of a seminar I was teaching in Seattle, a woman approached me in tears. She confided to me that she'd never had (or at least remembered) a dream that wasn't a nightmare. She'd worked very hard to teach herself to block memory of her dreams, because they were so frightening. She was afraid to go to sleep because of them. My heart broke for this beautiful mother of two young children. I thought, "She's sleep deprived enough as it is without the dreams making it worse!"

Nightmares are dream stories that are primarily driven by a sense of fear or horror. When nightmares become lucid dreams they are, I think, among the most powerful dream stories we create, simply because they offer unlimited potential to transform patterns. And yet they also offer the possibility for big trouble! It's tempting in a lucid nightmare to become a superhero and just kill or destroy or demolish the image that is "creating" the fear. This is a time when it's very important for the dreamer to be working from a most impeccable spiritual groundwork. It is not the image that is creating the fear; it is a pattern of reaction the dreamer has developed because of some aspect of his or her personal history. To make meaningful change, the pattern must be addressed, not the dream image.

To become the superhero is to allow the personal ego to take control of the dream. That may work for children as a tool to help them stop having nightmares. It does not serve a spiritual practitioner. It's just another way of avoiding the truth of the energy behind the fear. It's important, when one becomes lucid in a nightmare, to consciously go into the energy that the mind interprets as fearful. It's important to get to the actual energetic experience that is evoking the fearful images. Within the dreamer's lucidity he or she can see the truth behind the energy and dispel the fear.

One possibility is that the fear is rooted in the physical body of the dreamer. There may be aspects of the dreamer's personal history of abuse, trauma, or molestation that are imprinted in the dreamer's body and get activated under certain circumstances in the dreamtime. In other words, when our dream fibers uncoil themselves and connect with the source, sometimes those fibers are rooted in places in the body that also hold fear. If that's the case, the awake and skilled dreamer can change the pattern, reweave the energy, and adjust the unconscious reaction. This will result in a change in the dream story, and it will also result in a change in the waking reality of the dreamer, as well as a healing in the physical body. This is very different from simply allowing the dreamer's ego to "kill the monster."

BEING CHASED BY THE LIGHT

Another possibility in nightmares is that the dreamer is being pursued in dreamtime by the Light itself. As I've said before, we may pretend to be afraid of death, but our biggest fear is really self-actualization: maximizing our potential as humans. As we clear the psychological patterns that have kept us safely in the mundane, the ordinary, the little self, our potential may suddenly turn around and chase us. It won't stop until we're caught. If our ego selves are afraid of our divine selves, these kinds of dream experiences can register as nightmares.

One student at a seminar approached me after class. She has experienced a recurring nightmare since childhood. It's always exactly the same.

> I'm on a stairway. I'm outside a big white building. I start to ascend the stairs, and then I see them. There are five women, all dressed in white. They're waiting for me at the top of the stairs. I'm gripped with fear. I turn and run as fast as I can, although my legs are not working well. It's like trying to run through water. I look over my shoulder. They're running after me.

This woman has never become lucid during this dream, and so it remains the same. Clearly, there is a configuration of energy that she encounters during these dreams that her mind interprets as danger. She runs every time.

In my opinion, this is another kind of ego fear. The women in white may just as well be angels as sources of danger. In fact, the white building and the women in white sound very much to me as if she is approaching (ascending) some very high teachings. But part of her knows that the consequences of receiving high teachings may be very powerful. It is not unusual at all to find deep fears of "knowing too much" in women.

I asked the dreamer to create a ceremony in the safest place she knows: her home, her garden, the beach. In that place, she is to stay awake, and call up the images of the dream again. This is a way of learning to become lucid in dreams. We can redream them with intention while awake if we enter them in very humble and holy ways. I asked her to use every ounce of courage she could muster. "This time, don't run. Continue to ascend the steps. Ask the women what they want and what gifts they have."

Indeed, as I suspected, we learned from her redreaming ceremony that she had been running from her own wisdom all her life. This is not surprising, nor is it uncommon. We will discuss this in more depth in the next section. For now, it is simply important to know that redreaming a recurrent dream is often the best way to move more deeply into it. This is different from "taking control."

THE COMPASSIONATE DREAMER

I started this section on nightmares by mentioning the woman at the Seattle event who had only remembered nightmares. Surprisingly, she doesn't fit the category of dreamers who have physical fear imprinted in their bodies, nor does she appear to be running from her angels. After I questioned her for a while, I learned that she had had a good childhood, supportive parents, no trauma or abuse, had a great marriage, and loved being a mother (albeit a tired one). Her therapist had been trying to help her find the shadow or darkness inside her, the disenfranchised part of herself that creates these dreams. She was terrified that there was some sinful part of her that would be revealed through her dreams. She feared that she shouldn't be allowed to raise her children. What a shame, I thought. Why look for and invent evil parts of ourselves and call it therapy?

I asked her to share an example of the dreams with me. Here's what she told me:

> I'm watching a war scene. The killing is brutal, savage, bloody. Women and children are being gutted alive. Men are forced to watch and then beaten to death. Even though I know I'm dreaming, there's nothing I can do to stop the images.

It was particularly interesting that this dreamer could work well in lucid, clearly translucent, dreaming. I asked this young woman if she were familiar with the term *compassionate dreamer*. She said no, but her eyes widened in recognition as I explained that some people work in the dark labyrinths of dreamtime *just because they can*. I suggested that her blessed life had given her a vessel strong enough to see evil for what it is: errors in the human system, flaws in the human understanding of the dynamics of creativity versus destruction. I suggested to her that by becoming the dispassionate witness, she was contributing to the raising of human consciousness. I asked her to contemplate the amount of compassion she brings to these dream experiences.

Tears flowed freely down her cheeks as she listened to my suggestions. She did have the physical vessel to work with the forces of evil in the dreamtime, but she unfortunately didn't have the vocabulary to understand her work. Her interpretation of these dreams as nightmares has abated. Her fear that she is evil and shouldn't be a mother is gone. Her work in the dreamtime is more familiar to her and she is now better able to express herself and to actualize her spiritual imperative in the waking world.

This woman is one of the reasons I decided to write another book on dreaming. I realized that many people have experiences of this nature, and yet they have no information and no vocabulary to articulate the amazing spiritual and mystical revelations that are available to them every night.

PRACTICE PRAYING

In December of 1994, I sat at my father's deathbed. My sisters and I took turns being with him around the clock the last four days of his life. Just before dawn on December 17, I was alone with him. I experienced a profound and palpable change in the energy in the room. I knew that his dying time was near. I won't go into the details of his actual death, except to say that for me it was a mystical experience that changed the way I perceive life, death, and spiritual growth. As a result of the last hour of his life, I took on a new career, a new philosophy, and a new life path.

The first few months after my father's death, all of my dreaming was lucid. Every night, night after night, I walked into the dream with full consciousness. My awareness never shut off. This was five years after I had more or less recovered from the dreaming period described in the first chapter of this book, so watching the dreams carefully was an integral part of my daily practice.

I was at a spiritual teacher's house. All of his students were there. They were rearranging his furniture. There was a big controversy about where to put his bed—what direction should his head be? I tried to get interested, but I couldn't. The teacher was participating fully. He seemed deeply involved in all the decisions. But occasionally he would pass by me, stop, and whisper something in my ear about the evolution of consciousness or the true meaning of vibration. The paradox was funny, but when I laughed, all the students looked at me with fear in their eyes.

Because I knew this was a dream, I looked for the illusion. I thought, "Oh, in the dream you can go for the inappropriate or the ecstatic—the silly or the profound." I put my arm around the teacher, as if we were lovers. The rest of the students nearly passed out with horror. I thought, "This is how I can love Daddy now that he's dead. I can love him without fear of others' thoughts. There's no limit to love in the dream. There's no socialization here! There's no reason to stay in my own skin."

As I thought that, my skin dissolved. Everyone in the dream scene, including the teacher, froze and stared in disbelief. Each cell in my body crystallized into a microscopic speck of glitter. I laughed, and the laughter awakened me. I was not in bed asleep at all. I was kneeling by the side of my bed in prayer.

This kind of experience came night after night. I prayed constantly for the next few months—when I was awake, and when I was asleep. During this time I received a vast body of information from the dreaming realms about how soul consciousness works through the dreams to inform and support the dreamer's contract with life and form. It was intense and profound. The lucidity in the dreams made the entire experience otherworldly, and yet deliciously alive and grounded.

It didn't last. I didn't have the vessel in place to sustain that level of attention for more than a few months. But the repercussions have lasted and altered my life. Now my prayer is that the next time I enter that dimension of awakened consciousness, I will be able to sustain it, ground it, live it, and *be* it.

Now when I achieve lucidity in my dreaming, my first movement is to my knees. Prayer in the dream is powerful work. Praying during dreaming magnetizes the holy. Practicing prayer in the dream creates a reverberation that influences everything and everyone. It definitely transforms the dreamer's perception, and it therefore transforms the dreamer's story.

> *Pass into sleep in the concentration—concentrate with the eyes closed, lying down and the concentration must deepen into sleep—sleep must become a concentrated going away from the waking state.*
>
> —Sri Aurobindo[5]

Making lucid dreaming a part of one's spiritual practice is, to me, its authentic use. Anything less than that turns the dreamtime into an exercise for the false self, and diminishes the true potential of the dreaming. Through practicing being awake all the time, we awaken. Through prayer, we actualize!

collective dreaming

the second stage

The next stage of dreaming opens many doors and many new possibilities. This stage is frightening for some people. In fact, sometimes it's so frightening that dreamers consciously choose not to enter it. I assume, since you're still reading, that you're not one of those.

The stage that I call collective dreaming is a feminine stage. The spiritual aspects of first-stage dreaming unfold in fairly masculine ways. First-stage dreaming is directional, goal-oriented, and aimed toward certain ends. The ends, of course, are that the dreamer's mind and belief systems will open and soften, that his or her psychological and emotional blocks will transform, and that the dreamer's awareness of illusion will heighten. When those things happen, the dreamer is ready for another dimension of experience.

This second stage is not linear at all. It is not goal-oriented, nor does it involve specific tasks. This stage is round, spherical, spiraling, feminine. While the first stage involved integrating information and making changes within the personality and ego of the dreamer, this second stage involves accepting the reality that each dreamer has access to intuition. It requires receptivity on the part of the dreamer more than action. It is a highly necessary stage, because unless we recover the feminine qualities of intuition, receptivity, patience, and wisdom, our goal-oriented, linear, task-focused masculine lifestyle will continue to weaken us.

In the first stage of dreaming, one is tested to see if the dreaming vessel is strong enough to carry more Truth; to bear more of the wine of divinity. In this second stage, one's faith is tested. All that is really necessary for the dreamer to "master" second-stage dreaming is faith: a profound, intuitive, fundamental faith in one's ability to know.

Second-stage dreaming is about accessing information. At this stage, the dreamer's mind decodes messages it has received in the darkness. As the personal mind writes the dream story, it simultaneously unfolds (like opening a letter) the energy the dreamer encountered and deciphers the information carried in that energy.

Depending on many factors, not the least of which is the dreamer's connection to the moon during dreaming, one may literally pick up information that exists in the morphic fields of dreaming. Morphic fields are defined by scientist Rupert Sheldrake as "fields of information." They are "non-material regions of influence extending in space and continuing in time."[1] Data and information do not disappear when a form breaks down; rather, they continue to resonate as an invisible organizing pattern of influence, holding the structural and ideological information of a form. Morphic fields not only hold or store information, they transmit that information through space and time. These fields explain why ideas may occur simultaneously to people in different parts of the globe. In other words, an idea doesn't originate in the individual thinker. It resides in an invisible field of information to which the individual thinker attunes his or her mind. Several people may tune in to the same transmitted idea simultaneously.

Sheldrake uses a scientific, somewhat sterile phrase—morphic fields—while Rumi cuts to the deeper truth when he refers to "the secret heart of heaven." For Rumi, Truth is stored in a place that only the pure of heart (the naked, unashamed, liberated lover) can access. When the dreamer/lover reaches the stage of development which demands that one approach the darkness with purity of heart, he or she is allowed access to the information of love. This is second-stage dreaming.

Sheldrake, at least to my knowledge, has stopped short of discussing the idea that we encounter these morphic fields, these informational domains, most clearly in our dreaming. I'm suggesting that in second-stage dreaming, that's exactly what we do.

The Aboriginal people of Australia explain it slightly differently. They say that when we encounter a new idea, a new song, a new design in a dream, we've come into contact with an ancestor who has a creative desire. We, the dreamers, are the conduits through which the ancestors can create. And that ancestor may be speaking to several of his or her children simultaneously.

When we relax our own personal will during our dreaming time, we pick up information out of the morphic fields, out of the wisdom of our ancestors. Our minds write a story that can teach us something outside our range of typical awareness. This is second-stage dreaming.

THE PITFALL

Each stage of dreaming has a profound and serious pitfall. In the second stage, the danger is egotism. When you begin to pick up information in the dream, it is very tempting to believe it's because you are powerful, or because you are spiritually advanced in some way. At this stage some people start religious groups, move to separatist communities in the name of spiritual growth, or take other actions that demand external validation for their insights.

> *Dreams are not all mere dreams. . . . Many are records or transcripts of experiences on the other planes into which one enters in sleep, some are scenes or events of those planes.*
> —Sri Aurobindo[2]

Of course, in the long run, it never works. True spiritual unfolding does not allow for the misuse of power in any sense of the word, nor does it make special exceptions for people who decide that they are enlightened. Do not be fooled by people who are "spiritually successful." That success is temporary. It is really just public attention—not true success at all. Real spiritual success is silent.

THE SAFETY NET

Once again, the safety net within the pitfall is spiritual practice. If you adopt a conscious practice of clearing your emotions, mind, and body, you won't decide that you're all powerful. Look for children in your dreams! They are often indications that your spiritual practice is working and that your childlike innocence is intact.

Second-stage dreaming is formidable because it asks the dreamer to stop being self-indulgent and self-absorbed and to realize the true collective nature of the dreaming spaces. In addition, it asks the dreamer to trust the information that comes in dreams. This may mean shattering a lifetime pattern of discounting intuited information. It may demand that one stop believing that dreams are all about one's personal psyche. It definitely means that the dreamer must stop giving power to outside authorities.

> *Remember the Mother . . . before sleeping; for the more you get that habit and do it successfully, the more protection will be with you.*
>
> —Sri Aurobindo[3]

Second-stage dreams may be compared to labor contractions, which feel constricting but are actually expanding the opening in the body so that new life can emerge. Second-stage dreams demand that you realize that your dreams are what gave birth to the world.

telepathic dreams

To love is to know, and to know is to love.

~RAMAKRISHNA[1]

TELEPATHIC DREAMS ARE DREAMS IN WHICH WE PICK UP INFORMATION about something that has happened in waking, concrete reality. To qualify as telepathic, this "something" must be nonlocal to the dreamer, meaning it cannot have happened to the dreamer or within the dreamer's realm of awareness. In other words, it doesn't count if it's something you may have overheard on the radio or glimpsed in the newspaper but did not consciously register in your overt thinking. It only counts if it's something about which you have no clue.

For example, let's say you dream that you go to a hospital and you see a friend for the first time in five years. Then, the next day, you get a letter from that friend telling you that he has applied for a job at a nearby hospital. That's a telepathic dream. You simply picked up some information about the friend. The fact that you saw that person actually working in the hospital may mean that the probability of his getting that job is very high. If he gets the job, this dream was both telepathic and prophetic. Almost all dreams, except the most mundane, may fit into more than one category. This is because as you evolve spiritually, you actually live in multiple dimensions and you perceive more than one kind of information.

Telepathic dreams come only to lovers. I am not referring to people who are in love with each other, but rather to people who are in love with life, mystical lovers. When Ramakrishna said "To love is to know, and to know is to love," he literally meant that one cannot truly know another unless love is present. That's true also in the dream-time. You cannot open the door to information without the key pos-sessed by the lover. These dreams are dreams of the heart, and must be recognized and treated as such, or they will simply cease to come.

Before I go more deeply into examples of telepathic dreams, let's discuss the red flags on this level.

DANGER! POWER DREAMER LOOSE!

As with all types of dreaming, telepathic dreams carry a certain danger presented by the dreamer's ego. If, at any point along your spiritual journey, you divert your attention away from growth and toward per-sonal power or gain, it will be as if you have drawn the "go directly to jail" Monopoly card. What I mean is that all along the path we have opportunities to act without integrity. When we do that, the dreams immediately revert to stage one. We have built in self-regulated checkpoints moderated by the soul.

If you have a few telepathic dreams that give you truthful informa-tion, you may decide you have a line on "power," and start to exploit it. "Ah, now I'll be really smart and successful because I'll pick up all these secrets in the dream and know stuff that other people can't know." This bloated false self will then instruct the waking you to ask for specific information in the dreamtime. You'll try to become a dream spy.

All the ancient texts about dream schools refer to a technique known as "incubating the dream." This involves asking for certain in-formation, usually information about healing, to come through the dream. Unfortunately, the ancient texts don't talk enough about the spiritual development necessary to safely and accurately incubate dreams. I think these early dreamers assumed it was a given that one must have achieved priest or priestess level before this kind of ability develops. Dream incubation happened only under the most elevated ceremonial circumstances, in a temple, after days of fasting and medi-tational preparations, under the tutelage of a dreaming master. Only a *lover* can dream these dreams.

However, a few telepathic dreams may inflate you to the point that you think you've been granted special permission to "search and seize" Truth. The further danger, then, is that you'll automatically interpret every dream as a tele-

> *I may say that consciousness and receptivity are not the same thing. One may be receptive, yet externally unaware of how things are being done and of what is being done.*
>
> —Sri Aurobindo[2]

pathic dream, and you'll predetermine that you are *right* about whatever you think you know because you saw it in the dream.

Slow down there. Telepathic dreaming is not to be manipulated or exploited or used for personal power. In fact, it *will* not be used that way, and if you start trying to misuse it, it will undermine you, giving you all sorts of dead ends and cul de sacs to travel.

As radical as this sounds, I recommend that you postpone asking for information from a dream until you know beyond a shadow of a doubt that every shred of temptation to manipulate and misuse energy is thoroughly eliminated from your system, and that you are a *lover*. I, for example, never ask for specific information in the dream. I'm not evolved enough. However, I work to be receptive and to remain available to any gift the dreamtime has for me.

Remember, second-stage dreaming is about faith. You must develop the faith that when you go to sleep, the energy of the Void is pure and good, right and regenerating. It needs *no instruction* from your waking ego.

Instead of asking for information, I recommend that each time you experience a telepathic dream that proves to be authentic, you simply make a note of it in a journal. Take a page in the back of your journal and head it "Telepathic Dreams." Each time you receive a telepathic dream, note the date, location of the moon, other aspects of the moon (phase, relativity to other planets, whether it's in the same sign as your birth moon or sun, etc.), and look for your personal dreaming patterns. You'll soon discover that you have telepathic dreams at certain times of the month under certain lunar conditions. Now you know something important: You know when you tend to pick up accurate information out of the cosmos!

Then, the next time you know the moon to be repeating that pattern, you may go to sleep thinking, "Oh goodie. Tonight I'm going to learn something I didn't know before!" The more open and receptive you are, the more accurate and direct the telepathy will be.

DANGER! MR. FIX-IT AT WORK!

A second danger with telepathic dreaming is that you'll become concerned that you need to "do" something about the information. We live in a control-it-and-fix-it world. (At least we like to believe we are in control.) Have you noticed that most casual conversation between people centers around fixing each other? If I don't feel well and I mention it to a friend, she starts giving all kinds of advice. If I have a complaint or problem of any kind, and if I mention it to another person, that person feels an imperative to solve the problem—or at least to identify with it. Author and medical intuitive Carolyn Myss refers to this as *woundology*. We connect and bond with each other by finding common symptoms or wounds! And then we get busy trying to fix each other. We define ourselves as "good friends" by how much effort we put into fixing our broken friends. Because this behavior identifies us with our brokenness and freezes us in a dynamic that requires brokenness, it's absolutely psychically unhealthy, but all too common.

This woundology really emerges when people start recognizing their telepathic dreams. We think that if we dream something, we need to act on it. We think there's no other reason for having dreamed it. We're concerned that if we don't *do* something we aren't being good dream friends. We are often irresistibly attached to our dreams and the information that comes from them, and we want to prove our worth and our rightness.

This is flawed thinking. Remember that this stage of dreaming is really about developing feminine receptivity. This level of dreaming is about knowing that we know. It is a gift, reminding us that we are much vaster than we think. These dreams are affirmations. They come strictly to remind us that we are not separated from the implicate order of all things. They come to remind us that everything that occurs in perceptual reality is rooted in the unseen realms. They come to validate that we have the same acuity in the unseen as we do in the seen, if and only if we become receptive to the information.

These dreams are to be celebrated and enjoyed. The proper response to them is gratitude, not action. There's nothing to fix.

WHAT IF THE INFORMATION IS BAD NEWS?

My mother has always been particularly talented in telepathic dreaming. Unfortunately, she was raised in a generation and in a part of the country that treated the ability to dream as "witchy" and something to fear. She has lived most of her life caught in a pull between the harsh judgments of her world and the profound reality that her dreams give her real and accurate information. She had three or four close girlfriends with whom she literally communicated in the dreams. Once in a dream she heard her friend Mildred call her name and ask for help. My mother woke up from the dream and saw that it was 3:00 A.M. She decided she must call her friend the next morning. However, before she made the phone call, Mildred's son called to say that she had died—at 3:00 A.M. This was an unexpected death that shocked and grieved my mother deeply. My parents immediately called to tell me of Mildred's death, and during the conversation my mother told me of her dream. My dad, who was on the extension phone, made a comment—something like, "Mother's just being witchy again." By the end of that phone call my daddy had been well scolded by his baby daughter!

This kind of dreaming was familiar to all the women in my family. Both my sisters also receive information in dreaming. However, none of this was comfortable for my dad. He half-admired it and half-mocked it. It just didn't fit into his belief system and he didn't know what to do with it. One night he got his "just rewards." He was in the hospital recovering from open-heart surgery. He awoke in the night, having trouble breathing because the tube in his throat was irritating him. The nurse, unable to understand his drug-garbled talk simply gave him a pain shot and put him back to sleep. Meanwhile, my mother dreamed at 4:00 A.M. that she heard my dad calling her for help. She got up, bathed, dressed, and went to the hospital. They wouldn't let her in to the ICU until 8:00, so she waited patiently in the family room. My dad's response was "Where were you at 4:00 A.M.? I couldn't breathe and I needed your help." She said, "I know. I had a dream and I've been waiting outside for almost four hours to see you." That one made a believer out of him.

In some ways, these telepathic communications between close girl-friends or spouses are believable, even to the most skeptical. Everyone knows that an intimate relationship leads to that kind of intuitive knowing. But when this kind of information comes in the dream, it is not always limited to one's most intimate relationships; remember, dreaming is nonpersonal. Often, we dream circumstances and situations that are totally foreign to our immediate circle of friends.

One restless, hot summer night, I saw a troubling scene in a dream. I awoke the next morning, knowing that the moon had been in my telepathic configuration the night before, but I certainly didn't want this particular dream to have been telepathic or prophetic.

Vic was driving a car up a steep incline. We were in the Angeles National Forest somewhere. I was in the passenger seat—Ben, Sara, and a friend of Sara's were in the back. On a curve, Vic was going too fast. We hit a patch of ice and began skidding sideways. I heard Vic's voice say, "Are we going off the edge?" The point of view changed and I saw the car fly out over the edge of the cliff.

Back inside the car now, I said, "We're going to die. Whatever happens, I'll be with you. Close your eyes and let's be peaceful in our last seconds." I opened my eyes a few moments later and saw that we were in complete darkness—as if we were in outer space. We seemed to be falling forever.

I opened my eyes a second time. We were no longer alone. We were connected to another car with five more people. I looked out and saw the Earth, far below us. It looked like a patchwork quilt. I thought, "That cliff was really high."

As we neared the Earth, my family held hands. And then we landed, softly and without even a jolt. It felt that we'd been surrounded by an energetic field that protected us from the impact. I was amazed.

I got out and saw that the kids in the other car were lined up in a single file, marching like robots toward some nearby houses. Are they dead? I kept saying, "Can you believe this? Not only did we not die, but there are people nearby to help us!" I was practically leaping with joy, trying to get them to see how fortunate we were. I leapt and jolted myself awake.

As I said earlier, this dream was disturbing to me because it was very "real." That's one characteristic of telepathic dreams; they feel real. Because you are picking up information that is already in form, there's a density to these dreams that is recognizable (when you're used to it). This dream had that "real" feeling.

I had this dream very early on a Sunday morning in August of 1999. I puzzled about it all that day. It was eerie. Then, on Monday morning, when I read the morning headlines, I saw the news story. There had been a rave (an outdoor concert) in the Angeles National Forest that weekend. Very early Sunday morning, a car with five teenagers who were returning from the all-night event skidded off a cliff. They all died.

This is a typical "bad news" telepathic dream. For some reason, I tuned into the tragedy, possibly as it was happening, or at least within an hour of its happening. Was this also a shamanic dream (see Chapter Fourteen) in which I was assisting the kids in having a peaceful death? Perhaps. Was there anything for me to *do* with this information? No. This was a dream in which I saw, or perceived in the dreamer's way, an event. It was a dream that came on a telepathic night for me. It was a dream that simply affirmed that my consciousness and my awareness were expanded beyond the typical band of my limited boundaries. It is a sad dream, because the event was sad. Sad things happen in our world, and the more we can extend our compassion and acts of loving kindness into the sadness, the less fearful we will all be of death and sadness.

The main reason I use this dream as a telepathic example is that it offers the dreamer the opportunity to "believe." If you prefer to stay in the first stage of dreaming and either write dreams off as "just dreams," or keep them strictly within the limits of your own psychology, then it would be very easy to completely discount this dream as coincidence, or to redefine it altogether as a dream about a personal ego death that's occurring within my family structure. On the other hand, if you're a dreamer on a spiritual path, you can see this kind of dream as a letter from the level of soul. This dream speaks to the interconnectedness of all beings, to the unity of the death experience, and to the ability we have as dreamers to connect on the most subtle, compassionate levels of consciousness.

My teenage daughter, who was in the car with me in the dream, knew about the rave in the Angeles National Forest that weekend. She was never a part of the "rave culture," so she had been at home that night, but classmates of hers were there. Perhaps the mystery passenger in the backseat of my car in the dream story was an acquaintance of Sara's who was at the rave. In some unknown way, as a mother within a community, even though I had no conscious knowledge of the rave, I was connected. My fibers were pulled by the tragedy. This was not coincidence. This was not about me, nor about my family. This was a telepathic dream, sent as a gift to remind me that we are all One.

DREAMING EACH OTHER'S REALITIES

In telepathic dreams, we often peek into each other's lives in the most unusual and nontraditional ways. It's spiritual eavesdropping. Because telepathic dreaming can be incredibly intimate, it is very important for the dreamer to treat the information of these dreams with the highest of ethical standards. Often the information of these dreams is no different from being asked to keep a secret. Since only *lovers* receive these dreams, it is important to act in absolute alignment with Love in the treatment of them. When we see each other's realities, we must see with the eyes of Love.

At the end of 1999, I taught an online dream class. There were twenty women involved, and we tracked our dreams for the last six weeks of the year—the century, really. Our intent was to see what the future may bring based on our commonly shared dream images. The women were from all over the United States and Canada. They did not, for the most part, know each other. I knew some, but not all of them.

One of the participants, Annette, a woman I had known a very short time, sent me a private e-mail describing her upcoming trip to Africa. She was scheduled to travel with a small group of people led by our mutual friend, African shaman Malidoma Some. She had just received a letter about the lodgings, the itinerary of the journey, and the protocol of Some's village. Through this letter she learned that she would be staying in a motel that had running (although rarely hot) water, but only during certain hours of the day. The letter outlined a rigorous schedule of ceremonies and rituals she would be expected to perform. Annette, who had some health difficulties, wasn't at all sure she was "up" for the trip. The prospect of trying to rest and recover from her illness in difficult (probably dirty, possibly bug-infested) sleeping quarters, having few luxuries like water and toilets, didn't sound inviting. Also, the busy and demanding schedule made her question the appropriateness of the trip at this time in her life. She and I discussed this at length, but only privately. No one else in the online course knew of her plans or her concerns.

Judith did not know Annette. Judith lives in Texas, Annette in Illinois. They have almost nothing in common. The day Annette and I were flinging letters back and forth to each other about the Africa trip, Judith posted the following dream on the class forum:

> The setting was like a motel or dormitory. We were a group of people studying and celebrating. The accommodations were less than desirable; seedy and inconvenient. However, we were all glad that there were no cockroaches!
>
> A young good-looking African-American man was talking to me about the above celebration. While he was talking, he was working on filling his pipe. He had an elaborate concoction of tobacco that he put in his mouth and chewed on for a while and then placed in a bowl and mixed with some other substances before placing it in his pipe. (Alchemy?) He offered the pipe to me to smoke before he smoked it.

Annette and I were both astonished to see this dream. In my opinion, Judith dreamed into Annette's concern, projected her dream fibers into the circumstances, saw Annette's future trip through the eyes of the *lover,* and pronounced it "inconvenient but without cockroaches." In addition, the Malidoma figure seemed to be alchemically changing things within the dream. Judith had no connection with Malidoma, nor any other young, good-looking (or old and ugly for that matter) African-American teachers. Nor was she planning to take a journey of this ceremonial/celebratory nature. Partially because of this interesting encouragement, Annette did make the trip and lived to tell about it. In fact, it was a transformational experience for her. One part of Judith's dream story, however, was inaccurate. There were cockroaches in Annette's room—big ones.

After years of working with dreamers, hearing their dream stories, and being privy through my counseling practice to the private lives of many of them, I am absolutely convinced that we experience this kind of dreaming all the time. We don't realize it because we don't talk about it. We dream each other's lives. Someone is dreaming your life. You are dreaming other people's lives. That's another reason why it's a good idea to develop a spiritual practice around your dreaming. The "cleaner" you are, the "cleaner" the dreamers you will attract into your realm of influence.

DREAMING EACH OTHER'S DREAMS

Another member of the 1999 online dreaming class, Cassie, shared this experience with us:

> I dreamed of exotic and brilliant-hued flowers pushing through the snow. Some of them were an intense indigo blue.

Even though it was wintertime, there had been no forecast of snow before Cassie went to bed. In fact, the days had been clear and sunny. The next morning when she woke up, however, the ground was covered with snow. She was delighted and amused that she had dreamed of snow! Now, technically, even though she didn't "know" it had snowed, we wouldn't call this a telepathic dream because, on some level, her physical body, comfortable though it was in a warm bed in a warm house, could have sensed the change in barometric pressure and temperature. But that's not the most interesting part.

> The dream flowers had been so vivid and real that I found myself looking for them as I went up the driveway to meet my neighbor for a dog walk. Her first words were: "Can you believe this snow? Last night I even dreamed there were these gorgeous flowers blooming in the snow!" As I stared at her, another neighbor drove by and stopped to say hi and com-

ment on the snow. Then she said, "Last night I dreamed there were these amazing flowers coming up out of the snow! Weird, huh?" Neither of these women is at all new agey. It was then I realized something was up.

Indeed, something was up. What was it? We may never know exactly. But that's the point of many second-stage dreams. They're not about anything other than faith. They're about telling you that we are all interconnected. You have access to a wide spectrum of information. You can see and participate in creating other people's realities. You can see and participate in creating other people's dreams. It feels very feminine, doesn't it? These women communicated with each other on the most subtle, telepathic, intuitive levels. They clearly also communicated with Mother Earth, the weather, the flower people, and, most mysteriously, the frequency of color as it exists in the dream. On this very special night, these dreamers resonated with the flowering, the unfolding of life, and brought forth amazing, vivid, gorgeous images. Cassie's sense that the dream was real, so real that she actually looked for the flowers in the snow, gives us another clue that this was telepathic dreaming.

Color in the dream is very interesting to me. What have we encountered when our dream stories involve vivid color? We haven't "seen" color in the traditional, physiological sense, because there is no light hitting the retina of the dreamer. Instead, the dreamer has experienced a frequency within the darkness that translates to his or her mind as color. It's a frequency of the soul, a frequency that vibrates us into life. The dreamer has encountered a vibrational field that is the invisible precursor to color.

> *The soul . . . is the firmament of the whole organism. By saturating the body with its power, the soul achieves and carries out all its dealings with us. We become, in this way, gardens in bloom. . . .*
>
> —Hildegard of Bingen[3]

In most spiritual traditions, the word *flowering* is a metaphor used to describe the opening or unfolding of the soul in form. Flowering is the evolutionary drive. It is that aspect of life that moves us to experience ourselves in higher and higher states of consciousness. It is imprinted in the atom.

We constantly unfold our soul's intent for us. This intent is universal and collective in nature. From the soul's perspective, each individual is an eternal flower in a great garden.

Cassie and her neighbors dreamed an unfolding, a flowering, a vivid, amazing, gorgeous frequency. They used the unexpected snowfall as the background image of the dream (even though they were consciously unaware of the physical snow) and created a collective vision celebrating the beauty of life as seen in nature. It is truly moving. We "expect" this kind of experience from women who live in dreaming societies (Yaqui, Hopi, Aborigines, for example) but not from urban-dwelling women of Northwest America!

Here's what I said to Cassie about this dreaming:

> Your vivid flower dream experience was what I call an "atta girl" dream. Every once in a while you get these experiences that absolutely prove that life/dreaming is way more than you think it is. You've been doing something right, so the dream angels decide to reward you with *proof*. Then it's gone.

DREAMING THE IS-NESS

Second-stage dreaming puts you directly in the *is-ness* of life. You are One with what is. You are there as it happens, before it happens, after it has happened because the dreamer in you lives outside of the four dimensions of height, width, depth, and time/space. There are more dimensions. String theorists tell us there are ten and/or twenty-six. Mystics describe thirteen to sixteen. The esoteric schools speak of twelve. Who knows how many there are? I have no idea. But one thing I do know: The more sophisticated you become as a dreaming practitioner, the more of them you will come to know.

clairvoyant dreams

I sleep, but my heart watches.

~SONG OF SOLOMON 5:2

IN THE SECOND STAGE OF DREAMING, ONE ACHIEVES A LOVELY AND loving state of being. The heart begins to open, for the dreamer realizes that it is through the eyes of the heart that he or she is seeing the dreams. Only the lover's eyes could pierce the veil of the unmanifest and see what is to come.

This next level is what I call clairvoyant dreaming. The term *clairvoyance* typically refers to one's ability to perceive that which is not seen. The word is commonly used to describe someone who can locate objects that are hidden from sight, or who can intuit personal messages for other people. I use the term in a slightly more expanded sense. Clairvoyant dreams are those in which we perceive something before it happens. Usually clairvoyant dreams make themselves apparent within a couple of days. In fact, very often, the event from the dream occurs the very next morning.

The perceived event is not only unseen because we don't know anything about it (as in telepathic dreams), but it's unseen because it only exists in the realm of probability when we dream it. Our consciousness actually perceives something that is on the verge of happening. However, the fact *that* we dream it drags the event from one level of probability into a much higher level, similar to the way a computer mouse drags data from one file into another. Our dreaming creates a pathway of sorts that makes the manifestation even more probable.

To see something in a dream before it happens denotes a particular talent. One's heart must be open to the realm of possibility without attachment. To see something before it happens fills the dreamer with wonder and gratitude.

As I previously discussed, telepathic dreams feel real because there's a density to them that causes the dreamer to believe that they are actually happening. Clairvoyant dreams, on the other hand, have a much more "dreamy" quality. They are more symbolic, more etheric, more shadowy or wispy. We awaken from them sure that we've had a dream, which makes their coming true before our very eyes all the more uncanny. The experience of clairvoyant dreaming is humbling.

AH, YES! THERE IS DANGER ON THIS LEVEL, TOO

Like telepathic dreams, clairvoyant dreams carry ego traps. In fact, they carry the same dangers of ego inflation as telepathic dreams. With clairvoyant dreams, there's an even stronger sense of "I should do something about this!" Even with relatively mundane clairvoyant dreams, the temptation to try to make them mean something is strong.

A girlfriend called recently and said she'd dreamed a traffic jam the night before. When she awoke, she didn't think much of it, because traffic jams are certainly not unusual in the Los Angeles area. However, later that morning she found herself in an identical traffic jam. She called me, a little nonplussed, asking if she should have taken a different route: Shouldn't she have *done* something?

Her call left me pondering why we so often feel the need to *do* something. I assured her that her dream was simply reminding her that she has nonordinary levels of knowingness. This is about being and knowing, not about doing. Our waking mind's resistance to being and knowing is mighty, isn't it? For how many thousands of years now have we squelched our intuitive ability? By now it's become "natural" to quickly and thoroughly overpower and overrule the subtleties of being with the boldness of doing.

Clairvoyant dreams also hold one more danger—one that weighs even more heavily for many dreamers.

THIS IS WEIRD

Clairvoyant dreams often scare the dreamer. To dream something before it happens is downright spooky for most people. I can't count the number of times people have come to me for private sessions demanding that I teach them how *not* to dream. They are so tortured by the idea that they can see the future, they've literally developed fear around their own gift. The danger, of course, is that the fear will actually prevent the dreamer from moving forward on his or her spiritual path. When we're too much in our head, dreaming only makes "sense" through the fear of misunderstanding. To be fully in second-stage dreaming, one must "lose his or her mind."

> *After you take off your head*
> *the sunlight is much brighter*
>
> —Russell Salamon[1]

Fear of dreaming is an interesting aspect of the spiritual awakening. Often, dreams that frighten people are not ghost dreams, death dreams, or nightmares. They are actually relatively mundane. It's the fact that they *come true* that is so frightening!

My sister Marsha lived in a small West Texas town when she first noticed her talent for clairvoyant dreaming. She was a single working mom with her hands full. Between working full-time, mothering two young daughters, cleaning house, and cooking, she found herself trying to maintain a superhuman schedule. She was extremely grateful to a local gardener who came by every so often to mow her lawn. She paid no attention to his schedule, and just joyfully wrote him a check whenever he stopped by.

One night she had a dream:

> The gardener knocked on my door. He said, "I can't mow your lawn today, but I have someone to do it for me."
>
> The next morning I thought it was a strange thing to dream! That afternoon, the gardener stopped by, knocked on the door and said, "I can't mow your lawn today, but I'll do it tomorrow."

An astonished Marsha remembered the dream as he said that, and wondered why he'd said the "wrong thing" and why she'd had that dream. Her busy life pulled her attention away from the dream and the incident, and she forgot about it. However, the next day the gardener knocked on the door again and said, "I can't mow your lawn today, but I have someone to do it for me." That really stunned her. It even frightened her a little. She had many questions: What was that dream trying to say to her? Why did it take two days for the gardener to get his lines right? If this is an important dream talent, why is it wasted on such a mundane experience? Is this important or is it just weird?

These kinds of dreams are very important, strictly because they teach the dreamer to trust the psychic nature of her dreamtime. These dreams teach us that we live in an interconnected, interdependent, interactive world. Even our most ordinary dreams often tell us that. Why? Because we forget so often!

LAWS OF THE MOTHER

In his brilliant book *The Return of the Mother*, Andrew Harvey says the sacred feminine is defined by its three basic laws. The first is the *law of knowledge of the unity of all life*.[2] If we are to truly awaken the sacred feminine in our personal lives and reintroduce it to our religions, our societies, and our traditions, we must first grasp that all life is connected. We must know within our own experience that all life operates under the spiritual principle called Unity. Clairvoyant dreams are designed to shock us into seeing this. When we dream an event before it happens, what are we to believe except that everything is connected? How can we conclude anything else?

Harvey's second law of the sacred feminine is the *law of rhythm*.[3] He says, "The sacred feminine awakens us to the knowledge that the universe has its own laws and harmonies which are already whole and perfect, and which, if we are to live wisely, we have to intuit, revere, and follow." If we track our dreams according to the location and phase of the moon, we soon learn that we dream in accordance with the cosmic law of rhythm. Clairvoyant dreaming awakens us to the law of rhythm because it comes to us cyclically—at specific times of the month, based on our individual receptivity to the energies of the moon. In other words, not everyone dreams clairvoyantly on the same night. You dream clairvoyantly on the nights when your unique configuration of energy best fits with the cosmic rhythm of the flow of information.

Finally, Harvey names the third law of the sacred feminine, *the love of the dance*.[4] Again, I quote him: "I think it is essential when we talk of the restoration of the sacred feminine to make clear that what is being restored is a totally unmorbid, healthy, exuberant, sensual, ecstatic vision of life." When we dream clairvoyantly, we are dreaming the ecstatic dance of life. We are seeing what is ready to take form, and then we watch it take form. By forcing us to remember the future, our clairvoyant dreams *demand* that we have a respect for the fact that we live within a universal structure that is outside our linear and rational comprehension.

This level of dreaming is profoundly feminine. At its core it evokes the sacred feminine within your own life. Learning to see clairvoyantly, whether awake or asleep, is available to every human being. The dreams will not stop until you either learn to receive their gifts, or you cut them off with your fear!

MAKING NEW FRIENDS

Many years later, after Marsha had become more comfortable with her dreaming talent, she had a dream that involved a fellow faculty member, someone she knew only casually.

> I was leaving a party when I saw Julie talking to a man. I decided to go to the rest room, and Julie followed me. I noticed, and told her, that she had blue lipstick all over her chin. She started crying and told me that she was embarrassed because everyone who had seen the smeared lipstick probably guessed that she had been kissing the man that she had been talking with. I tried to reassure her that nobody noticed the lipstick, that I had not noticed it myself until we came into the rest room where the lighting was brighter.

A few days later, Marsha found herself sitting next to Julie at a faculty meeting. She laughingly told Julie about the dream. Julie didn't laugh, nor did she comment. A few weeks later Julie confided to Marsha that she was indeed involved with a man in an extramarital affair. Now, typically, this kind of dream might scare someone off—getting busted by a casual friend's dream could be off-putting. But Julie realized that she had the opportunity to create a friendship. Along with clairvoyant dreaming comes an imperative toward ethics and confidentiality. Julie apparently watched Marsha for a while, and realized that she'd met a trustworthy person who would not betray her. A large part of opening to the sacred feminine involves unbendable loyalty and allegiance between friends. One who dreams into another person's reality must also respect that reality as holy, sacred, and not to be judged or diminished in any way.

Julie doesn't remember her dreams often. But she jokes that she doesn't need to because her best friend does it for her.

KEEPING UP WITH OLD FRIENDS

My most overt clairvoyant dreams involve keeping tabs on old friends. It is not unusual at all for me to dream about someone I've not seen in years, someone with whom I've lost contact almost altogether, only to have them call me the next day and validate whatever I dreamed about them. In a way, this is also telepathic dreaming, because I do see accurately into what has already happened to them.

Most of my clairvoyant dreams have involved seeing into one person's life at a time. This one was unique because it appears to have been about several people.

I was staying with my friend Cristina. I woke up early one morning, knowing that I needed to find another place to stay that night because her boyfriend was coming for the weekend. I took a walk and ran into an old friend, Dennis.

Dennis and I were so glad to see each other that we spent the whole day chattering, lunching, walking, catching up. We popped from location to location, setting to setting, in continuous chatter. I was delighted to hear how well he was doing on every level of his being.

Suddenly, I looked at the horizon and saw that the sun was setting and I remembered that I hadn't moved my stuff out of Cristina's apartment yet.

I was really concerned because I didn't want her apartment to be messy
when her new boyfriend arrived.

You won't be surprised to hear that Dennis called me the next
morning. I hadn't heard from him in at least five years, and in fact
about three years earlier his Christmas card had come back un-
claimed, so I wasn't sure where he'd moved. As often as this happens,
it still amazes me and I still squeal with delight, which is exactly what
I did when I answered the phone and heard Dennis's voice. We talked
and chattered, touching the sweet moments of our twenty-year
friendship like a rock skipping across a lake. Indeed, I was thrilled to
hear how wonderfully he was doing in every respect. I was especially
glad to hear about his spiritual and emotional growth.

Then I told Cristina. She was excited also. In fact, her new boyfriend was coming that weekend. And ironically, she had an ex-
boyfriend named Dennis with whom she'd been feeling the need to
communicate. Just the night before she had written in her journal that
it would be a good idea to try to find her Dennis.

What more proof do I need? We dream each other's realities. If we
don't know it, it's simply because we don't talk about it. After the
phone call from Dennis, which was weird enough, I could have just let
the dream go. If I hadn't told Cristina, I would never have known
about the deeper connection.

FORESEEING TRAGEDY

Of course, one of the reasons many people fear the ability to dream
clairvoyantly is that they don't want to see tragedy. It feels to some
dreamers as if they invoked or in some way helped create the tragedy
by dreaming it.

The Cristina I mentioned in the dream before is a college profes-
sor and a very powerful dreamer. She had the following dream in the
fall of 1999.

I dreamed that I was at a funeral with a lot of people, held outside the back
of a cathedral. It was an interesting Baptist/Protestant church, but in a

Mexican-looking town. We were having to have the funeral over and over. There were all sorts of people there. Went to find my friend Jeanne, and I discovered that I had to climb to the top of a really tall structure made of wood to find her. She was in a small room at the top of the structure/tree house sort of wooden building, lying on a bed naked fanning herself from the heat, saying she was burning up.

This dream occurred the night before a bonfire structure, which was being built by students on the Texas A&M campus, fell, killing several students. Cristina has several friends, including Jeanne, who were professors at A&M. When she heard about the accident she, of course, wondered why she had this dream. She could not have changed the course of events, so what was the point?

Again, this is an example of the spiritually evolved dreamer's ability to be of assistance in the dream. Cristina eventually realized that she had to go to the funeral over and over in the dream because the grieving process for her friends was so intense. It is my feeling that her participation was also about helping the young people in their dying process through her prayers, her meditations, and her contemplation.

THE ONLY PRAYER

If the only prayer you say in your entire life
is "Thank You," that would suffice.

~MEISTER ECKHART[6]

One of the deep challenges of second-stage dreaming is learning to be in gratitude for the gift, and learning not to be in judgment or guilt for what we see.

Clairvoyant dreaming, if it is properly understood, and if its power is thoroughly integrated into the dreamer's psyche, brings the dreamer to a state of walking gratitude. Usually, there is nothing to do about these dreams, and nothing to be except thankful for them. These dreams are the gift of spirit, and they are the result of (as well as the impetus for) spiritual growth. The dreamer who is blessed with clarity of vision is truly a gift to other people. Of course, sometimes there is a doing imperative in the dreams. I have certainly been known to change my schedule or plan for the next day based on a dream that I was sure was clairvoyant. But for the most part, these dreams are not orders from on high.

Meister Eckhart, a thirteenth-century Christian mystic, was clearly a dreamer. In his sermons he refers often to the "masters of spirituality" who come to him and teach him. He does not call them religious leaders, theologians, priests, or professors. I think these are Eckhart's dream teachers. I find over and over again in his readings admonitions about maintaining oneself so that clear vision and clear dreaming are possible. This book is sprinkled with quotations from Eckhart. I want to discuss this one in detail.

Eckhart says, "If the only prayer you say in your entire life is 'Thank You,' that would suffice." He's telling us that life is a gift from God, and that's all we really need to remember to live it fully and well. It pleases God that we are thankful for our lives. Clairvoyant dreaming, for me, is the reminder that life is a gift. Each time I see into the unmanifest, I realize that life is much more than I could possibly imagine. My mind, my imagination, my thoughts, as limitless as they are, are still inadequate in their ability to comprehend the vast gift of life.

When I'm asked, "What should I do about this dream?" I reply, "Pray." I mean that on every level. To see the unmanifest is a sacred gift. We pray "Thank you" for these dreams, for this gift, for this knowing.

prophetic dreams

Should there be a prophet among you,
I make myself known unto him in a vision,
I do speak to him in a dream.

~NUMBERS 12:6

I CALL THE THIRD LEVEL OF SECOND-STAGE DREAMING PROPHETIC dreaming. These are the dreams in which you see the future. They differ from clairvoyant dreams in two ways. First, clairvoyant dreams are more immediate, manifesting within a day or two, while prophetic dreams manifest anywhere from a week to a year or more later. Second, prophetic dreams are much more symbolic and stylized than clairvoyant dreams. One has to really work on figuring out the riddle of a prophetic dream.

It is easy to understand why prophetic dreams present themselves as puzzles or riddles. When you dream into the future, you're dreaming a probability factor. As Tenzin Wangyal Rinpoche points out, "In a dream of the future, the cause is present, and the propensity toward a certain result is present, but the actual dream story is a product of the dreamer's imagining."[1] You are sensing energies and collective (or personal) choices as they exist when the dream occurs, and you're seeing their potential conclusion. However, there can be no certainty to these dream stories, because the dreamer cannot know what kinds of changes may occur to alter the potential outcome. Especially when we are attuned to a potential future event, we must be very alert to the instability of the dream images.

Dreams refer to the unborn, to the darkly felt
inclinations toward the new world, a not-yet world.
~BRIAN SWIMME AND THOMAS BERRY[2]

Swimme and Berry didn't break dreaming down into different categories, as I am doing, so this comment refers to all sorts of dreams. And in a way, all dreams reflect the movement of the dreamer's consciousness into the not-yet world. However, prophetic dreams are particularly unique in that way. When the dreamer unfolds his or her dreaming fibers, which tune into specific circumstances or energies that are attracting several possible future outcomes, the dreamer's concrete mind has a challenge in writing a story that adequately represents it. The dreamer must measure the possibility of certain outcomes and factor in the possibility of those outcomes being changed by choice. This results in a dream story of a labyrinthine and symbolic nature!

WHAT IS A PROPHET?

Because organized religion has imperialized the word *prophet*, many dreamers resist owning their prophetic talents.

> *Why have the true prophets again and again been reviled, slandered, betrayed, even killed? Because the true prophets reveal to us exactly what we could be, if we only worked and prayed and struggled, humbly and passionately enough. . . . This we cannot bear because we cannot bear truth, and so we mock and kill them.*
>
> —Rumi[3]

Edgar Cayce, a rare modern example of a socially accepted prophet, proved himself by being so accurate in his predictions that few could deny his gift. Cayce, by the way, was called the sleeping prophet, because he received his information in the dreamtime! In the twenty-first century, however, most men and women who are prophets are called psychics.

The word *prophet* carries too much spiritual implication. Why then do I call these dreams prophetic rather than psychic? Let me explain.

Author Gregg Braden's book *The Isaiah Effect: Decoding the Lost Sci-*

ence of Prayer and Prophecy offers an interesting blend of scholarship
and personal experience in the study of the gift of prophecy. He defines prophecy as the ability to witness the future as the consequence
of choices that are being made in the present. In his vocabulary, a
prophet is a master of energy who can slip back and forth between
possible futures and then record the resulting experiences. He discusses prophets ranging from biblical figures such as Isaiah and
John in the Book of Revelation, to the Hopi and Mayan elders, to
Nostradamas and Edgar Cayce. In each case, he points out that
most prophets begin with prophecies of apocalypse and destruction
and immediately follow them with prophecies of a peaceful new
world. Braden suggests that those are not linear prophecies as many
literalists assume (first we'll experience apocalypse and destruction,
then we'll experience a new age of peace), but rather they are two
possibilities of the same future seen by the prophet simultaneously.
The collective choices we make determine which of them we will
experience.

His suggestion for how these parallel prophecies come about is
very interesting. He describes future possibility as parallel waves of
energy, or parallel roads or tracks into the future. Occasionally, because of choices made in the present, one of these roads may whiplash
into a curve, making it veer very close to or possibly touch another
road, before veering off again and back to its original track. Physicists
call those points in time and space, those points when two possibilities
touch, choice points. Braden suggests that prophets, people of clear
vision, have the ability to project their consciousness into those choice
points and see the resulting possibilities. One result looks dark and
menacing, while another looks bright and regenerating, and a third
may be more neutral. Braden doesn't explain why most of the
prophets present the destructive option first, polarized and contrasted
later by the more hopeful picture. He doesn't discuss why prophets
tend to choose the polarities and not go for the middle ground. I suggest that it may be due to the personal propensities of the prophet
himself. Many times people with the gift of prophecy don't have the
support system that keeps them balanced. I imagine our collective fas-
cination with the shadow side of the human condition also encourages
the pessimistic versions of prophecy.

WHAT IS A FALSE PROPHET?

Herein is the danger of this level of dreaming. If you do own your prophetic nature, it's very important that you balance it. A false prophet is a person who believes his own press. A false prophet is someone who uses his or her prophetic talent for personal gain. A false prophet is someone who does not know the power of the spoken word, and who speaks carelessly and wrongly.

Remember, this second-stage dreaming is a period of inflation or expansion. You are learning that you have powers. You are learning that you have access to information that you're not supposed to have. You are developing latent talents. The temptation to use that information for personal gain is huge. The even greater temptation is that you'll decide that you are the Source of this information and these talents.

People are extremely suggestible, and many are more than willing to turn their power over to anyone who will take it. Sometimes, when I'm giving a seminar, I can actually feel these projections. Dreamers are so happy to hear someone state what they know to be true, that they unconsciously decide to project their picture of their own divinity onto me. Now, a self-crowned prophet *eats* that projected energy like food. The results are disastrous for everyone concerned. False prophets are lying to themselves and to their prey.

AND IT CAME TO PASS AS HE INTERPRETED IT

Another problem at this level of dreaming is that too many prophets interpret their own visions. They do not go to an expert to offer their visions for analysis. They don't have dream circles.

Tamar Frankiel and Judy Greenfeld, two members of my dream circle, in their book *Entering the Temple of Dreams*, speak to this issue. They remind us of the Jewish teaching about interpreting dreams. This teaching is based on a famous Torah portion (scripture passage) regarding Joseph's ability to interpret prophetic dreams. Joseph, who had been sold into slavery by his brothers, had interpreted the dreams of some of his fellow slaves. His interpretations had been correct, and the dreams had manifested, giving him quite a reputation. The Bible says, "And it came to pass, as he interpreted to us, so it was" (Genesis 41:13). Biblical students know the rest of the story: Joseph was called to interpret a dream for Pharaoh. Joseph's accuracy in seeing the meaning of the dream saved the Pharaoh's people from starvation. His reward was that he was elevated from slave to a position of power in the government.

The Talmud, a Jewish text documenting time-proven rabbinical teachings about the scriptures, concludes from this story that we must always interpret dreams *for the good*, for "all dreams follow the mouth. . .the mouth meaning the interpretation given to the dream."[4]

In addition, the Zohar, a thirteenth-century document exploring the secrets of Jewish mysticism, tells us that when we have a dream we must not hold it; we are to share it with friends so that we can receive the benefit of their good wishes and blessings.[5] Joseph was a dreamer, but more important, he was spiritually evolved enough to hear the truth behind the images of the dream. Indeed, it was for his ability to hear the Pharaoh's prophecy that he was rewarded. Pharoah was a prophetic dreamer who had the wisdom to ask someone else for interpretation.

Crystal Cave Woman showed me the cave paintings left by ancient dreamers. Years later, my dear friend and teacher Heather Valencia generously expanded my understanding by instructing me in the age-old (and still practiced) Yaqui dream circle form. Since then I've made it a habit not to interpret my own dreams. I have a "circle of Josephs" with whom I share my stories. In dream circle we use the ancient practice of deep listening. I ask each dreamer to carefully develop the ability to hear each person's dream as if it were a letter from the level of soul, a level of consciousness that has human healing, wholeness, and holiness as its focus. We must understand that every dream is a message from divinity.

This is why I call the third level of second-stage dreams prophetic: because the true prophet knows to trust the information of the dream but not to interpret it. The true prophet takes the dreams and visions to a council of wise people. A true prophet takes full accountability for the truth of the dreaming energy, and listens deeply to the possible interpretations of the dream story. The psychic, on the other hand, reports his or her visions frankly and honestly but without deep, spiritual accountability. The true prophet knows the impact of dream, vision, and word on society and the consensus reality, and carefully measures his or her actions accordingly. Both prophet and wise council are necessary in this level of dreaming.

First let's look at a few prophetic dreams, and then I'll explain further the imperative of the modern-day prophet.

THE NEW NEIGHBOR

With all this biblical talk, you're probably expecting that every prophetic dream is of apocalyptic proportions. That's not the case at all. Indeed, we also see the future in seemingly unimportant ways.

One September I had the following dream:

> I was at the Santa Fe house clearing it out for the new owners. I had some workers there creating a spiral design on the floor with the old bricks. I loved the way it changed the energy in the house.
>
> I saw a new neighbor. Her life's work was that she grew and arranged calla lilies. She had some of the most beautiful callas I'd ever seen. I wondered exactly where she lived. I wasn't aware of any other houses for sale in the compound.

For many years my husband and I owned a second home in Santa Fe, New Mexico. It was a very sweet and very magical little adobe house built in the early 1900s. It was small but efficiently designed so that even with the whole family there, we had space and privacy. It had a garden that was absolutely heavenly. However, for many reasons we had decided to sell it. At the time I had this dream, it had been on the market almost a year and we had not received a single offer. It was a mystery to everyone, and my husband was getting agitated and concerned about the cost of maintaining two homes. There was nothing wrong with the house. It was not priced inappropriately. It was, in fact, charming, inviting, magical. And yet no one wanted it.

After sharing this dream with my dream circle, I decided to go to Santa Fe and spend some time alone in the house in order to perhaps rearrange the energy in some way. Because of the demands on my schedule, I couldn't manage to get there for about six weeks, but during the last week of October, I went and spent a week alone there. I cleaned, fluffed, smudged, rearranged furniture, and talked to the walls. As I drove home the next week my car phone rang. A woman had come to see the house that morning (after I had left) and had made an offer. Within hours it was in escrow. Six weeks later I went back to clean it out for the new owners.

I knew nothing about the buyers, and since they didn't show up for the closing, I didn't get to check them out the way I'd hoped. It was important to me that the house go to a steward who loved it the way I had, but I had no way of knowing or controlling that! Then, a few months later, the woman who had bought the house called me. She said she'd been looking for three years for "her" house in Santa Fe. She knew there was a specific historically important house there for her, but until she walked into mine she hadn't found it. She had changed real estate agents just before her October trip out to Santa Fe, and the new agent showed her my house immediately upon her arrival! During this phone conversation, she mentioned casually that one of the reasons she bought the house was because of the garden. She is a landscape designer.

What was that? I dreamed the calla lily lady, the new neighbor, and couldn't figure out where she lived. That's because she lived at my house, but I couldn't see that yet, because the dream occurred when she was still in the realm of probability. I had to rearrange the energy in the house, she had to change real estate agents, and we had to be there at the same time before it could all happen. Apparently I dreamed into this woman's desire for a house with a garden like mine. Apparently I saw the potential, based on the energy present at the time of the dream, for her to buy the house. Apparently there was something "wrong" with the energy in the house that needed the adjustment of the dreamer to make it ready to sell.

Now, this dream wasn't about grave social issues. It wasn't about seven years of plenty and seven years of famine, like the Pharaoh's dream. But it was an experience of my seeing clearly into the potential future. It does give me as a dreamer permission to trust my clarity of vision, and it deepens my personal faith in the truth of the information of the dreaming.

A PROPHECY FOR YOURSELF

It is very difficult for a dreamer to see his or her own future, even when it's clearly presented in a dream. Often, when I'm writing a book or an article, I'll call someone to ask for permission to use a certain dream as an example. In the process of journal searching to look for the dream, the dreamer will be surprised to find multiple examples of prophetic dreams that he or she had but either didn't remember or didn't recognize as prophetic at the time. These personal prophecies are extremely difficult to identify until after they have manifested.

Richard shared this dream experience with me.

> I was in the western United States, standing at the edge of a deep canyon. There was a man-made arch bridge connecting the two sides of the canyon and overlooking a deep gorge. I stood at the entrance of the bridge.
>
> On the other side of the bridge I saw a figure dressed in white moving toward me. I was pulled to move toward her, and we met in the middle of the bridge. She said, "I have reconnected with you at last. My name is Lenora." We embraced. It was like two souls connecting.
>
> I brought her to my side of the canyon, and as we touched our feet on solid ground, the bridge collapsed. We knew our souls would love each other for thousands of years.

Richard did not know what to make of this dream. At first glance, from a psychological and/or transpersonal perspective, it appeared that his own masculine and feminine nature had met, embraced, and crossed the emotional or psychological chasm that may have kept them apart. An inner split may have been healed through that dream story.

However, two years later he met Lenora. The woman he had seen in this dream actually came into his life. Their connection was profound, strong, electric, immediate. They married.

This dream turned out to prophesy Richard's own future. And the prophecy was even more profound than he knew on his wedding day. It turned out that Lenora's emotional intensity created a chasm between them. They loved each other deeply, they knew they were connected on the most profound soul levels, but they could not live to-gether. They divorced but continued to struggle with the paradox of their undying love versus their undying incompatibility. They married a second time, and divorced a second and final time. The deep gorge of emotional dissonance could not be bridged as long as these two lived in the same house—the same side of the canyon. Their deep respect for each other ironically required that they *not* live together as husband and wife.

Self-prophecies are hard to read, hard to comprehend, hard to understand, except in retrospect. Looking back, Richard sees the absolute truth of his prophecy on every level. When he brought Lenora to his side of the chasm, the bridge collapsed. She couldn't live with him, and this dream had told him that. Yet even if he could, he wouldn't change a moment of the way life unfolded his dream. Perhaps if he'd known then what he knows now, he would have done it differently, and ruined the whole beautiful story!

YOU'RE KILLING ME!

Not every prophetic dream gives the dreamer/prophet clear messages. Even in retrospect, after the prophecy has manifested, sometimes the dreaming prophet has questions about whether an action should have been taken. My sister Marsha shared this one with me in October of 1998. Keep in mind as you read it that she had not seen either of the men in this dream for over thirty years.

> I was at a resort. I had gone with a man. At first I thought it was my first love, Fred, but later I realized it was Jerry (another high school friend). I wanted him to spend the night with me, but he thought it would jeopardize his chances to "win" me. I ended up spending the night with Fred—or someone who looked like Fred.
>
> In the middle of the night the phone rang. Jerry was calling. He told me I was killing him. I tried to apologize, but he was too devastated to talk to me.
>
> I went into the bathroom and when I saw myself in the mirror, I was young with black hair, and did not look anything like myself.

When my sister shared this dream with me, she was still uncomfortable with some of my dream teachings. She was more at home
with a Jungian/psychological approach, so that's the direction we
took. I suggested that she dialog with her higher Self and find out why
she doesn't know her own reflection. (However, I also suggested that
seeing someone else's face in the mirror, for me at least, indicates that
I'm having someone else's dream. She never commented on that suggestion, so we instead interpreted the dream from a psychological
perspective.) We discussed the broken heart issue in the dream, agree-
ing that betrayal in love is as devastating as a heart attack.

About six weeks later Marsha learned that Jerry had died of a heart
attack exactly one month after the dream. My immediate response
when Marsha told me was, "I wonder whether the woman you saw in
the mirror was Jerry's wife. I wonder if they were estranged. I wonder
if he was trying to 'win' her back from another man." As much as Marsha didn't want to admit that the dream had possibly prophesied
Jerry's death, she felt a profound shudder when she heard of it.

In wild curiosity, I looked up the astrology of Marsha's dream. She
had the dream on a night when the moon was in Virgo, and it was aspecting Pluto (god of the Underworld). Further, Jerry had died exactly a month later—on a day when the moon was in Virgo aspecting
Pluto. Also, Marsha pulled out one of her old yearbooks and looked
up the woman Jerry had married. Indeed, she had dark hair, and she
had the face that Marsha had seen in the mirror in the dream.

The astrology of this dream and the resultant outcome is important. Our prophecies often manifest on future days in which the
moon's aspect and phase is identical to the night we had the dream.

We will never know, of course, whether Jerry's wife was "killing
him." If they were estranged, the dream may have also been telepathic. However, Marsha definitely picked up on the possible result of
Jerry's life energies and choices.

THE PROPHET'S RESPONSIBILITY

This invokes the ultimate question of the prophet: What is my responsibility? What should I do when I prophesy? Is it my job to call
everyone I dream about and warn them?

First, it is the dreamer's imperative to know his or her patterns. If you ignore the prophetic aspect of your dreaming because you prefer to look at it through a less spiritually evolved lens, you lose the lesson and the gift of the dreaming. Next, after sharing the dream with your trusted circle, you must listen deeply to the possible interpretations. Marsha will certainly never again avoid looking at the possible prophetic nature of a dream with the moon in Virgo aspecting Pluto. That may be a pattern unique to her. If you prophesy, you must find your own pattern and configuration.

Calling Jerry to tell him he might die, or to tell him his wife was having an affair, would certainly have been inappropriate for Marsha. This kind of dreaming is not designed to give the dreamer carte blanche to interfere in people's lives. However, something as shocking as this leads us to ask some important questions about the responsibility of the prophet.

Matthew Fox, one of the most visionary theologians of our time, is both a mystic and a prophet himself. In his book *Sins of the Spirit, Blessings of the Flesh*, he speaks of prophecy as belonging to the fifth chakra, the throat. According to Fox, it is the imperative of the prophet to speak his or her truth through the throat—the healthy person's instrument of truth. Dr. Fox comments that dreams of the throat are often dreams of the prophet's finding his or her voice.[6]

I agree. And yet, the true challenge is "What do I say?" Is it appropriate to project my interpretation of a prophecy onto someone else? Certainly, this is a very delicate subject, and one that tortures many prophetic dreamers. My answer is fairly simple: You must speak what you *know* and only what you *know*. Obviously, the details of a prophetic dream may not be absolute, nor are they clearly defined until they occur! It would definitely have been inappropriate for me to find a calla lily expert and demand that she buy my house in Santa Fe, just as it would have been inappropriate for Marsha to decide and announce that Jerry was dying, or for Richard to ignore the flesh and blood Lenora when he met her, denying the prophecy he'd dreamed.

> Whatever can be truly expressed in its proper meaning must emerge from inside a person and pass through the inner form. It cannot come from outside a person, but must emerge from within.
>
> —Meister Eckhart[7]

What is appropriate, however, is to trust the energy behind the dream. The prophet must redouble his or her attempts to clear systems of belief that are clouding vision. The prophet must work creatively to express Truth through the way he or she lives life. The prophet must become more authentic, live closer to the Truth, peel away any shred of illegitimate behaviors or thoughts. The prophet's job is to live more and more from within—more and more from the core of his or her own being. A prophet is a mystical activist!

Sometimes this also includes speaking out against any social or governmental barrier that prevents us from living this way. Matthew Fox encourages us to "speak out to interfere" when we see that something is obstructing justice.[8] He himself is a leader in the Environmental Revolution, and he speaks often and loudly in support of Native Americans, African-Americans, women, homosexuals, and people who suffer at the hands of society, in addition to his strong stance on nature and the rights of Mother Earth.

This last level of second-stage dreaming (like lucid dreaming, the last level of the first stage) is a test for the dreamer. It is a test of faith. Do you believe? Can you handle the deepest truth of yourself: that you *know?* Are you ready to be accountable for the fact that you are a prophet? Your primary responsibility is to own the gift.

transformative dreaming

the third stage

In the third stage of dreaming an even more profound transformation takes place within the dreamer. The changes that have occurred in first- and second-stage dreaming (changes that bring one to the door of the third stage) have, for the most part, been evoked by the dreamer's choices and actions. Third-stage dreaming, however, comes not at the request or by the invitation of the dreamer. Third-stage dreaming comes as a surprise.

Every level of third-stage dreaming should arrive with a sign that says "warning, do not enter." While third-stage dreams aren't as frightening as second-stage (because by now you've fully accepted the strangeness of having dreams manifest before your eyes), they are much more profoundly and drastically impactful on your life. My entire dreaming experience described at the beginning of this book could be called a massive third-stage initiation.

> *The price for Truth is oneself, and not many*
> *are prepared to pay the whole price.*
>
> ~LLEWELLYN VAUGHAN-LEE[1]

Third-stage dreaming comes when one fully steps onto the path of compassionate service to life. The whole self—physical, mental, emotional, and spiritual—enters the sacred kiln again for a final firing, and the heat goes to its maximum temperature in order to burn away any remaining weaknesses, fears, flaws, doubts. Only the strong survive.

At this point in the process of spiritual unfolding you have worked hard to purify your psychological misunderstandings. You have been diligent in learning to trust the communication with the level of soul. You have demonstrated that you are prepared to walk a true mystical, spiritual path. And at this point, your dreaming Friend says, "Okay. You are chosen because you *have chosen* to follow your heart."

And then the real work starts. Andrew Harvey's *The Way of Passion* is a wonderful book describing the process of the annihilation of the false self (ego) as it occurred in Rumi's life. He explains beautifully what happens during the process for most mystics: The Friend, Great Dreamer, your personal guardian angel, or whatever name you give this force, works to destroy anything and everything that is destroying you. However, that doesn't look as you may think it should. You've probably imagined most of your life that your enemies are external to you. In this phase, you may be surprised to find that your destroyers are internal aspects of your own false self: your greed, your self-importance, your sense of separation, your dissociation, your vanity, your deluded sense of rightness, your profane way of seeing yourself, your neuroses, your desperation to be in control, your fear, your unconscious projections, your attachment to outcome. These are the aspects of your life that will now fall apart. And in that falling apart, there is a heart opening that is unbelievably profound. It feels like a heart breaking because there is so much loss during this time—or at least the false self interprets these destructions as loss. But in truth, you find that your ability to love increases in direct proportion to your ability to shatter.

The experience of this annihilation of the false self, the imagined self, does not generally feel good. It hurts like hell. Sometimes it hurts like physical illness. In my case, for example, it appeared that I was very sick. And yet my body did not respond to chemicals, drugs, or alternative healings. It was the mystic's disease—an *un*ease with everything in life that is not true.

Sometimes these periods come masked as divorce, death of a loved one, financial disaster, career crisis, rejection from a lover or guru, traumatic physical accident, betrayal on the deepest levels, or nervous or mental breakdown. However it comes, you'll know it's a part of your spiritual journey because your dreams, your letters from the soul, will change.

SEEING THE DREAM

In third-stage dreams, the sense of the source of dreaming shifts. One feels more like he or she has *seen* the dream, or *received* the dream, rather than having created the dream. As I mentioned in the first chapter, when my dream teachers showed up, I simply surrendered to the experience they were designing for me. I had *no* feeling of connection to the creation of these dreams. In other words, I couldn't connect what was going on in my psyche or any part of my waking life with what I was learning and being given in the dreamtime. And I was too tired to do anything but surrender.

This stage of dreaming requires absolute surrender and receptivity. Second-stage dreaming also required receptivity in order for the dreamer to tune into the information of the morphic fields of dreamtime. However, receptivity takes on a whole new face in third-stage dreaming. At this stage, one must be less like a radio receiver (the second-stage type of reception) and more like an open window. In third-stage dreaming, there's an involuntary emptiness in the dreamer, usually caused by something totally beyond the dreamer's sphere of influence, that renders the dreamer open and available.

This sense of the external origin of the dream gives you a new relationship to it. Now dreaming becomes a literal visit into other realms, other dimensions, other spaces. Dreaming takes on a sense of traveling, voyaging, trekking. When you awaken from a third-stage dream you know you've been somewhere.

THE PITFALL

The danger in third-stage dreaming is overwhelming. I want to strongly emphasize the power of evil forces, and the probability that they will present themselves to you in this stage of development. They may lose you forever if they don't grab you now.

Of course, in the widest spectrum of Truth, evil does not exist. Everything is God-ness and nothing exists that is not God-ness, goodness.

However, we aren't living on the widest spectrum of Truth. We are living in a duality, and in that duality we experience polarities. In the duality/polarity consciousness, evil is a real force of which we must remain aware, and with which we must dance. When your false self shatters on this step of spiritual development, there are moments of absolute chaos in your life, in your mind, in your heart, in your emotions. During those moments, the dark forces can and will present themselves to you. You'll be tempted with every imaginable possibility, ranging from wealth and fame to death (which is sometimes an attractive option to someone whose life is falling apart). In first-stage development, you were asked to open your restrictive and belittling beliefs. To do that you had to undergo a radical self-inventory. In second-stage, you were asked to learn to trust your intuitive self, which required putting away systems of belief that belittled your deep knowing. In this third stage, you're asked to transform yourself into a vessel strong enough to hold the light of God. To do that, you must see and recognize the undeniable face of evil.

In *Sins of the Spirit, Blessings of the Flesh*, Matthew Fox reframes and redefines the energy we call evil and places it in a context that helps you understand its source, its reason for being. I suggest that you keep a copy of this book nearby at all times, especially during third-stage dreaming and your own annihilation period. Refer to it often. Chapter Six, "What the Mystics Say About Sin Including Rumi, Kabir, Julian, Eckhart, Jesus and Paul," reminds us that every mystic has gone through it, and every spiritually advanced human has survived it.

There are two other pitfalls at this level, and they polarize each other. The first is self-proclaimed martyrdom. These are the people who have been sicker, been betrayed more, been more financially devastated, been more emotionally destroyed, and been more depressed than any other. Sometimes, when I talk to self-styled martyrs, I get the feeling that they are actually in competition with me or with each other for the Pity Prize. Through pain, the false self can speak, saying "We're so special. No one has ever hurt like we hurt. Look at how spiritually evolved we are because we hurt so much." It's a deadly trap.

The second pitfall is the opposite of martyr but is equally as deadly. It's the evangelical pitfall. If one has a physical illness during this time, or is in any kind of definable pain, he or she often finds temporary help: a vitamin therapy, a crystal therapy, a physical therapy. In order to validate his or her desperate searchings, the seeker becomes an evangelist, trying to get everyone he meets/knows/ever heard of to also try the therapy. I can't count the number of phone calls I've had from well-meaning friends who, after one visit to a doctor, a therapist, a nutritionist, a chiropractor, an herbalist, have decided that I must go see this person because he or she will heal me. Those phone calls have nothing to do with me. Those phone calls are cries for help: "Please, I've fallen into the evangelical pit. I'm desperately trying to get someone to fix me, and I need you to fall into the pit with me!"

These pitfalls are common, and absolutely predictable. You *will* fall into them—one or both. But you *do* have a safety net!

THE SAFETY NET

What would that safety net be? You guessed it: spiritual practice. You simply must continue to pray, meditate, practice your movements, whatever you have adopted as your daily practice. These spiritual practices go hand in hand with the dreaming. The more you clear your system of lies, errors, misunderstandings, energy blocks, emotional hang ups, and desperation, the more cleanly you'll enter the dream space. Your teachers and healers will be magnetized to you in the dream, and your process will move smoothly and at the rate it needs.

When you find yourself wallowing in self-pity or verbally competing with someone for the Pity Prize, first laugh, then pray or meditate or do a few gentle stretches or movements. When you pick up the phone to make a call to convince someone else to go see your doctor/therapist/healer, first laugh, and then pray or meditate or do a few gentle stretches or movements.

DON'T STOP NOW

At this stage of dreaming many people stop, put on the brakes, disconnect altogether. The pain is too severe. The price is too high. The evil is too dark. The mirror is too distorted. The fire is too hot. At this stage many dreamers opt to close down and arrest their spiritual growth.

I feel that is primarily due to the fact that our society closes us down and shuts us out. So few people know about these kinds of initiations, annihilations, and transformations that, when they occur, there is absolutely no recognition of their profound importance. With no vocabulary to articulate the process, there is no understanding; there is only fear. I'm certain that I would have closed down if I hadn't had the wise and unconditional support of my husband. He never once indicated that he thought I was crazy, weird, making it up. He never once indicated that the burden he was having to bear was not worth it. While he couldn't explain what was happening, he *knew* something was changing me from the inside out, and he was in no way willing to judge or diminish the experience. Not many people have the luxury of that kind of support.

We must start supporting the spiritual awakening of our brothers and sisters. We must gain the vocabulary to help them articulate and understand what is happening. We must know what is happening within ourselves. The hardest part is holding on. You are being literally, cellularly rewired. You are becoming Love. Let yourself be Loved to death!

healing dreams

What does God do when he loves one of his servants?
He afflicts him. If the servant endures
with stamina and sincerity, God chooses him.

~RUMI[1]

HEALING DREAMS ARE THOSE IN WHICH THE DREAMER IS EITHER healed by the dreamtime experience or is able to heal someone or something else through the dream. In the dreamtime, healing and being healed are one and the same. The reason for this is simple. When we are healed on a spiritual level, meaning when the lines of communication between our embodied selves and the level of soul are completely open, we become accountable to and sensitive to the collective agony of the world. When we participate in healing someone or something other than ourselves, we lend our spiritual development to the collective so that the world might be healed. This is not intended to be a grandiose statement, indicating that the dreamer's responsibility, goal, or imperative is to change the world. It is intended to state a very simple truth: As each human being reaches higher, more subtle and more sublime states of consciousness, the whole world benefits.

What is healing? At this level of spiritual development, healing means much more than "curing" or "alleviating symptoms." Healing means *whole-ing*. It means rearranging the energy of a person or a circumstance so that it reflects a clear image of his or her divine nature. Healing means bringing something or someone into full alignment with the level of soul, while also rooting them more deeply in the level of form. A truly healed person is fully embodied, fully present, fully available to the realm of form, and yet fully in communication with the Divine. A healed being is one who experiences unity consciousness and sees the interconnectedness of all beings and all actions, awake or asleep.

In an earlier chapter I mentioned that the first stage of dreaming is masculine in nature, in that it is goal- and task-oriented. The second stage of dreaming is feminine, because it involves opening the doors of communication and intuition and being highly receptive to the information of the dream realms. Following this analogy, the third level of dreaming can be compared to the sacred marriage between the first two. Now the dreamer becomes fully integrated, fully healed. This marriage, this integration, this unity appears on all three levels of third-stage dreaming, but most important, it occurs as the dreamer heals and is healed.

Let me give you an example of how this works.

EVOLVING INTO HEALING

The pain she felt at the death of a loved one initiated Maria's movement into third-stage dreaming. John had been her spiritual teacher and her personal companion for years. In many ways, her world fell apart when he died. His death was particularly unique, because he died consciously, with open mind and open heart. His dying process, which lasted for several months, actually reached very high spiritual dimensions, because his conscious suffering created a healing for Maria and many of his other students. Maria was at his bedside in the last moments of his life. The loss of his physical presence pained her deeply.

She shared with me:

> For five years I have had a recurring dream (at first several times a week, now less often) of just hanging out with John. We are eating, or visiting, doing nothing special. Then I suddenly realize: "He's dead, I saw it. He can't both be here now and be dead." I would always awaken at that point.

In the first year or so after his death, Maria felt the grief deeply. These early dreams were first-stage dreams. She was reliving her relationship with John, and being asked by the dreams to expand her belief systems. You see, her belief in death as a physical separation was still dominant on some level of her being, and therefore she woke up when the belief in death as separation occurred to her during the dreamtime. Her profound experience with John's conscious death had taught her on another level that he was not dead, but transformed and transfigured. The difficulty in integration between the old belief and the new experience showed up in her dreams. The dreams persisted.

> About a year ago, the dream was the same, except I now didn't wake up. I would say, "Oh, it's okay, I'm dreaming," and not wake up.

As Maria's spiritual vessel became stronger, and her lucidity became clearer, she was able to stay with John in his dream visits to her. Her newly fired vessel, so to speak, carried more of the wine of Truth, and she became comfortable with the information or feelings the dream experience may have for her. This ability to become lucid and stay with the dream, allowing it to unfold without her ego's needing to control it, took her into second-stage dreaming. She was able to sit patiently, passively, receptively within the dream, being more fully awake, aware, and alert. This subtle change in the dream marked a huge growth in Maria's spiritual development.

But we're not through yet.

> Then the last two times I had it that same thing happened, and then I thought, "I think I will ask him about this. I think it is the brain unable to grasp what Essence knows, but I'll ask him if there is something else to it."
> Then I don't have the nerve to ask him. I don't know why—if I am afraid of being stupid, if I am afraid I will awaken, or what.

Eventually, Maria fully embodied the healing these dream visits from her beloved held for her. She became lucid, and realized that she could learn, develop, grow by being with him in the dreamtime. She no longer needed to passively sit, but she could actively engage with him. She sees him not as dead but as living in the realm of Essence. She understands that the human brain has trouble grasping information from Essence. Now her spiritual vessel has strengthened itself to the point that she is ready to ask the questions and explore the boundaries of her mind! This healing catapulted her into third-stage dreaming.

Eventually, Maria was able to ask John, in the dream, "What's going on here?" She wrote to me:

> I can't put it into English exactly, what he told me, but the gist of it was that he is now in both (or more than one) dimensions at once. He did not "die," spiritually *or* physically. In the dream I completely "got it," but even as I write this I begin to question. . . .
>
> Also, not in language but in some other way of understanding, he tells me, or I realize is maybe more like it, that it is up to *me* to get to a place where I can comprehend both. If I expand my comprehension, I can be aware of all of it, paradox, no conflict.

Maria's and John's post–physical-death relationship exemplifies how the dreaming urges the dreamer forward on his or her path of spiritual growth. Because her love for him transcends human form, that love can and will continue to magnetize her ever more fully into her own divine nature.

Healing dreams take many forms. As I mentioned earlier, third-stage dreams feel like journeys into another realm or visitations from another realm. They feel as if something is being done "to" the dreamer, not without his or her permission, but certainly something from an external source that is more powerful than the personal mind could possibly create.

These visits from John are real visits. Maria is not imagining a relationship that is gone. She experiences John's presence, and heals from his being there. It's not uncommon for widows or widowers to encounter their loved ones in the dreamtime for many years after death. In some cases, of course, this is because of the emotional tie between the two, and these may be first-stage dreams in which the dream is asking the dreamer to move on. In a case like Maria's, however, since the months prior to death were spent in conscious preparation, these dreams are third-stage dreams.

HEALING THROUGH MUSIC

Another common healing experience comes with the occurrence of music in the dream. When we hear music, or when we sing in a dream, what have we encountered in the blackness? We've contacted a vibration that surpasses typical sound waves.

In spring of the year 2000, I taught one of my online dream classes. Our intent was to examine our collective dreams around the time of the vernal equinox. Our focus was to determine what kinds of seeds we were planting for the next spiritual growth season. (Typically, in the Northern Hemisphere, we see spring and summer to be spiritual growth times when we are reaching toward the sunlight, while autumn and winter are spiritual deepening times when we are rooting ourselves into form.) Many of the spring dreams contained music.

Cassandra shared this one:

> I awoke very slowly, realizing gradually that I was listening to very beautiful music, which faded into the soft and gentle lapping of water on a shoreline. Even after the sounds had faded, I had great difficulty completely waking up. The sounds were only in the dream.

This was one of mine:

> I dreamed I was in a very old Volkswagen bug. It belonged to a young man who is a casual friend of mine. I was driving so that he could sing. He was playing his guitar and singing a beautiful song he'd just written.

Annette's dream seemed particularly powerful:

> Periodically through the night, I'd be awakened by a woman's voice singing "I have loved you with an everlasting love, I have called you and you are mine." . . . I recognized that my voice was very similar to the one I heard. As I awoke the final time I was at a microphone singing "Amazing Grace."

As we shared these and the many others that involved music that spring, we realized that together we were attuning to a new vibration.

Together, through musical resonance, we were planting seeds for a new harmonic. The dreams made us hopeful.

> *There is no doubt that the light . . . cannot work very much through us as we are. We do have to undergo a tremendous change. Even a great pianist cannot play the Hammerklavier Sonata on an out-of-tune piano; it just sounds absurd.*
>
> —Andrew Harvey[2]

During this dream class I was up unusually late one night and I happened to catch an interview on a TV talk show. The host, Charlie Rose, was trying to conduct a rather serious, relatively sophisticated artistic interview. The guest, Carlos Santana, would have none of it. Rose asked him a question about why music is such an important part of his life. Carlos, leaning back in his chair, almost too relaxed for TV, answered in a casual neo-hippie tone of voice, "Music changes the molecular structure of the room, man." Rose snapped back that this answer was new agey, woo woo, too-far-out-there. He leaned forward and very seriously reiterated more concretely, "How is it that music has carried you through your very difficult life?" Santana leaned forward, and face-to-face, almost nose-to-nose with Charlie, in a very serious tone of voice said, "Music changes the molecular structure of the room, man."

I think I actually woke my husband laughing and applauding as Carlos and Charlie Rose continued the interview. It can't be said any better than that. Whether the dreamer is hearing the music in the dream, whether she is singing it herself, or whether she's wide awake at a Carlos Santana concert—"Music changes your molecular structure, man." When you hear music in your dream, you experience a profound healing.

Judith was traveling with a group of her students to the sacred sights in Crete when she had this dream.

> I dreamed of a Goddess figure who was playing a musical instrument like a harp or a cello that was made from the body of a live, young boy. He was chubby and maybe four or five years old. In the first scene he was curled on his side and the strings of the instrument stretched from his forehead to his toes with a bridge in the middle of his body. The scene changed and he was on his back with his hands behind his head, his feet together, knees

apart, little genitals waving in the breeze. The music was incredibly beautiful and he had a very self-satisfied look on his face.

At the level of healing dreaming, we are restored to our most innocent selves. I don't mean to indicate that we become child*ish*, but
rather we become child*like* in our capacity to learn, our willingness to
participate with the Divine, and our ability to be played. We become
attuned to the level of soul, and we become the instrument of the Divine. Allowing ourselves to be played and thus healed, we perfect our
instrument so that it can be a part of the orchestra, so that we can participate in the collective dream with impeccability and attunement.

HEALING THROUGH NATURE

Annette is an unusually strong dreamer who consciously walks a path
of prayer. Dreaming has led her into the most elevated and sublime
stages of spiritual growth, and her sharing in our dream circle always
nudges other people forward. She offers this healing dream to any and
all:

A few days ago in a dream I was told that all I had to do in life was to put
my back against Nature, anything in Nature, and allow the information of
Creation into my spine.

I've been discussing the power of dream circles throughout this
book. Now I want to take the opportunity to show you the wisdom
that comes from such circles. Lindy is a beautiful young woman,
about twenty years younger than Annette. In addition, she doesn't
know Annette. They have never met except on the Internet. And yet,
here is what Lindy had to say about Annette's dream.

"To put your back against nature and allow the information of Creation into your spine seems to point directly to the relationship between our bodies and feminine Mother Nature. Since nature is a vast
spiritual entity that our culture has chosen to ignore, the dream seems
to be saying that to line our bodies up with it is to remember its power
and to realign with this major feminine force.

"The spine, in particular, seems responsible for bearing our life force. Any distortion in our spines (which may derive from the stresses of our masculine culture, including the stresses we experience from this culture's emphasis on looking with the visual eye and not with our intuition) may interrupt our life force and thus our spiritual flow. The dream might be suggesting that to align the spine with nature (or perhaps simply to be present in nature) is to line up intelligence with intelligence and through that, our life force could flow unobstructed and we probably would 'know all.' Perhaps the dream suggests that it is in nature that we can find our own true nature."

Such is the wisdom of a dreamer. Lindy entered the dream not as a psychological event for Annette, not as a personal message to Annette for her own use, but as an energetic dynamic between the level of soul and the level of human intelligence. Lindy's words amplify the gift of Annette's dream by making it a healing dream for any and all who hear it deeply. Deep listening, the kind of listening one must develop to hear the healing dream, requires a nonpersonal, profoundly spiritual ear.

Lynette experienced this same kind of healing through the spine and nature in her dream, and she also realized that it was an experience to be shared.

> I am sitting at the back of a cave with others. The cave has a wide opening looking out onto a vista. There is a series of scenes looking out, somehow these are moving toward the end of the world. Even the cave seems to slowly get smaller as earth falls away from the entrance. At one point, I consider my life and am thankful for my body, my life/physical existence. I sit in a sense of deep gratitude. I feel myself letting go. Peace. The cave begins to tilt up. Totally relaxed I melt into the cave wall behind me, the earth, becoming one with it, yet totally intact, moving through it, yet part of it. It is sensual, wonderful. I think I'm dying. I come out on the other side of the cave wall into a different place and call back to the others in the cave.

Lynette called back to the others in the cave to invite them to the same level of merging with the Mother, and emerging healed. At this stage of dreaming, one realizes that he or she is One with the Mother

Earth, One with the Father Sky, One with all sentient beings, and One with the level of soul. The Oneness is the healing.

HEALING THROUGH LIGHT

When we relax our control, and move freely without constraints into the Void, we may encounter the deep light of the darkness. The light of dreamtime carries a dynamic, an energy, a frequency that is different from sunlight. The deep light of the darkness has nothing to do with physical eyes, for it is an invisible light. It is the source of light, the sun behind the sun. When one encounters the light of the darkness, it can be felt throughout the whole body. I often find myself in a dance, of sorts, with the light of the dream. Grandfather Jack, my teacher from Chapter One, taught me how to see the light of each sentient being in the dream. Healing dreams push this ability to see a step further and allow the dreamer to feel the light in his or her own body. It's hard to explain or describe. You simply feel this light, more than seeing it. It feels as if the dying star, which spewed all the elements that now reside in your body, has reignited itself inside you. In this dream experience, I felt the light in every cell of my body.

> I had only been asleep a few minutes. Vic was not in bed yet. I was awakened (became lucid) by an intense laserlike light beam radiating from inside my head. I was aware of my breath, aware of my body on the bed. Yet not awake. The light slowly penetrated each cell of my body first my entire trunk, then my arms, then my legs, and last back to my head. As it filled my head, I asked, "What is this?" I heard a voice say, "This is the love of God." I said, "Okay, thank you, God. Please let it come in a dosage that I can embody." The intensity eased up a little. It had been just bordering between ecstasy and pain. When it eased up, it was only ecstasy. My heart was especially brilliant with an orangish glow. My legs were also quite bright. Eventually it stopped and I stood up. I looked at the sheets expecting to see a photographic imprint of my body. The light had been that intense. Instead, I saw a hologram of myself made of sparkling floating things.
>
> I looked at my physical body. It was still glowing, but it quickly dulled.

Dreams of this intensity don't come often. But when they do, the dreamer is never the same again. I didn't wake up the next morning looking any different, but I knew that a transfiguration had occurred. The dream came on summer solstice of 1999. This is the shortest night of the year, and therefore the longest day. This is the time when light rules. And yet the experience of the light, for me, was an experience in the light of the darkness, the invisible light sourced from inside the human brain, the light of the love of God. When a dreamer reaches the level of receptivity that allows the light of the darkness to penetrate her body completely, she is never the same again.

What healing occurred that night? For me, it was a healing of magnificent proportions, while it was simultaneously very subtle. The brilliant orange light at my heart tells the story. The dreaming fibers that reside in the womb married with the light of the pineal/third eye in my head. They met at the marriage altar in the heart. When the heart becomes the source of one's thinking and doing, the sacred marriage is sealed.

Tamar's experience with this light was similar, except the light that penetrated her body seemed to have an external source. Her dream journal reads:

> I'm in an elevator. The elevator goes up but instead of stopping at the top it keeps going. It flips sideways and starts swinging in huge circles. I'm frightened. Then the movement comes to a stop. The elevator disappears and I'm looking at a cloudy gray sky. An opening appears in the middle with feathery clouds and white light. I have a moment of lucidity when I wonder, "Is this one of those 'tunnels'?" It fades then appears again, with part of a white orb in the hole. Then again, with light purple and lavender clouds and light. I'm aware of my body, and I wonder if I am waking up, but no, I just hear my breathing and feel my position on the bed. The same image appears a few more times, with white or lavender light. Then I say, "Thank you, Hashem [God]" and fade into sleep.

The similarity between these two dreams marks a common trait of healing through light. First, in both dreams the dreamers were lucid and profoundly aware of the body, the cells of the body, matter. These are not dreams of escape from the body, nor of observation of an event. These are sensation dreams: dreams consciously experienced within the body. Just as with Lynette's dream of dissolving into the back of the cave, these light-healing dreams involve a profound physical sensation of the human body's merging with a beyond-human frequency or energy.

Second, in these two dreams and in Lynette's dream, notice that the dreamers remembered to invoke Meister Eckhart's prayer of gratitude. Healing requires gratitude. It requires humility and gratitude. When the dreamer is lucid enough to remember to pray during the unfolding of the dream itself, the body and soul of the dreamer become one unified field. The body alters itself chemically to more clearly match divine energy, while the spirit alters itself energetically to fit more perfectly with the body/vessel. This kind of radical, unparalleled experience deranges and then rearranges the dreamer.

HEALING ANOTHER

Sharing similar dreams with others, as we did in the music dreams, is one way of healing each other through proper use of dreamtime. When several dreamers have similar images or occurrences during the same night, a shared experience results. However, sometimes a more direct exchange of energy also occurs between dreamers during sleep.

Ginny, a medical doctor, felt out of place in her field. A few years after she "recovered" from the physical and mental trauma of medical school, she underwent a spontaneous spiritual opening that never stopped. She no sooner integrated one opening experience than another would come. It became difficult for her to practice traditional Western medicine because as she opened she became more sensitive to the deeper causes of her patient's symptoms. She studied acupuncture, homeopathy, and energy healing in order to treat people in a wider range of therapies. However, the more she broadened, the more she opened spiritually. It seemed to be a never-ending cycle. Eventually, she became depressed, feeling she was on a treadmill going nowhere.

Sometimes, when we think we're doing the right thing, we're actually trying to choreograph and control our own spiritual journey. After a certain degree of opening, it is impossible for the human ego to know how to design the voyage. At some point, we have to give away all pretense of control.

One day I saw Ginny in her office and realized through our discussion and through her body language that she was in a deep depression. My heart went out to her, but I knew there was nothing I could do. Sometimes healing is painful.

A few mornings later I made the following note in my journal:

Most of the night I worked on Ginny. I placed hands on her as well as called on angels to surround her and help. She seems quite ill, and I could feel the depression, like a chemical stew, in her body.

The next morning I awoke with a strange sense of peace. My husband and I laughed and teased each other at breakfast. (I'm usually grumpy in the morning, so the playfulness was surprising.) I felt a new ease in my own body. Mid-morning, Ginny called to tell me about the amazing dream she had the night before. In her dream I had come to her with several angels. The dream lasted all night, and she felt as if we had rewired her central nervous system. She felt better that morning than she had in ages.

When a dreamer has compassion without investment in result, he or she can visit loved ones (sometimes even strangers) in the dream-time and effect a healing. I realized that I felt particularly good that morning because I had spent ten hours in the vibration of healing energy the night before.

After that day, Ginny began to change her life. In the four years since that dream, she divorced her nonsupportive husband, sold her home, closed her practice, and moved to another state to help create a holistic healing center. Now she's doing her real work. Now she's more fully alive than ever before.

WHAT AM I TO DO WITH A HEALING?

Even in third-stage dreaming, even after we've immersed ourselves entirely into the fire, surrendered totally, and abdicated fully to the process, sometimes we still want to do something about our dreams.

Here's what there is to do: memorize the feeling. Memorize the ecstasy of the dream healings.

As our lives are falling apart, our health is shattered, our finances are in ruin, our loved ones have left or abandoned us, while all that seemingly devastating and deranging stuff is happening in our waking lives, that's when the healing dreams come. We feel ourselves being rewired in the dream. We sense a transfiguration that is leaving no stone unturned, no cell ignored. Our molecular structure is being changed, man.

These dreams are sensational. They are body dreams. We feel them on a nuclear level in the very center of our cells. Every molecule in our bodies is awakened, cleared, enlightened. But it doesn't happen all at once; it comes gradually, and only in small doses. Our job as healers and patients is simply to remember the feeling. When we awaken, when we walk the treacherous path of the vertical waking world, we need to be able to recall and re-create the feelings, the sensations, the wildness of the healing energy as it surges through us in the dream.

OH YES, THERE'S DANGER HERE, TOO

It's tempting to wake up from a healing and demand that everything be okay, which is the danger of this stage. We feel a sense of entitlement: the pain should be gone, the fat should have melted away or the unexplained weight loss should have reversed itself, the depression should have lifted, the headache should have dissolved, the fatigue should have transformed. These demands must be recognized for what they are: inappropriate and immature understanding of the relationship between form and spirit. Form is slow, dense, gross. It's much more efficient to observe the waking body and its integration of the healings in the same way we observe a lucid dream. Let the healing unfold in its own timing, remember the feelings and the sensations, re-create them in your imagination. Soon you'll find the balance your life needs.

This is also the stage at which delusional dreamers ordain themselves as the "healers of the Earth," or worse, as God's personal healers. They suddenly see what's wrong with everything, and decide they know how to fix it. They begin to study every kind of healing technique, in order to master it. They don't recognize the personal desperation behind their behaviors. They don't understand that they cannot personally fix anything.

YOU'RE AN OLD ROLLING STONE

The dreaming will not abandon you now. You're over the edge. One of my favorite country lyrics appears in a Randy Travis song: "Too Gone Too Long." He is telling an ex-lover who has abandoned him that it's too late to come back home now. He sings, "You're an old rolling stone who's rolled over the hill." By the time you've come to third-stage dreaming, you're over the hill, honey. Now the light is chasing you. Now it's just a matter of time until you fully embody your soul's intent for life.

> *Is there anything that God doesn't have already that you could give Him? Is there anything that God could need that you could possibly provide? All you are here for, and the entire meaning of the Path of Love, is to bring before God a heart bright as a mirror, so God can see His own face in it.*
>
> —Rumi[3]

teaching dreams

*When you long enough, the Divine spirit can
descend in dreams and teach you directly.*

~ANDREW HARVEY[1]

TEACHING DREAMS, AS HARVEY SAYS, COME WHEN YOU LONG ENOUGH.
When you long for nothing but Truth, divine spirit can give you direct transmissions. Sometimes, when a teacher appears in a dream, he or she wears a disguise. My teachers came with varying personalities. They didn't appear in the image of Jesus or Buddha or other enlightened beings. They came looking like regular folks: grandmothers, a grandfather, a mermaid.

What are teaching dreams, and why do we have them? These are third-stage dreams designed to give the voyager information for his or her new life. Remember, during third-stage dreaming, your waking life is undergoing radical redirection. The life you have known endures a complete transformation, and you start to live a life that is in alignment with your soul's intent. The teaching dreams come during this deconstruction period to lay the foundation for the reconstruction. Teaching dreams keep you sane during this time. Believe me, when I was struggling with my health, if my dreams had been as devastating as my waking life, I would have gotten up and walked into the ocean with the Mermaid that day she offered.

You may not grasp the importance of a teaching dream for many years; indeed, you may not even understand the message for a long time. However, through that teaching you are being transformed into something more magnificent than you can imagine. Let me give you a marvelous, funny, and yet incredibly poignant example.

THE HOUSEWIFE AND THE TURKEY

When he was first born we called my son, Ben, "Buddha baby." He was big (almost ten pounds at birth) with an enormous head, and he was incredibly peaceful. He appeared to be very wise. Everyone commented on it.

One night when Ben was barely five years old, I dreamed that I was preparing him to be baked as our Thanksgiving dinner. He was to be the turkey! In the dream he gave me instructions as to how to cook him so that he would be the best meal ever. When I finished my kitchen tasks, he realized he had some time before he had to get in the oven, so he padded off on his little turkey legs to go out and play.

As you can imagine, I was appalled at this dream story. I'll never forget the stunned, drop-jawed looks on the faces of my dream sisters the night I presented it at circle. In fact, during that circle, Ben came into the room, as he often did, and sat in my lap for a while. We all giggled lightly, picturing him as a fully stuffed and ready-to-bake turkey.

For years I wondered about the deeper meaning of this dream. What had I encountered in the blackness that made my mind write such a story? We came to some understandings in circle about how a mother "cooks" a child, prepares the child for the fire of life, ideally brings a child to well-done status before sending him out into the world. We also, of course, discussed the fact that some children know more about parenting than parents, and the wise mother/cook practices deep listening with the child in order to know how to be his or her parent. All those messages were presented in the dream. But there was more, and I knew it. I simply couldn't access the deeper truth that evoked the images.

And then one day I read a funny little poem by Rumi called "The Housewife and the Chickpea." The poem reports a conversation between the housewife, who is at her stove preparing food for her family, and a chickpea, who is being cooked. The chickpea feels profoundly indignant that he is being afflicted and asks the housewife why she hates him so much that she would hurt him in this way. But the housewife calmly pushes the pea back down into the boiling water. She admonishes the pea to cook and cook well, and not to be so self-pitying. She explains that in order to be "good" one must be cooked. She clarifies for the chickpea that his job is to intermingle with life by becoming food for life. She mercifully reminds the chickpea that only through boiling can he lose his separated self and his personal existence and dissolve into the Greater Being that he is destined to become. Her final words encourage him to become that new self:

> Become food, strength, and fine thoughts;
> You were weak as milk; become a jungle lion![2]

This poem rattled my core. The dream story of Ben as a turkey contained the same teaching, although in my case it was the turkey teaching the cook rather than the other way around. My teacher, my son, reminded me that in order to "mingle with life" one must be life's food. If we are to fully embody our soul's intent, we must prepare ourselves so that we are the best meal life ever ate. We must offer ourselves so fully to life that we become the banquet, the strength, and the fine thoughts on which a human incarnation thrives.

The real wisdom within my dream story came when Ben waddled off to play. Remember, during my dreaming time I was shown that dreaming is the direct connection we have to the Creator. The Dreamer's Creation Story reminds us that it is the human child's job to play, because the real contribution the human makes to universal consciousness—to that connection with the Creator—is a highly developed imagination. Ben showed me through this dream that he was fully prepared to be life's food, and that he knew that his real "flavor" resulted from his ability to play, to dream up his reality, to develop his imagining skills, to become fully human.

During my elevated dreaming time, everything about "me" dissolved, which resulted in a deeper connection with the Creator. I had no future that I could picture, and since my memory had been wiped out, I had no past. The teaching dreams that came contained a new body of information. Through integrating that information, I became life's food.

TEACHING DREAMS HAVE ECHOES
OF OTHER LEVELS OF DREAMING, TOO

It is often hard to categorize a dream definitely. Is a dream that demonstrates healing a "teaching" dream or a "healing" dream? As the dreaming levels unfold and become more complex, dream stories may contain aspects of many types. However, categorizing them becomes less and less important as the dreamer becomes more and more sophisticated.

When Tamar shared this next dream story with me, I saw in it traces of psychological dreaming, prophetic dreaming, as well as teaching dreaming.

It seems there's been a class or training session. Now we have to climb an extremely steep incline that feels like firm foam rubber covered with an off-white fabric, like a thin terry cloth. It's very hard. Some people get punished (pushed?) when they can't or won't climb. Maybe I do, too, but I'm up again and trying to make it. We have partners. Mine is slightly ahead of me and taking tiny steps. We're able to see the top now and there are two words there, spelled out on little round balls, one letter per ball (like lottery or bingo numbers).

H E A V E N
C O L O N I Z E

[The words are written in this way, like "Stop Ahead" is written on the street.]

It's quite clear to me [in the dream] that it means go to heaven and colonize it. Don't do it alone, but with others.

The spiritual journey often feels like a difficult climb. This dream story has a testing quality, which I consider to be a psychological element of Tamar's personal struggle. Certainly foam rubber and terry cloth aren't as formidable as a rock cliff, but it's clearly been a difficult journey for Tamar, one that requires tiny intentional steps.

This dream also contains a prophetic element. What does it mean to colonize heaven? How would an advanced spiritual disciple interpret a dream imperative like this? Colonize has a rather negative connotation based on our Western history. But let's use the softer and more literal meaning of the word. "Colonize" originates from the Latin word *cultum*, which means to till or cultivate. Is Tamar's dream telling us to cultivate heaven? Are we to create our colony of artists, our colony of spiritual practitioners, our resonate group of fellow climbers, and cultivate a heavenly community? In this case, as Tamar and her dream sisters reach what would appear to be the end of their climbing journey, they get a hint of what's ahead (like the "stop ahead" signs painted on our streets to alert drivers to what's coming). Tamar's climb takes her to a heavenly opportunity.

Finally, this dream contains echoes of my Outward Bound Man dreams. Tamar is also learning and physically memorizing the tricks of navigating the Dream Weave. Tamar's weave is a mountain made of terry cloth–covered firm foam rubber, rather than the jungle-gym form my dream stories took. Nevertheless, this is a teaching dream for Tamar. It is teaching her something about the necessity, importance, and power of negotiating the Dream Weave with others. Tamar experienced firsthand the collective nature of dreaming by realizing that the work of colonizing heaven must be done with her fellow voyagers.

BEING THE SCRIBE IN THE DREAM

Earlier I spoke of Jeanne's dream in which she was simply the witness of a dream that began like this:

> I am in a Roman city thousands of years ago, and simultaneously at this time. Robert is with me, along with other friends in the dream. The stone streets, buildings, public baths, are all sepia brown, and the images I see are, sepia, too.
>
> I move back and forth in this dream, between being in and among the images of the scene, and being outside of it, seeing it on a sepia-colored blueprint map of the city.

Well, that dream continued in a way that showed Jeanne's personal spiritual advancement. As I said in the introduction to transformative dreaming, there is a sense in these dreams that one "sees" a dream more than that one "has" the dream. Jeanne's "seeing" of this dream became more obvious as she continued:

> Robert hands me a pencil and says, "Here, draw people walking through the scene from here to here," as he points to streets that are at one corner of the map and traces curving streets that lead to the center plaza.
>
> I take the sepia-colored pencil and draw a beautiful image of a man in ancient Roman garb quickly and with ease. Then I sketch another person. A woman. A third is a tall man who stands before me, with an embossed emblem on the fabric of his tunic.
>
> Eventually, Robert and I walk back to the city streets and find ourselves on a university campus.

Jeanne pointed out to me privately that she has many dreams in which she is handed pencil and paper and asked to draw, take notes, or in other ways scribe the dream teachings. I remembered that Crystal Cave Woman always had drawing tools and sketch pads. I also remembered that from time to time other members of circle have reported being asked to take notes in a dream. These kinds of teaching dreams ask the dreamer to bring the body of information from the dream closer to manifestation by making it more concrete—by writing it down. In ancient days, the scribe of a temple was an extremely important person who objectively charted the events of human cultural development. Similarly, scribes in the dream chart the dreamtime's cultural development. By transposing the images of the dreamtime into the "more concrete" language of the scribe's notes and drawings, the dreamer helps create a road map, a blueprint, for other dreamers who may reach these elevated altitudes!

Tenzin Wangyal Rinpoche comments that there are numerous examples of very high Tibetan teachings and vast bodies of Tibetan knowledge that have come through such teaching dreams. The scribes of these dreams may experience the teachings night after night after night, until the dream teachers are confident that their messages have been accurately and adequately recorded. These teachings are called "mind treasures" in the Tibetan tradition.

In any dreaming tradition, these teachings can only come through a dreamer who has reached very specific levels of personal development. Wangyal Rinpoche states, "In order to receive these kinds of teachings in a dream, the practitioner must have developed certain capacities, such as being able to stabilize in consciousness without identifying with the conventional self."[3] In other words, one can only qualify as a scribe in the dream if one can receive the teachings with a clear mind, with no personal investment as to the content of the teachings, and no ego attachment to the wisdom of the teachings.

This is the true test of whether you have had a teaching dream. Are you at a state in your own personal development and spiritual evolution that you qualify as a dream scribe? Do you feel possessive about the teachings as they come through you? Are you clear and sound and stabilized in your mind? Is there pride in your sharing or not sharing of the teachings? Only you can answer these questions.

THE DREAM UNIVERSE CITY

The last line of Jeanne's dream story is highly typical of a teaching dream. So often our teaching dream stories are described as being on university campuses. This most likely results when the mind tries to find placement for the teaching dreams, and what better place to learn than in a university?

Jeanne's university is similar to most of these dream universities. They all have ancient architecture reminiscent of Roman, Greek, or perhaps Sumerian cities. The stone buildings glow, as if made from marble or alabaster, but with a lighting source that emanates from within the walls. The libraries of these universities are unique. Often the seeker of information simply enters the library and asks these amazing luminescent walls a question, only to have the answer delivered immediately. And finally, these universities are also total environments for the inhabitants, where they live, work, eat, and play.

I've come to call this university my Universe City. I go there often. In fact, I have an apartment there. I even have a dream place where I hide the key. I call myself a perpetual student. Here is a selection of some Universe City dreams, mine and others:

Judith and I are both students of Matthew Fox, so this university dream of hers not surprisingly begins:

Matthew Fox, Will (my husband), and I were climbing a large stone staircase—I thought it was in Greece. Will went off to do something academic. Matt and I were going to feed some horses. We were carrying a bucket of feed between us. The feed was strange-looking. Matt then had to go off to do something businesslike and I was left alone to feed the horses.

Jennifer's dream story didn't include the description of the university, but it contains two very familiar teaching dream themes. Many of us have the oh-no-I-forgot-to-study-for-the-test dreams! It's also common to find highly unusual courses offered at dream school!

I was at school, supposed to be taking a math exam I had not prepared for. I hadn't attended any classes all year and knew none of the formulas, math being the one subject you can't bluff your way through. I'm very worried. Then I remembered: Hey, I've already graduated, I don't need this credit! And I relaxed.

I noticed a poster on the wall advertising a course taught by Pleiadians. It was a golden poster, all about star knowledge & prophecies & wisdom from the Pleiades. I stood there looking at it, wishing I'd signed up for that course. There were cryptic symbols all over the poster, and I suddenly realized I knew what it all meant, but I couldn't express it. It was saying something about the fate of the planet. There was a small year 2000 calendar on the bottom of the poster that I was staring at as the dream faded away. . . .

This library dream is typical of my trips to the Universe City Hall of Records:

I was taken to a room in The Library that has walls "alive" with information. You speak to a wall, and it displays data like a huge computer screen.

I show my friend how to use the library. It is encoded. You go up to a large piece of art on the front wall. This is like the card catalogue. You get fairly close, you throw your eyes out of focus. Then you're able to see the golden words. They float to the surface like 8 Ball toys.

We did that and saw that the books he needed were in section seven. We went to section seven. I showed my friend that on the shelves are the mundane books. If you want the sacred books you have to find the slot through which they could be passed. It's an "invisible" slot in the wall. I wasn't allowed to tell my friend where it was. You have to find it yourself, telepathically. It's very hard to find because it's in another dimension. If you find it, you stand in front of the slot and mentally ask for the books.

The sacred books come through the slot one at a time. You use one, return it, and another will come. If you misuse one or try to take one out of the area, you'll be banned from ever using the facility again.

The teaching and library stories that we hear so often in dream circle are memories of very real journeys into dreamspace. In the invisible gridwork we call the Dream Weave, there is a great data bank, or a great depository of records past, present, and future. After a dreamer has developed the mental clarity and spiritual stability to incorporate the higher teachings, he or she can go to that dream school to learn. The information is presented to or seen by the dreamer, and it is sourced outside the dreamer's own personal field of knowledge. Ironically, the dreamer may or may not wake up in the morning with specific information to write down in a journal. These three dream stories, for example, don't contain specific memorable data. That's because often what is imprinted into the dreamer during these dreams is not linear, logical, or cognitive. The act of going to the Universe City, however, indicates that something has been added to the dreamer's knowingness and it will be accessible when needed.

Each of these example dreams have third-stage qualities. Judith ascended the ancient stone stairs with her teacher, with whom she was going to perform a fairly mundane job: feed the horses. This dream indicates that she is operating as a peer, or on the same level with the teachers, now. She's graduated, ascended. Jennifer remembered that she's already graduated from the typical waking educational system, and therefore was immediately presented with an opportunity to attend a cosmic class. I learned how to access and assess information from the data bank of the cosmic library.

It is higher education at its most elegant. The dream stories are often presented in the university format to make it clear to the dreamer where he or she has journeyed during sleep.

WHO ARE THE DREAM TEACHERS?

I struggled with this question for years. When I teach seminars or give lectures, people often ask me who I think the teachers are that come to us in the dream. Sometimes our Higher Selves are the teachers. Some dreams are messages to ourselves from ourselves. However, I define those types of dreams as first-stage dreams, because they are usually coming from the level of soul as a request for change within the belief structure or behavioral patterns of the dreamer. When one dreams on the third-stage level, the teachers do come as visitors from another realm, but not as recognizable persons from our charted history.

This next dream came on a night when the moon was aspecting (creating an imaginary angle in the sky with) Neptune. Esoterically, Neptune is considered the "dreamy" planet. It carries the qualities of imaginal energies. Neptune, the god of the sea, had the ability to appear and dissolve in a holographic, dreamlike way. When the moon is aspecting Neptune, a dreamer's experience is often connected to the collective dream, to the Great Dream of Mother Earth.

I was teaching a course on dreaming at Esalen. There was another spiritual teacher there, and I had heard wonderful things about him. I arranged my classes so that I could also take his. He looked like he came from India.

The first time I saw him, his light and the purity of his body and love energy completely overwhelmed me. I almost lost consciousness. I fell to the floor absolutely and thoroughly agonized over my love for him.

He did not let me lose consciousness. Instead, he held me and sang to me. It wasn't a chant or any big religious mantra. It was a simple tune with simple lyrics.

> *You know that you make*
> *the birds sing*
> *You know that you make*
> *the butterfly's wings*
> *You know that you make*
> *the flower's sweet smell*
> *You know that you make*
> *the ocean tides swell*

You know that you make
me love you

I'd never heard such a beautiful song. I was devastated and deranged by my love for this man. Nothing else mattered or made any difference.

I staggered back to my room to recover. The room had been ransacked. Everything was overturned, clothes were strewn, the bed was on its side, items were missing. I didn't care. I turned a chair right side up, sat down, and began to sing the song. Other verses involuntarily sprang from my mouth.

You know that you make
the ant dig its bed
You know that you make
the rose open red
You know that you make
the mockingbird sing
You know that you make
the bumble bee's sting
You know that you make
me love you

I saw out my window that his students were gathering for *darshan*. I rushed so I'd be there in plenty of time. But I was late anyway. I tried to step in quietly, not to disturb those who were already meditating, but again the power of his light overwhelmed me and I began to stumble and lose body coordination. I was a complete and total wreck: a complete and total devotee.

I began to chuckle thinking how upset everyone in dream circle would be. I've told them so many times not to follow anyone else, to be their own spiritual authority, and now I have a guru. I woke myself up laughing.

This dream was long, and powerful. The teacher of this dream was simultaneously not anyone else, and not me. This teacher was a master dreamer, or perhaps a composite of many enlightened teachers who work on the dreaming levels. This teacher was an entity so far beyond my own spiritual development or my mental ability that I literally could not maintain coordination and physical control in his presence. And yet he would not let me lose consciousness. He sang a song to me that indicated that I was the Cause of his Love. Who was he? Who are all those dream teachers?

Tenzin Wangyal Rinpoche answers this question beautifully. "What is a true master? It is the formless, fundamental nature of mind, the primordial awareness of the base of everything, but because we exist in dualism, it is helpful for us to visualize this in a form."[4] Yes, these teachers are formless, primordial awareness. It is the dreamer's mind that needs to project form and structure onto them, so that the lessons can be concretely received.

This new guru is not an external spiritual authority. This new guru exists on the plane of causation as a formless aspect arising out of the cosmic soup of all potential. Our teachers come, finally and fundamentally, to remind us that if we could only lose investment in being physical beings, if we could only transcend duality and need for control, and simultaneously if we could only awaken our consciousness, we could reach levels of light and Love beyond our present abilities of comprehension. Our teachers come to teach us that we are loved because we are Love.

Who are the dream teachers? Where is the Universe City? The true, authentic, bona fide, legitimate dream teachers are Love in form. The location is in the realm of the formless. You may test the veracity of your teaching dreams by testing the teaching. Is it pointing you toward actualizing your divine self? If the teaching does anything other than take you to your most loved and loving self, it is a figment of the false self's imagination.

This dream completely deranged my body, my room, my "stuff," and my antiguru beliefs. It showed me the root of my origins. It sang to me the song of my song.

CAN YOU FAIL DREAM SCHOOL?

On all levels of dreaming, and in all stages of spiritual growth, there is the possibility that one can take a wrong turn, misinterpret a signal from spirit, or make an error in judgment that results in a backing up and starting over.

People who are in the middle of their shattering, and in the midst of their third-stage openings often desperately need validation. So they teach. They think, for example, that being sick qualifies them to be a healer. They think that their diet is right for everyone, that their therapy is The Truth, that their system is universally applicable. The temptation to become the Teacher is profound.

I ran into (and paid a lot of money to) dozens of these people as I scavenged the entire Los Angeles area looking for my magical healer. More often than not, I found people who were more dysfunctional and neurotic than I. I'll never forget the day I took my friend Lynn with me to meet my newfound miraculous teacher. (I admit it. I was being evangelical, hoping Lynn would validate me by spending a bunch of money on the same course.) Anyway, no sooner did we go into his office than he literally broke down in tears, telling me he was having troublesome mother issues again, and he ripped off his shirt to show me a back covered with oozing sores. Then he asked *me* if I could heal him. The irony was not lost on Lynn.

I'm making the point lightly, but it is actually a very serious concern. If you begin to teach what you think you've learned before you've fully integrated the teachings, fully tested their veracity, and fully earned the spiritual credentials, you could hurt other people and yourself.

MAKING AN "A" IN DREAM SCHOOL

If the dream teachers came into the dreams, wrote an outline or syllabus on the blackboard, had us copy it, and then came back a few nights later to test us, dream school would be easier. As I mentioned at the beginning of this chapter, third-stage dreams come so that we may have a foundation on which to reconstruct our lives. The test comes as we put the teachings into practice. To make an "A" in this school, one has to live the teachings in such a way as to demonstrate their Truth. Happiness, peace of mind, acts of loving kindness, compassionate state of consciousness—these are the credentials you receive when you graduate from Universe City. If you're experiencing anything less, you'll be required to take the course over.

TWELVE

oracular dreams

> ... *the earth has always been talking to us, but many*
> *of us have lost our sensitivities to sound and to*
> *vibration, so we do not hear her. Through sound she is*
> *telling us exactly what is going to happen next.*
>
> ~JOSEPH RAEL[1]

IN ORDER TO FULLY UNDERSTAND ORACULAR DREAMING, ONE MUST know a little about the history of the oracle. There are many myths and tales about the ancient use of oracular divination. As far as I can discern, the oldest is the Gaia story. I will borrow from author Merlin Stone's work to describe this story to you. If you have oracular dreams, I suggest you read all of Merlin Stone's books, but particularly *When God Was a Woman*.

Gaia is the primeval prophetess and most ancient feminine deity. She is Earth herself. She is the oldest of all the Holy Ones. She is said to have given birth to the heavens and the oceans, and to all the beings that reside therein. In prepatriarchal days, shrines to Gaia were plentiful, and they were considered the holiest of all the pagan sacred sites. Priestesses who devoted themselves to Gaia sat at her altars, and through a trancelike communion with her, they prophesied the future and brought forth her decrees, which arose from deep in the earth, deep in Gaia's body.

The most sacred of her shrines was at the foot of Mount Parnassus at Delphi. A sacred cave positioned there has long been revered as the location of the oracle. This cave is sometimes called the navel of the Earth, sometimes called Her Womb. People came here from all over the Mediterranean world to hear the divine word of Gaia, as spoken through her initiated priestesses. Often the divine words of the oracle were interpretations of or responses to dreams brought by seekers of the Truth. From as far as civilization extended in all directions people came with questions, people came for healing, people came with pure desire to know the Truth as spoken by the oracle.

Greek myth maintains that Apollo and his men conquered Delphi and took control of the rites that occurred at the Delphic shrine to Gaia. His voice was louder than hers, it is said, and over the centuries, the ability to hear her soft resonant voice was lost to the human ear.

The quotation at the beginning of this chapter is from Joseph Rael, also known by his students as Beautiful Painted Arrow. He is a modern mystic of the Southern Ute and Picuris tribes of the American Southwest. He lived in New Mexico in the early 1990s, although he traveled extensively, sharing his wisdom with people all around the world. He often told a similar Gaia story as it exists in the oral tradition and language of the Tiwa, an indigenous pueblo population of the North American continent. Similar stories may be heard in Africa, Australia, and Indonesia. It is well known around the world that at one time in our history we knew how to receive transmissions of Truth directly from our Mother, the Earth, Gaia.

Echoes of that time still remain for some of us, through a process I call Oracular Dreaming.

> *So plunge into the truth,*
> *find out who the Teacher is,*
> *Believe in the Great Sound!*
>
> —Kabir[2]

Oracular dreams are usually, though not always, auditory dreams. They come most often just as the dreamer drifts into or out of the blackness prior to deep sleep or prior to awakening from deep sleep. Have you ever just barely drifted off to sleep and then been suddenly awakened by a very clear voice saying something to you, only to jerk your eyes open and see no one there? You have been contacted by the oracle. That was the voice of Gaia, reminding you that your greatest wisdom comes from deep listening.

EATING THE ROSE

I had heard the voice oracle all my life, but only in the most superficial way. Several times a month, even in earliest childhood, particularly when I lay down in the afternoon for a nap, I heard a very rich, cellolike androgynous voice call my name. At first, of course, it frightened me. It was not a voice I knew, and yet it was deeply familiar. Eventually, the voice became so familiar that the fear vanished. For a while, then, I admit that the voice evoked a vague sense of guilt in me. I felt guilty because I was napping when I should have been doing something else, and I interpreted the sound of the voice to be a scolding tone. Finally, though, in my middle and late twenties, I realized that The Voice was neither scolding nor trying to awaken me. The Voice was reminding me to pay attention to the dream. I learned to become lucid during dreamtime as a result.

About three years after my first bout with "mystic's disease," I had the opportunity to take a ten-day Kalachakra (heart opening) initiation with His Holiness, the Dalai Lama. It was a deep privilege for me to be afforded this experience. While it was an open-to-the-public event, I was hardly aware of anyone besides myself and His Holiness present in the room.

During the initiation, he spoke of the heart as a rose. He spoke of the process of spiritual evolution as a flowering, a never-ending opening, like the rose that finally shatters its bud/container/ego, and then opens, perfuming the world with its unparalleled beauty.

> *There are many whose eyes are awake*
> *And whose hearts are asleep*
>
> Rumi[3]

My thoughts during those long days (ten hours each day, ten days in a row) often drifted back to my illness/dreaming period. I could see that while I had been given profound teachings through my dreams, I had not been given the passion to live the teachings. My mental body, my emotional system, my health, my career, and my way of experiencing life had been shattered, but my heart had not been opened. My bud was still tightly sealed. I had no clue how to open my heart. Yes, I loved my husband, my children, my nearest and dearest friends and relatives. But I wasn't "in love" with life. I didn't know how to be Love.

On my way home one night, during that initiation, my right foot firmly encountered a very solid concrete curb and I sprained my ankle. But I wasn't about to miss a single moment with His Holiness, and so I got a cane and hobbled to my chair the next morning at the prescribed time. I sat down, almost in tears from the pain. First the monks chanted for a while, and I lost myself in their droning voices. Then His Holiness entered the room. As he entered, and we stood to greet him, I felt a strange sensation in my ankle—a rattling/cracking kind of feeling. The pain left. The pain was gone. By lunchtime, the swelling and bruising were gone. I walked without a limp, without even muscle memory of the injury. I was astonished.

Our day always ended with His Holiness answering questions. We wrote them on pieces of paper and passed them to his interpreter. That day I wrote an explanation of what had happened to my leg, and asked His Holiness to explain this kind of spontaneous healing. He listened to the question, paused for a brief moment deep in thought, and then answered simply, "I have no idea."

The humility of that response reduced me to tears. Even if it were true that he had no idea (which I doubted), no one in authority ever claims *not* to know. You don't sit on a stage in front of people and say "I have no idea." It's un-American! The tears that flooded down my face at that moment were the rain that opened the rose of my heart.

That night I had the following oracular dream.

> I heard the Voice say, "Now you may eat the rose."
>   I went out into the garden and chose a small, perfect pink rose and ate it.

That was the first time the Voice had ever said anything to me other than call my name. My experience with His Holiness and my new relationship to the oracle had a profound effect. The sincerity of my tears broke the tightly closed bud around my heart, and I felt a force of loving energy invade the trunk of my body with every breath. It was a spontaneous opening, a spontaneous healing, and a spontaneous knowing. Life and love became synonyms that day.

The oracular dreams tell us where we are in our spiritual journey, what's coming for us, and how we are to proceed. When we've sent our dreaming fibers (which come from our womb, our own birthing place) deeply into the Womb of Gaia, she speaks to us directly, and with unveiled Truth.

BEING AND VIBRATION

Joseph Rael's teachings were not really traditional Native American spirituality. He taught that sound, vibration, and energetic frequency are the "place where God hides." Beautiful Painted Arrow taught that silent sound is the foundation on which all form is built, and audible sound is God's saying "yes" to life. His little manifesto, *Being and Vibration*, never leaves my bedside. It is the one book for which I reach any time I need inspiration, gentleness, peace.

In 1992 I had a dream that technically doesn't qualify as an oracular dream, because it was Joseph's face and Joseph's voice speaking to me. But the dream explains the oracle to me:

> Joseph's face came up out of the darkness. He said, "Each sound comes directly from the principle it is nourishing."

What an amazing dream experience: just a head and a voice speaking a deep Truth that could occupy one's thoughts for a lifetime. Sound nourishes spiritual principles. Sound is the food that says "yes" to the principle ideas that create life. The Dream Weave is made of silent sounds, inaudible postulates, out of which all form is woven. When we encounter the naked Truth of the oracle, sound becomes the oxygen that fills our lungs with Love/life.

Oracular dreams are truly letters from the level of the soul. They are riddles that lure us into life's deepest meaning. They are the soul's way of nudging us, urging us forward on our quest toward radical living.

> *In a dream, in a vision of the night, when deep sleep falleth on me, in slumberings upon the bed; Then He openeth the ears of men.*
>
> —Job 13:15

HEARING THE ORACLE FOR ANOTHER

Of course, a priestess made the ancient oracular statements to a seeker. This distinction needs to be understood, so that you'll not confuse the oracular potential of your own dreaming. In the prophetic dreaming chapter, I mentioned that it is very important for the prophet to seek the wise council of his or her trusted circle before interpreting a prophecy. The same is true with oracular dreaming. One must seek council. This is a spiritual cross-check system. In our society we are carefully trained to think badly of ourselves, to go for the "what's wrong with me" interpretation, and to gravitate toward the "I'm broken, fix me" state of mind. For this reason, it's a little risky for anyone, no matter how evolved, to be the sole interpreter of divine message.

In fact, sometimes our messages come through our dreaming brothers and sisters rather than directly to us. I know it's sometimes easier to really "get" a message that comes to me from someone I know, trust, love, respect, than it is from a direct transmission through a dream.

This was the case with Tamar's dream.

A voice said, "Tell Phyllis not to worry or be upset by her dreams. They have very important messages."

Then I saw a printed page with II Kings at the top, in the style of a version of the Torah that I use.

Then the voice continued, "Like the messages to the kings of Israel."

This brief dreaming experience contains many interesting elements. First, it was clearly a message for a friend that came through Tamar. Phyllis was new to dream circle, and she was tortured with guilt for coming (her husband thought she was at temple). She started coming to circle because the messages she received in the dreamtime were clearly more than "just dreams." They were both awe-inspiring and deeply frightening. It made perfect sense that Tamar, a highly sophisticated dreamer—in fact we could call her a priestess of the dreamtime—would receive such a message for Phyllis.

Also, my dream circle consists of women from a wide range of religious backgrounds and belief systems. It is truly an ideal ecumenical circle, with many faiths and spiritual systems represented. Tamar is Jewish, and probably understood Phyllis's position, fear, and beliefs better than anyone else in the circle. The oracle chose a priestess from whom Phyllis could hear and trust the message.

Finally, this dream is an interesting example of the visual as well as the verbal oracle. Often oracular dreams have a visual aspect, and in those cases the visual is as important as the verbal.

THE VISUAL ORACLE

Sometimes the verbal aspect of an oracular dream is diffused and hard to understand. Sometimes the riddle comes in the form of a series of unusual visuals, with little or no sound to accompany it. We discovered an especially talented visual oracle dreamer in one of my dream classes.

Annette's visual oracle dreams come in threes. Three visuals, and the dream repeats itself three times. The first one she shared puzzled us.

> First someone was tugging at my hair. No visual, no sound, just sensation.
> Then I felt someone trying to put a crown on my head
> And finally, I saw a lion.

This information was a little cryptic for the circle, so all we could say was it sounded like she was being crowned queen of the dream jungle.

On another night she saw three very interesting but interconnected symbols

> First, I saw just an @
> Later, the @ became the center of a spiral that seemed to move out from it.
> Then the spiral ceased to be circular and took the shape of a heart.

One of the dreamers in the circle saw the significance of the three images repeating themselves three times as being a very modern, technovisual oracular dream. Perhaps the oracle was using the imagery of the Internet to let her voice be heard in a new way.

After taking the council of her circle, and then contemplating the meaning of the images, Annette realized that these dreams, first the crowning, and then the cyberspiral that becomes a cyberheart, to be an imperative to establish a dreamer's network on the Internet. After all, her name is "a-net."

THE MUSICAL ORACLE

Earlier I described musical dreams as healing, which indeed they are. But some of them are also oracular. The difference is that the musical oracle is tone reminding us on a cellular level of our divine origin.

> *Bring roots, because your hair*
> *will not hold you here.*
>
>   —Russell Salamon[4]

In his must-read book *The Direct Path*, Andrew Harvey describes a dream experience in which he stood in a cloud of light ecstatically singing with a million-voiced choir. He said, "I was given to understand that I was hearing the voice of my soul as it parted from the Source to enter embodiment. . . . I realized that the whole meaning of my life would be in 'reentering' consciously that divine music here on earth in a body. . . ."[5]

This story particularly delights me, because it so beautifully describes not only the oracular dream but also the idea that the level of soul is not personal. The million-voiced choir singing in the cloud of light is indeed a dream of the analogy I used earlier in the book of the light beam being the soul as it leaves Source to enlighten the path for the tree. Andrew's million-voiced choir is unity consciousness singing itself into form. A dream such as this comes not to call us out of our bodies, out of our lives, out of our form, but to anchor us more fully in life.

This dream reminds me of one I had when I was seven months pregnant with my daughter, Sara. I went to a yoga class, and, believe me, I was ecstatic when the instructor said the class was finally over and we could lie down for *savasana* (which I translate as naptime). Just as I got comfortable on the floor, the ceiling opened and a host of heavenly beings peered into the room singing the most glorious song I'd ever heard. They were celebrating the near-birth of this baby. I felt that the hundred or so angel-beings were soul siblings of my baby, and that they were particularly joyful that she had decided to take an incarnation.

The musical oracle comes to remind the dreamer of his or her divine origin. It comes to attune the dreamer to his or her tone/ song. It comes to initiate the dreamer into an even more expanded consciousness—the one that is to come in fourth-stage dreaming. The musical oracle is a special gift of song from the soul.

THE DANGER SIGNALS

As with every level of every stage, oracular dreaming is not without its dangers. There's a fine line between a mental illness style of hearing voices and true oracular dreaming. It's very tempting to just hear voices telling you what to do, when to do it, who to trust, what to say. I frankly wish I had a nickel for every time someone has called me with a message they've gotten for me from their "voices."

If you have oracular dreams, it's very important to have a circle of wise, *sane*, trusted dreamers with whom to share. Deep listening is the key. Act rarely. True oracle doesn't ask you to do anything or say anything that is invasive to another's process, harmful to yourself or another, or in any way deceitful. True oracle only guides you toward more and more authentic living. True oracle does not involve escapism or denial, nor does it criticize or correct. True oracle reminds you of the truth of yourself and the interconnectedness of all beings.

PASSING THE HUMILITY TEST

In addition, humility is key to successfully avoiding the pitfalls of this level of dreaming. Humility may be defined as "the true authentic knowing of the essential self." Humility is tied to the word *humus*, earth. To know oneself is to embody spirit into matter, to bring light into earth. If you are in touch with your essential self, it is impossible for you to inflate, lose your mind, become delusional. An honest, innocent, humble manner is necessary at this level of dreaming and spiritual growth. In fact, one cannot pass the test of the oracle without it.

Elaine passed the test.

> I am handed a white sheet of paper, folded in half. I open it and on it is
> written a message that says I have successfully completed number two and
> I now walk hand in hand with God. It is signed "Deborah."
>   The writing is small and appears to be written in a charcoal-colored
> pencil. I reread the letter and wonder why this has been given to me.

To complete number two is to finish with duality thinking, to move
into unity consciousness, to walk hand in hand with God. Elaine was
raised in an Orthodox Jewish home, but in her adult years she chose
not to practice traditional Judaism. Her roots, however, remained
within the Jewish faith.

Deborah was a ruler in Israel during biblical times. Tradition tells
us that she lived under a tree and received her knowledge from it,
much like the Buddha. The legend of Deborah's tree identified her
with the mystical Tree of Life as studied in the Jewish teachings of
Kabbalah. By expanding this idea slightly, we can see that Deborah
was a priestess of Gaia, hearing her voice not from the cave but from
the deep roots of the tree embedded in Gaia's body. In the Bible,
Deborah is often called a prophetess. It makes perfect sense that
Elaine, an elder in our dream circle, would get her oracular diploma
from Queen Deborah.

Elaine's humility will carry her forward into the fourth stage of
dreaming, and it will support her philanthropic work. She wonders
why the paper is given to her, never inflating her ego, never becoming
delusional in her self-concept. We all walk hand in hand with God,
do we not? Elaine has simply reached the stage of knowing it. She
now becomes our Priestess of Gaia, as initiated by Deborah, the
prophetess.

A GIFT OF THE NIGHT

Cassandra is one of the most prolific and talented oracular dreamers
I've ever met, and she has shared many oracular dreams with me over
the years that I have known her. Some of them were funny and absolutely indecipherable to me. Once she heard the following message:

It's not enough to write about BMWs, you have to ride in one (or own one), too.

Cassandra is not a "beemer" sort of girl. She lives in snow territory, she lives in a rural setting, she has an Earth First consciousness that doesn't exactly fit with the tone of this dream. I couldn't comment!

It wasn't until she shared this one with me that I realized she didn't "get" her talent.

I had been participating in some sort of ceremony. At the end, the voice said, "This is a blessing, not of record, but of night. This is a blessing, not of origin, but of night."

Cassandra ended the reporting of this dream with a rather frustrated, "Who is that Voice?" I told her of the oracle, and reminded her that the Voice is the ancient Gaia, the oldest wisdom, speaking to us and through us. Here is Cassandra's response, which came a few days later.

Dear Connie,

Thank you.

I have usually dismissed that type of dream and have been irritated at its cryptic nature. To acknowledge those dreams as oracular has been a personal earthquake for me at a very deep level. And I am coming to understand it is a sacred blessing.

A blessing, not of record (not written before, not part of history, not static/fixed)

but of night (tonight, this night).

A blessing, not of origin (childhood, past, ancestry)

but of night (the present, ongoing, fluid now).

And what is this blessing of the night?

It is the dream.

PART FIVE

philanthropic dreaming

the fourth stage

I call this stage of dreaming philanthropic because now, after entering Love's kiln and going through the last firing, and becoming the finished vessel, after surrendering yourself to the wine maker, and becoming the wine, your process changes. You are now in service to others. You no longer need the dreams to be about your psychological or spiritual process.

The dreaming changes altogether now. You have become the ultimate philanthropist, giving not only your money and your time but also your greatest gift, your life, to serve. The Tibetans refer to this stage as the ability to receive dreams of clarity that can come only as the result of consistent continued disciplined spiritual practice in the dream.

> *Nothing resembles God in all creatures so much as repose.*
>
> —Meister Eckhart[1]

Very few people ever get here. There are, of course, radical and unusual circumstances—for example, when an enlightened being consciously takes an incarnation and is born with full memory of who he or she is. But under ordinary circumstances it takes years of developing one's spiritual muscles to reach the fourth stage. For the average person, arriving at fourth-stage dreaming prior to age sixty-five or seventy is extremely rare and can be accomplished only by the most devoted disciples of the spiritual path.

However, there is good news. Sprinkled throughout your life, you glimpse fourth-stage dreams. It's like a sneak preview, or a reminder that your journey has never-ending rewards.

I don't claim to be in fourth-stage spiritual development. In fact, almost anyone who does is probably fooling himself or herself. If you're in it, you don't need to proclaim it. When someone comes to dream circle and presents a dream that we recognize as fourth-stage, we all just sort of stare at each other for a moment. We fall together into a breathless silence, a communal awe, a collective wonderment. When a dreamer brings a fourth-stage dream, she shares it openly with circle, because she knows that it is not "her" dream, but rather a gift to the circle, a letter from the soul.

One unique feature of fourth-stage dreams is that the dreamer's mind doesn't seem to be writing a story. In fact, in place of a story, the dreams are often simply images. The dreamer's consciousness has expanded so far beyond the personal self that he or she seems to align with a new lexicon, language, and visual verbiage that just *is*. The dreamer may awaken with clear impressions but no story to tell.

Another, and perhaps more telling, feature of a fourth-stage dream is that the dream needs no interpretation. It is an event, not a metaphor. If the dreamer remembers a story, it isn't symbolic, but instead a journalistic-style reporting of an event. A fourth-stage dream, for example, may consist of meeting a person who makes the dreamer feel deeply loved. This kind of dream needs no validation or evaluation. It's simply a direct experience with the Divine.

If first-stage dreaming is masculine, second-stage dreaming is feminine, and third-stage dreaming is about the sacred marriage of the two, what is fourth-stage dreaming? I use the words of my teacher Beautiful Painted Arrow to describe it. In fourth-stage dreaming, one becomes a Mother/Father being. At this stage, a constant birthing/parenting/dying/and rebirthing occurs.

At this level of spiritual unfolding, we recognize ourselves as cocreators of the universe. Just as Mother/Father God constantly gives birth to the universe, we constantly give birth to God. Through our eyes, God sees. Through our mouths, God speaks, tastes, sings. Through our fingers, God touches. Through our ears, God hears. Through our dreams, God imagines. When we truly know this in the core of our essential selves, we become Mother/Father beings.

THE PITFALL

There's jeopardy here, too. This may be the most lethal spiritual pitfall of all. Remember when I said that second-stage dreaming holds the potential for misuse of power, the most dangerous of all the pitfalls? Fourth-stage holds the potential for withdrawal. When one reaches fourth-stage development, philanthropic dreaming, one has to look at the agony of the world with open eyes and an open heart. Indeed, one has to become fully available and accountable to human frailty. It's easier to turn away. It's easier to stay at home, living quietly, passing the time meditating, puttering in the garden, praying, dreaming. I call this pitfall lethal, because you run the risk of "killing" your spiritual development. You desire to be alone, cloistered, in prayer. You feel that solitude is your "right." But at this stage, more than at any other, the mystic must become the voice of wisdom for the community.

THE SAFETY NET

Of course, your spiritual practice will be even more important to you in fourth-stage development. If you have a rich and nourishing spiritual life, you will know now that what you've been seeking was in you all along. You'll know now that you are divine, that you and spirit and soul and God and unity consciousness are all one, interactive and interdependent. You'll remember who you are on the most profound and truthful levels.

ceremonial dreams

Ritual is the principal tool used to approach the unseen world in a way that will rearrange the structure of the physical world and bring about material transformation.

~MALIDOMA SOME[1]

THIS LEVEL OF DREAMING IS PARTICULARLY MYSTERIOUS AND MAGIcal, because the dreamer/spiritual voyager gets the opportunity to cocreate the framework through which a form can manifest. In other words, as fourth-stage dreamers, we literally work with other dreamers and beings from other realms (angels, for example) on the Dream Weave to cocreate blueprints or architectural drawings, if you will, that function as the structural beginnings of concrete manifestation. Any idea or structure that is ready to manifest needs to find its best expression or form. In ceremonial dreams, we help create that framework. We are not the architects, but rather the draftsmen of these blueprints.

"Creating a blueprint through which a form can manifest" is a good definition for ceremony. As Malidoma Some points out in his book *Healing Wisdom of Africa*, when we participate in ritual, we create the structure through which a form can manifest, and we are also able to go to the unseen realms to correct damage or disturbances that exist in our world. The morphic field from which potentialities and ideas are drawn exists outside the realm of form. After an idea that resides in potential has reached a human mind, there are specific steps involved in bringing that idea into concrete realization. Ceremony is the first step. Through ceremony, order is imposed on chaos and rhythm is projected into disorder.

A ceremonial dream occurs when, in the blackness, we interact with an idea that is in the process of becoming a concrete reality. If we are at the fourth stage, we may be magnetized to this kind of group work. It's like being periodically inducted into a club whose purpose is to bridge the "as above" to the "so below." In this case, the "as above" corresponds to the morphic field of ideas, while the "so below" refers to the arena of actuality. We participate with other dreamers of a similar level to create an energy field that enables manifestation.

The dreamer who reaches this level may have some sense that there is a Great Plan in the universe, but has no specific overview of the design. These ceremonial dreams feel good, though, because the dreamer who has reached this level of development knows that life is a collective process. These dreams assure the dreamer that he or she is not alone, not working without guidance from a wiser hand, and not needing to be invested in the outcome.

He or she knows that spirit and matter are not antagonistic toward each other, but are indeed interrelated, interconnected, and undeniably interdependent. Experiences of ceremony in the dream reinforce this knowledge.

Of course, those who work in ceremony in the dream often participate in waking ceremonial work, as well. Yet dream ceremonies are slightly different. When we create a waking ceremony or ritual, it has certain limitations because it is of human design. The results are limited to the imaginative powers of the humans participating in the ceremony. In the dreaming, the participants don't usually know the full intention of the ceremony. The work is bigger than the human mind can fathom. These ceremonial intentions reside outside our limited consciousness. We are the workforce, simply participating.

THE STEPS OF A CEREMONY

Whether dreaming or waking, ceremonies involve certain steps. To make this clearer, imagine something you've created—it could be something you'd consider "creative," like a poem or a painting, or something that's very mundane, like a business form to use at work or a soup to serve for dinner. After the idea occurred to you, you took specific steps to manifest the idea. You must have (at least mentally) stated your intention to do this thing, and then organized the steps in the most efficient order. Then you gathered the tools or supplies needed, chose the space (Shall I cook in the kitchen? Shall I write in the office?), and began the work. At the point when you actually begin the work on a creative project, something else takes over; the book or the soup or the product takes on a life of its own. As mundane as that kind of activity may sound, it actually follows the steps of high ceremony: statement of intent, calling in the energy or powers or helpers, gathering the tools, setting the space or building the altar, and then allowing the form to manifest.

In a waking ceremony every participant agrees on a specific intent and a desired result. In a ceremonial dream, we usually do not know the actual intent or result of the ritual. We may not know what kind of soup we're making, because we are working in a Mindspace that is bigger than our human consciousness. Usually we wake up remembering nothing other than our part. The whole picture is not available to the individual dreamer, but the sense of trust, the faith that one has done the right thing, is definitely there.

For this chapter, I've chosen dreams that demonstrate the composition of a ceremony in order to give you a structured concept of how ceremony and ceremonial dreaming work.

THE WOMEN IN FLOWING AQUA GOWNS: STATING THE INTENT

The first step of ceremony is the statement of intent.

Theresa is one of the few card-carrying, fourth-stage dreamers I know. She began her serious journey toward fourth-stage dreaming years before this dream, when she went through a particularly difficult separation and divorce. It was a devastating experience that shattered her life as she had known it, her family structure, and her personal sense of self. But as it happens for all people of courage and power, she allowed the "trial by fire" to open her mind and her heart.

This extreme loss motivated her to search tirelessly to find her essential self and to establish a sense of self-worth. This dream came as an indication that she had been successful. It shows that her physical, emotional, and mental vessels were now ready to contain spirit.

I was on a huge bus with a group of women. The bus had been traveling all night. At dawn, we arrived at our destination. I was one of the last off the bus because I took so long gathering my things. As I emerged, I saw that we were in high desert terrain.

In front of me I saw two very different groups of women lined up facing each other. I joined my group from the bus. I found myself in the front of three lines. My daughter and two of my friends were behind me in the other two lines.

We were facing a group of women in beautiful elegantly flowing aqua gowns who were also arranged in three lines. They were clearly women from another realm or dimension. There was a sense that they were higher beings.

The women from the bus were invited to "cross an invisible line" that separated the two groups of women. I knew that if I did this, I would be joining them. I knew that it was a major decision. I also knew that this was a profound commitment, like entering a mystical covenant that was at that point unknown to me.

I looked back. I deeply wished that my daughter and my two friends would join me and cross the line. However, I knew that because of their marriage, my two friends probably wouldn't be able to make such a commitment. I sensed that my daughter was wavering, but leaning toward going.

I knew I had to make the decision, and did so. I crossed over the line and faced the aqua-gowned women. I realized that I'd just stepped into a spiritual community. I still didn't know exactly what it was, but I sensed that it had to do with the women's work in the spiritual realms. I also had a sense that my daughter had come with me. There was a feeling of incredible expectation and anticipation.

This dream story is a classic initiation into ceremonial dreaming. After her long ordeal of searching for the truth of herself, Theresa was asked to join the community of women in flowing aqua gowns, and to begin her collective work with the dreamers who ceremonialize women's spiritual growth. By taking the step "across the invisible line," Theresa stated her deepest personal intent: that she was ready to move to a new level, a new dimension, a new way of being.

The color aqua is extremely important in this dreamer's experience. In the Void, Theresa encountered a higher level of feminine energy. She intuitively knew these aqua-gowned priestesses to be a spiritual community. They were dressed in a color that is not in the typical spectrum, not seen in the ordinary rainbow. In other words, she encountered a vibration that is not primary, and not secondary (in the traditional sense of our color bands), but is of another dimension. Aqua combines the peaceful and hypnotizing blue of the sky or the robes of Mary, with the lush verdant green of our Mother Earth. Rudolph Steiner, in his lectures on color, tells us that blue is the color of the darkness (outer space/as above) as seen through the light (the sun). Green is the color that results from matter (earth/so below) metabolizing the light (photosynthesis). From that perspective, these women were a spiritual community, and their clothing indicated that they were dedicated to the "as above, so below" principle. Theresa was inducted into an order of spiritual ceremonialists. The implied intention of this ceremony was her initiation into that realm.

This dream occurred after Theresa was postmenopausal—when her childbearing and child-rearing years were over. The dream brought her to a new level of understanding her spiritual development. She had graduated from the personal and psychological work of her earlier life; she had crossed the line into a

> *The holy spirit is in the revealed:*
> *it is below. It is in the concealed:*
> *it is above.*
>
> —The Gospel of Philip 59:15

community that is dedicated to spiritual growth and service in the world.

This was an experiential dream. Theresa actually experienced this initiation. If she had still been dreaming in the first stage, in the level of psychological dreams, she would have seen the women who didn't cross the line as immature, unripe, unready aspects of herself, still caught in life's distractions. But this dream story had a different feeling to it. There was an enormous amount of intuitive knowing in this dream. No words were really spoken. There was just the journey, the dawn, reaching the destination, and the telepathic invitation. From this point on, she held a new position in the collective spiritual work. She got her aqua gown.

THE MAGNIFICENT WILD BOAR:
ORGANIZING THOUGHT—THE INVOCATION

After the intention of a ceremony has been stated, the next step involves organizing the thoughts behind the ceremony and calling in the energies that will participate in the event. These can be unseen spirits, nature spirits, ancestors, animal spirits, and elemental energies.

Jeanne's dream story perfectly demonstrates how we take responsibility for very specific tasks.

> I'm at a lagoon at night. It's like the beautiful, gentle lagoons on the Big Island of Hawaii. Connie is about to have a dream circle. I'm supposed to do something though and leave the lagoon where all the dream sisters have gathered and go toward the coast.
>
> I come across a corral, a very small one, that is only about 12 feet x 12 feet just inland of the coast. In the corral is a magnificent wild boar. We gaze at each other for a long time. I sit so that we are the same height. He is massive, dark brown, with golden eyes.
>
> Eventually, I realize it's time to get to dream circle. I enter the doors to the lagoon and Connie greets me and asks me to hurry up; they have been waiting for me.
>
> I feel I have some other tasks to perform, but I want to go to the lagoon first for dream circle.

This dream brings up some interesting aspects of ceremonial dreaming. First, I want to point out that though I appear in the dream, this Connie most likely wasn't really me. Often dreamers encounter a teacher in the dreamscapes, and they put a familiar face on that entity. To really encounter other-dimensional beings, as Theresa did in her dream, is sometimes overwhelming. We only remember them as such when the dream is a true initiation, as Theresa's was. Jeanne has been in my dream circle for ten years and in dozens of ceremonies, dreaming and waking, with me in that period of time. In the Void, she encountered ceremony, and she most likely put my face on the Mistress of Ceremonies to make the experience more familiar.

Second, Jeanne's dream shows the importance of bringing other sentient beings into the process. This step of ceremony involves an invocation. It is organization of thought, but more important, it also involves invoking all the powers, all the ancestors, as well as all the thought forms who can add perspective and dimension to the ceremony.

Jeanne dream-knows that she is to go and meditate with the wild boar, the javelina. Because we don't know the full intention of this ceremony, we can only speculate as to why the corralled wild boar was to be a part of it. Best-selling author Jamie Sams, in her tapes entitled *Animal Medicine*, tells us that the medicine, or spirit gift, of the wild boar is "courage in the face of danger." Sams points out that when life becomes too comfortable, too corralled, we lose the adventure and therefore the magic of our journey. Encountering the wild boar, in waking or in the dream, restores the courage to face life head on.

Jeanne's period of contemplation, face-to-face with the wild boar, brings the boar's powers into the ceremony. Humans have obviously contained this boar. His golden eyes, however, carry the unconfined energy of the sun's rays, and they penetrate Jeanne's mind. When she has aligned her thoughts with his (put her self at eye level with him), she knows she has sufficiently invoked his presence, and she feels an urgency to join the circle and contribute her part to the ceremony. Other circle members may also have been in charge of calling other animal spirits, ancestor spirits, or land energies into the ceremony.

THE APOTHECARY: GATHERING THE TOOLS

It is often necessary to gather certain ceremonial tools and accessories, like candles, incense, flowers, icons, stones, water, earth.

Lindy contributes the next segment of the ceremonial dreaming in which we gather the tools to create the alchemy of the ritual.

In the dream I am an apothecary. Women are bringing things and identifying what their medicine is. I am responsible for knowing the medicine of deep-yellow butternut squash. It is then my job to convert all of the things brought to me into the medicine that has been identified.

Like Jeanne, Lindy doesn't know the whole design or intent of the ceremony. But her part is very distinct, and she is unquestioningly willing to perform it, because these dreams carry a sense of "rightness." There is never a fear, a concern, a need to control.

Also, in almost every ceremonial dream, color plays an important role. This is because when we encounter a frequency in the Void that indicates that we are in ceremony, that frequency also bears a striking resemblance to our sense of color. We could say that these dreams are the spectrum from which form originates. They are beyond our visual capacity. So our minds color the dream story for us. Like Jeanne's boar's golden eyes, Lindy's influencing color was the rich golden hue of the yellow butternut squash.

Steiner tells us that yellow is a "feeling" color. It brings joy; it warms us. He states that through yellow, "we become more attuned to our own 'I', we are, in other words, filled with spirit."[2] Think about a plant that is partially in the sun and partially in the shade. The leaves that are infused with sunlight, with yellow, are brighter, more vivid, more filled with spirit than are the leaves on the shade side. Yellow makes us more of what we naturally are. Steiner goes on to explain that when yellow is given the weight of matter, it becomes gold. From that perspective, like aqua, yellow/gold is an "as above (sun), so below (earth)" color. It is a perfect ceremonial dream frequency.

MANY WILD FLOWERS: SETTING THE SPACE/MAKING THE ALTAR

Ceremonies need a focal point. They may take place in a temple, but more often they occur out of doors or in an arena that is not typically used for worship. If that is the case, it is important to set the sacred space. It is usually marked off in some way, with flowers or a border. And there is usually an altar, which serves as an anchor, a place where the participants can focus their attention.

In an online dream circle, two dreamers shared very similar dream stories from the night of the winter solstice, which was the night of the most magnificent full moon we'd seen in a long, long time. This first dreamer definitely tuned into setting the space for ceremony.

> We are clearing a meadow for some sort of event. Men are sitting on a small fence on the perimeter of one side of the meadow, waiting. A big man on a huge tractor is about to mow the field. The meadow is full of turquoise-blue lupines and gladiolas. I say, "Wait!" and begin picking the flowers. My arms become full of them and I keep on picking them by hand with a sense of urgency.

The fence marked this ceremonial space, and the arena was about to be cleared for seating. But the dreamer knew the importance of gathering the flowers for use on the altar. This next dream gives us a little more information about the content of the ceremony, but still no real understanding of what the results may be.

> I was at a beautiful location just north of Santa Monica, California. The land had a beach as well as fields of wildflowers, mostly California poppies and yellow daisies. There were perhaps fifty or sixty dreaming women there for a week of dream camp. We created a magnificent altar with the flowers.
> We were divided into six groups, and each group choreographed a dance, introducing a kind of dreaming they represent. Then we were all in a big circle in the field of flowers—all dressed in our most elegant dreaming gowns—all glowing in the full moon—and all experiencing a like-never-before-felt inner peace!

I chose these two dreams not only because they both illustrate the aspect of ceremony that involves building an altar and setting the sacred space, but because they demonstrate that sometimes dreamers actually show up at the same ceremony, whether or not they see each other or recognize each other's role. In my dream circle, we find that dreamers often appear in each other's ceremonial dreams. Jeanne's earlier dream was an example. However, these two dreamers do not have a history of being in circle together. In fact, they had only met once a few months prior to the dreams. They did not know each other well, and they did not live near each other. This seeming coincidence, a full-moon winter solstice ceremony experienced by two dreamers in different parts of the country, reminds us that dream encounters are magnetized by the moon's influence on the dreamer's consciousness.

Most dream ceremonies occur outside, involving the elements, the plants, the animals, and the colors of nature. There's an aspect to these ceremonial dreams that is earthy, primitive, pagan. Theresa's location in the desert, Jeanne's at a lagoon, and these last two in fields of flowers all give us a dreamer's hint as to the kinds of ideas that may be manifesting through these ceremonies. Even Lindy's apothecary dream involved the plant world and the "medicine" therein. This is another significant consistency with ceremonial dreams: the realms of nature and the dimensions beyond ourselves work together to create the proper forms of manifestation.

Again, the colors of aqua/turquoise of the lupines and gold of the California poppies and yellow daisies are the dominant colors. It's always interesting to look at the spiritual significance of colors in any dream, but especially the colors of a ceremonial dream. These "as above, so below" colors are what I call the frequencies of the other side of the rainbow. These are futuristic colors, in that they are implied through the mixture and blending of the primary rainbow spectrum. These ceremonial dreams are definitely planting seeds for a future outcome.

THE BOWL TAKES A LIFE
OF ITS OWN: TAKING ACTION

After the space is set and the altar is built, it's time to enter the body of the ceremony. At this point the participants begin to take action. We have made plans, designed the ceremony, invoked the powers, gathered the tools, set the altar, but at this stage, spirit truly enters the arena, and we have no idea where the ceremony will go. Lorrie shared this story with our group.

> I dreamed of a circle of dreamers on a mountain (I know this sounds like old news, but it felt so different). We were sitting around a large earthen bowl which was bottomless. In turn, we each dropped a stone (the stones from inside the mountain) into the bowl while chanting in a very ritualistic way. Suddenly the bowl seemed to manifest an energy of its own, a life force which swirled in circles.

The bottomless earthen bowl becomes the focal point. It is the "so below" mirror of the great Void. Usually we imagine ourselves as moving out into the vastness of space when we approach the "as above" darkness. This ceremony, however, pictures us as sitting around a bottomless earthen bowl, reaching endlessly down into Gaia, which becomes a swirling vortex of life force.

And what do the dreamers bring to this process? Their voices (their personal frequencies) and stones to throw into the soup. The stones are the skeletal system of the Mother Earth. They hold the memories of the mineral kindom's creation, all the way back to the dying star who spewed the elements out into space. The stones are bringing the past into the potential future by blending themselves with the energies of this ceremony.

This dream reminded me of the many times I sat with a circle of women in Crystal Cave Woman's cave, working with the stones from inside the mountain, working to remember the ancient dream teachings. Perhaps Lorrie was one of those women there with me!

Again, Lorrie didn't know the overall picture, nor did she feel a need to know the expected results of this ceremony.

THE DANGER

As I mentioned in the introduction to the fourth stage, the danger at this level is that the dreamer will turn away from his or her responsibility to society. It would be easy for Theresa to dismiss her induction into the Aqua Ashram by saying to herself, "Oh, that's only what I do in the dream. It has nothing to do with reality." It would be equally easy for each of the dreamers I quoted here to think "That's nice" and forget about bringing the dream into their lives. At the fourth stage of dreaming, one is in a spiritual unfolding that demands action. In all the prior stages, I've warned against doing something about the dreams, because in those stages one doesn't usually have the wisdom to act appropriately. However, at the fourth stage, it is time for action: mystical action, wise action, informed action.

I do, however, caution against an action that tries to duplicate the dream ceremony. Ceremony creates the blueprint. Dream ceremony creates a blueprint in realms and with intent that we can't possibly reproduce. During my mystical dreaming period I sometimes re-created dream healing ceremonies, metaphorically stomping my feet and demanding to be healed—that is, demanding to feel better. It didn't work. It was a childish display of my own misunderstanding of the spiritual process.

It is much more useful to take your role in the ceremony seriously, and duplicate that in your daily life. For example, it will be helpful for Jeanne to bring wild courage into her daily life, while it would probably not be useful for her to either go out and find a wild boar with whom to commune or to have an active-imagination type dialog with a boar. In first-stage psychological dreaming, one might use an imaginary conversation with a dream character to help deepen a symbolic understanding of himself or herself. In fourth-stage dreaming it's more appropriate to become it, live it, manifest it, and let the manifestation be the understanding. Fourth-stage dreams, in other words, are more an experience of *being dreamed* than of having dreams. A fourth-stage dreamer is learning to participate consciously with the Great Dream of the planet.

Each ceremonial dream tells the dreamer what to do. Theresa, for example, knew, after her initiation dream, that her work in the world had then expanded to finding ways to work in spiritual communities with women. Jeanne's wild boar gives her permission to bring wildness, animal mind, unconfined courage into every dream circle. Lindy's apothecary dream indicates that she is an alchemist, and that her waking world work is to convert the ordinary substances of everyday life into their medicine, their alchemical gold. And Lorrie now knows that her position in the circle of life is one of deep importance, one that is situated so that she can view the vortex of life force.

At fourth-stage dreaming, the danger is not that we'll do, but that we'll not do. We must learn to become mystical activists, to re-create ourselves so that our *doing* and our *being* are one. We are no longer operating in duality—I and thou—consciousness at this level. We know that whatever we do in the world affects the world. We are responsible to the world, and accountable for it.

THE LABYRINTH: THE COMMUNITY HEALS

Again I turn to Malidoma Some's explanation of the meaning of ritual. He writes, "What the indigenous world offers to the modern world centers around the understanding of the concepts of healing, ritual and community."[3] According to Some, healing is a necessary part of human existence because we are vulnerable to biological and physiological instability. Ritual is the technology we use to address the subtle energies that create healing. And community is the way we remember the collective nature of life itself. Through our rituals, we heal ourselves, experience our communities, and rediscover the interconnected meaning of life.

The next dream came to me on what I call my Big Power Day. Once a year, near your birthday, the moon is in the exact same position (phase and sign) that it was on the day of your birth. For a dreamer, this is the most holy day of the year. This is the day in which you receive your Big Dream for the year. This was my Big Dream of the year 1998.

A spiritual leader called to ask if his tribe could do a healing ceremony at my house. I said, yes, of course.

Ten or twelve people arrived, mostly women. They changed into their sweat lodge clothes. A black woman came up to me. She was the one to be healed. She told me a dream about her grandmother. It was obscure and I couldn't make much out of it. She said until we connected the dream, we wouldn't know the form of the healing. I said I'd give it more thought.

More people arrived. There were circles of people chanting and praying in every room of my house.

I asked the leader if he needed anything: sage, tobacco, rattles. He said no, but he thanked me for honoring the protocol of ceremony by offering.

We went outside. My garden was larger than I remembered—acres and acres. To the left of the front door was a big mud labyrinth. It was marked with short adobe walls. People crawled through the wet, muddy passageways. There were several people in the process, including the woman who was there to be healed. She was caked with mud.

To the right was a water labyrinth located in a small lake. The water was an unusual turquoise blue, and colored balloons marked the labyrinth. People swam or treaded water to maneuver that one. I saw the mud-caked woman enter the water.

There was a third labyrinth in the meadow below, marked with big rocks. The meadow was beautiful green grass, spotted with golden wild-flowers.

Now there were hundreds of people on the property participating in the ceremony. Everyone needed to travel all three labyrinths—each brought a different metaphor for healing. I also noticed that no one was paying par-ticular attention to the woman who needed the healing. I dream-knew that this was the process for this community—if one person needed healing, they all went through all the steps of healing. No one was outstanding, no one singled out. Interesting community, I thought.

This dream encapsulates all the steps of ceremony. The statement of intent came with the initial phone call. Invoking the ancestors came through the woman's dream of her grandmother, and through the chanting and prayer circles that formed in all the rooms of the house. Gathering of the tools was implied as I offered to furnish anything the leader may not have. Each labyrinth served as its own altar, its own focal point of attention for the participants. And then, the people of the community took action. By maneuvering themselves through all the labyrinths, participating with all the elements, every person expe-rienced his or her healing. The colors of the "as above, so below" principles were there in the mud, the water, the grass, and the flowers. And the community was healed.

Although we don't know the full intent of this ceremony, nor do we know the outcome, I felt that the dream certainly planted the seeds for a new kind of community. Everyone was important. Everyone recog-nized the need to heal the whole community.

The woman who shared the dream of her grandmother gave us an oracular clue about this dream. *She said until we connected the dream, we wouldn't know the form of the healing.* This is a key, I think, to every ceremonial dream. Our job is to connect the dream to our waking reality and to contribute our part to the ceremony. Even though we cannot know in the dream the full intent of the ceremony, when we see the results manifest in waking life, we realize the power of our work.

I saw this dream as a personal imperative to continue to be, as my friend Heather Valencia puts it, hostess to Great Mystery. I know that my property, my garden, my Earth, is sacred land, here to be used for the healing of the community. My Big Dream that year asked that I continue holding the space. When I see a need for healing, I must go through all the steps myself. Otherwise I'm projecting and not participating.

Ceremonial dreaming is truly magical and mystical. It goes beyond any of the former levels, and yet it has aspects of all of them. If and when you are invited to participate in the ceremony of the dream, please do so with deep gratitude, humility, and love.

shamanic dreams

*This is how the mystic lives: seeing the magic, changing
the environment with the mind, and allowing actions,
even actions of the imagination, to have significance.*

~TENZIN WANGYAL RINPOCHE[1]

THE SHAMAN IN AN INDIGENOUS TRIBE LIVES BETWEEN THE WORLDS.
Usually he or she literally resides at the edge of the village between
the wild, untamed, out-there world of the jungle and the safe, domes-
ticated, in-here world of the culture. Most inherit their role by being
born into a family of shamanic lineage. In some cases, however, life
ordains the shaman when he or she survives some cataclysmic, con-
sciousness-altering, ego-annihilating experience, such as a life-threatening illness, a life-altering accident, or an act of violence.

The job of the shaman is to negotiate between the worlds, between
the seen and the unseen, between the ancestors and society, between
the not-yet and the manifested. The shaman is the indigenous mystic.
As we become more sophisticated on the dreaming journey, we also
become shamans of the dreamtime, mystics of the waking time. The
shaman/mystic is a healer, a magician, a wizard, an alchemist, an
herbalist, a minister, a ceremonialist, a master of divination, and a
Lover. No one loves life like a shaman/mystic, because no one sees the
fullness of the magical, mystical journey through all of life's dimensions like a shaman does.

A shaman serves life. A shamanic dreamer does the same. The actions and dreams of the shaman are philanthropic: They are always for
someone else, in the service of the whole.

Shamanic dreams involve total abandonment of the false self.

Shamanic dreams can only occur when the dreamer has completely surrendered himself or herself to the service of life. Shamanic dreams are visions. They sometimes occur when people are awake, in ceremony, or in altered states of various kinds. They also occur in sleep. Either way, they have a "different" quality to them. There's an intensity, a heightened state in which all the senses are more acute, the emotions detached, and the mind sharp.

INCUBATING DREAMS

Earlier in the book I spoke of dream incubation, an ancient practice that involves asking for specific information from a dream and setting up a ceremonial circumstance through which that dream can come. It is only at this elevated level of spiritual development that dream incubation is safe. It is only when you know that you are able to go into the Void free and clear of personal issues that you should incubate, or ask for a dream for another. Otherwise your own "stuff" will contaminate the clarity of the vision.

Ironically, most people who are truly capable of shamanic dreaming don't incubate or ask for specific sorts of dreams very often. They know that the dream or vision will come in its own timing, and to impose personal will into that arena risks distorting the purity of the transmission.

If you feel that you are dreaming on this level, I strongly urge you to get a teacher. More than any other kind of dreaming, shamanic dreams increase the danger of the dreamer's returning to the body with unwanted residue from dimensions other than our own. Never go into a shamanic dream without the proper protection. You must be totally and completely surrounded by divine light to work in the shamanic world of dreams.

At this level it is extremely important to be aware during dreaming. The more you practice the night-dream awareness, the clearer your dreams will be. In other words, you'll have fewer dreams that are shrouded with symbolic images, and more dreams that are direct experiences of the light, direct transmissions from the dimension of Truth. This awareness is not the same as the awareness in lucid dreams. It's not just an "Oh, yeah, I'm dreaming" awareness we're striving to achieve on this level. It's a fundamental integrity that runs through every cell of your being.

SHAMANIC PARENTING

A few years ago I stumbled into an awareness that I get a lot of the information about how to parent my children from my dreams. Let me give you an example.

My daughter, Sara, is dyslexic, which has made life in general and school in particular very difficult for her. She has no accompanying physical, emotional, or behavioral problems, so we have kept her in traditional mainstreamed schools, supported by educational therapists and tutors. Every academic year has been torture for her. Since I was always a quick study, it's been hard for me to know how to help her. I have no concept of how she learns, how her brain works, how she sees the world. In fact, there have been times when I've joined her teachers in feeling that she's just not trying hard enough. She was a freshman in high school when I had this dream:

> I'm in high school. I can't understand why I'm in high school when I think I remember that I have two master's degrees. It feels odd—this body. It's as if it's not mine. I feel fear all through my body.
>
> I can't remember my schedule. I get it out of my notebook to see what class I have next. I can't quite remember where the classroom is. I see on my report card that I failed my math class. I wonder how that happened.
>
> I talk to a girlfriend. She said she got an A in math. How can I fail when my best friends are passing?
>
> I finally find the class and sit down. Someone hands me a test. I look at it and can feel my brain popping—like some kind of chemical popcorn thing is going on. I have no idea what the questions are about. I can't remember what we've studied in this class.
>
> I wonder if I've stumbled into the wrong dream.

I wake up from this dream befuddled. I've never felt so confused or out of sync with myself. I often have school dreams, but this one was foreign to me. I considered the possibility that I was in the wrong dream, someone else's dream, as I drifted back to sleep.

The next day Sara and I were driving somewhere, so we found ourselves with the rare opportunity for a long uninterrupted conversation. She began explaining to me what happens when she tries to take a test. She mentioned that it feels like her brain is popping. I suddenly realized that I had shamanically shape-shifted in that dream, and for a very few moments I'd seen the world through her eyes. I didn't tell her, because it made me so sad to realize that she lives in such anguished confusion, especially when she's under the pressure of performing at school. For the first time I understood that stress and fear (created by tests) cause a chemical reaction in her brain that literally prohibits access to the part of the brain that may contain the information she needs.

My astrology books tell me that the moon was in Cancer the night of the dream. That is Sara's sun sign. Since Cancer is the home of the moon, it is not unusual to have dreams that bring up issues of home and mother under a Cancer moon. I immediately looked up all my Cancer moon dreams, and could see that I have the ability to peek into my children's essential natures on those nights. These are not telepathic or clairvoyant dreams where I pick up information about what they're doing. They are, rather, shamanic dreams, where my consciousness shifts into theirs. In these dreams I see the world through their eyes, I experience life as they live it. It's a marvelous parenting tool! I've never pressured Sara again to try harder academically. Instead, I've become her ally.

I did not incubate or ask for this dream. It came to me as a gift on a night when my consciousness could travel, unfettered by personal issues, into the eyes and mind of another person. I remained aware of self, which is why I awoke with the question of whether I stumbled into the wrong dream. But that awareness of self did not impede the clarity of the dream's vision.

SHAPE SHIFTING

Sometimes, when an indigenous shaman goes in search of information for the healing of a member of his or her community, it becomes necessary to shift the human consciousness entirely. The reasons for this are complex. Suffice it to say that the information he needs is outside the typical band of human consciousness. In such a case, the shaman can move his or her consciousness into that of an animal, a bird, a river, a stone—any form that has sentience. By extending my consciousness into my daughter's in the previous dream, I achieved a mini-level of shape shifting. Often, though, a shamanic journey or dream involves changing forms altogether, which is a very difficult and painful process, requiring enormous physical energy and mental courage.

Judith and her husband are the elders in a spiritual community in South Texas. Their tribe regularly participates in nature-based ceremonies. Judith had been on a very intentional and disciplined spiritual path for over two decades when she had this shamanic dreaming experience. She was, by the way, in nature on a vision quest at the time of the dream.

> I was in a very dim environment. Sort of hazy and foggy. I met a very, very old man who told me his name was Unchpa'a and that he was an "earth teacher." He was very humorous and laughed at me a lot. He told me to drink a tea that he was brewing over a fire. I did. It was vile.
>
> Then my body began an excruciating process of changing into a raven. I could literally feel my bones, muscles, and skin crunching and stretching and pulling my body out of shape. When it was finished, I was no longer "myself." I was a raven, and I flew to "visit" several members of the Earth Tribe. Some were coming to vision quest and others were just in pain. I didn't really do anything but fly into their bedrooms (they were all asleep) and send them raven energy.
>
> I didn't return to the place of the old man, nor did I return to my body. I woke up feeling like I had been "slam dunked" back into human form. I was very disoriented and confused about what had happened.

In the eight years that have passed since this experience, Judith has had a very interesting ongoing waking-dream relationship with ravens who appear as her allies during difficult moments.

Judith met a dream teacher and had tea with him, reminiscent of my Grandmother Teacup dreams. If the dream had stopped with her meeting the teacher and drinking the tea, we would have called it a third-stage, teaching dream. However, the dream seems to be saying,

"Because you know the protocol of meeting a teacher, drinking the tea, and allowing yourself to be receptive, you are now ready to move on." From that point on, the dream wasn't a story that needs interpreting and telling. It became a shamanic experience.

It's interesting that Judith didn't awaken with a big "A-ha!" She didn't come back into human form with the sense that she had a new power, a new ability, a new way to serve. She came slamming back, disoriented and confused. That's not unusual in shamanic dreaming. It's not a kinder, gentler path, the way of the shaman. It's difficult, painful, disorienting, disfiguring, wild, agonizing, mad, deranging. It's also fundamentally rewarding and permanently altering.

PREPARING THE WAY

The shaman travels the path before the people of his village. He or she forges the road and marks the trail. Sometimes, in the dream, we also mark the way for someone. We dissolve into someone else's future, and make their way easier.

Peggy had this initiatory experience at a time when she was particularly open to life's guidance. Her children were grown, she was single, and she was looking for her mission. She'd been without a clear picture of her direction for several years. And during those years her dreams had become so wild and outrageous that she hardly knew how to address them. She began coming to dream circle. As she presented this dream, we all went into a trancelike state with her.

I am lying very flat. My arms are crossed over my chest, breast area. My legs are crossed at the ankles. I can see the nightgown I have on and see my bedroom and I feel confused—am I in the dreamtime or waking time? I know I am watching myself.

I am filled with such terror. I have no recollection of this kind of terror. Black, hot, sticky, no smell.

I see I am enclosed in a glass oblong ball, vast in its size. I seem to be floating in something, a thin dark red substance. The terror is almost unbearable. I try to move but can't. I see myself try to uncross my arms and legs but I can't move. Time and again I try to move.

I try to scream but nothing is coming out of my mouth but gasps. My mouth feels so big, stretched over my teeth. I think time has stopped, I look at the clock by the side of my bed—it says 5:00 A.M.

At the moment I look at the clock and see the hour, I remember to say "Holy Father." I hear and see myself mouth the words, then I am screaming "Holy Father" over and over. With the words *Holy Father,* I break through the glass that is surrounding me with a *whoosh* sound. My head feels the pressure of the break—gently not painfully. I continue to say "Holy Father, Holy Father."

I open my eyes! Where am I? I am alone; no one is around, very quiet, cool, beautiful light. I think I have been here before. "Stay calm," I think to myself, "because fear will take you away."

Thoughts fly by like messages on the Goodyear Blimp. I can see my thoughts. I am fascinated. I experiment with sentences and watch them appear before me. I am laughing. Then I see the words, "Thank Holy Father that the terror is gone." The words are so easy to see.

I come back into my bedroom and waking time laughing.

Exactly two days after Peggy had this dream experience, her godmother died suddenly, in her sleep, around 5:00 A.M., of a brain aneurysm. Something in her head broke; the pressure broke—gently not painfully.

Peggy had not made the connection between this dream experience and the death of her godmother. When she came to circle that night, we made it for her. She was stunned. Could she have possibly been lifting the veil of death for her godmother? Could she possibly dream-know that such a death was about to take place? Could her nonattachment have elevated her into such profound dreaming states that she actually assisted the dying in her sleep? It certainly sounded that way to the members of the circle.

At dream circle we tell our dreams twice. The first time we go around the circle and every person shares her dream. That way we get an overview of the dreams, get a line on what themes and similarities are in the collective that night, and we get the opportunity, by listening to the language of the dream, to move our consciousness into a dreamspace. The second time we read our dream is when the circle is ready to make comments, draw connections, and point out synchronicities. I had glanced at my watch when we got to Peggy's dream the second time she read it. It was 9:15 P.M.

Peggy called the next morning. With a shaking voice she told me that a friend of hers in Florida had died the night before, shortly after midnight (which would be shortly after nine in California) of a brain aneurysm. While we were discussing whether a dreamer has the ability to go into a deathlike consciousness with or on behalf of someone else, a friend's death occurred.

Fourth-stage dreaming is definitely a step beyond. Beyond what? Beyond the beyond. A fourth-stage dreamer moves into levels of awareness most of us believe are impossible. As I stated in the introduction to this section, when you truly reach fourth-stage dreaming, you and soul and spirit and God are all one flow of energy. Your personal ego and personal will have dissolved into alignment with divine source. We can almost say there's no "you" left, other than the structure through which the soul can function. There is nothing to fear in fourth-stage dreaming, because fear is a human construct.

Peggy remembered to pray. She remembered that fear does not serve anyone or anything. Whatever the words, remembering to pray in the dream is the mark of someone who is highly evolved.

THE MODERN SHAMAN

It's not easy to be a shaman in Western society. The mental and physical demands of the fast-paced, technological world are nearly impossible to meet while engaging in the altered state of the shamanic world. Yet to be a modern shaman, one can't completely retreat to the desert or the mountain. The work of the shaman, the work of bridging the worlds, must be done in the city, in the community, in society. Authentic shamans are very rare.

Having said that, I've met a few. One is a Cherokee woman named Heather Valencia, whom I have already mentioned. Heather truly lives "at the edge," at the boundary between the knowable and the unknowable, between chaos and order. "At the edge" is the most creative space in the universe. Heather lives "at the edge" of consciousness. She knows the Lords of Chaos very well; she knows the Lords of

Order equally well. She negotiates with them both on behalf of her clients and her world. Heather, true to her shamanic nature, lives "at the edge" of civilization, just where her little city dissolves into a desert. Her book, *Queen of Dreams*, will appeal to anyone who is interested in trying to truly understand complexities of a modern-day shaman's life.

Heather has been enormously invaluable to me, both in helping me understand my dreaming and in helping me embody it. She knows, like no one else I've ever met, the importance, indeed the imperative, of developing the skills of living the dream. Remember Grandfather Jack, the shaman dream teacher who taught me to see that every being is made of light from the stars? Heather is his flesh-and-blood, female counterpart. Heather can see the light source of every being, and she can also see the shadow that every being's light casts.

Heather is more awake and educated to the processes of shamanic dreaming than anyone I know. She never loses sense of self, even when she is clear that she's inhabiting another form. Because she is a poet, an artist, and an amazing communicator herself, I am going to share this dream experience with you by using her exact words.

This dream came on a dark moon in Scorpio in October of 1992.

I have arrived after dream voyaging through darkness in a smoky pale white chamber. Seeing through the eyes of the Celestial Voyager, detached and apart, there is a stairwell at the bottom of which lies the crumpled form of a beautiful young woman —golden haired with a perfectly shaped Venusian form. Her waist is small and her hips are shapely. Her legs are long. Her bosom is full and naturally so. Her breasts move lightly up and down with her shallow breathing. Her aura is gray-green and dingy. She is praying and crying for her mother. There are ugly purple bruises on her limbs and track marks on her arms from needles.

The Voyager is able to discern the view of her present chamber as the young woman perceives it. A dirty city sky can be seen high above, but there is no way out of the courtyard she lies in. She lies aching on cement in this place with no doors or windows. The stairs lead up to a short hall with a locked door at one end and a door to the right opening into an office with no other doors or windows. The only furniture is a desk with a chair and a red phone.

A middle-aged woman with dyed wine-colored hair is manning the phone. There are two other young girls in the room. One leans on the desk, the other lies prone in the corner with a needle in her arm. The phone woman is like a prison guard.

There is no water anywhere. The dryness and uncleanness is stifling. The mood of the dream is deadly. The dreamer knows the girl does not have long to live without intervention. What keeps her breathing is a tiny blue ceramic bead on a black satin cord that she wears as a necklace. It carries a shimmer light of the dreamer's prayer magic in the form of Divine Mother Love.

The dream ends there, but Heather's explanation continues. She says: "My personal and innermost dream circle is made up of my Cherokee cousins, originally from Oklahoma, my Yaqui niece from Tucson, who is the head dreamer of her generation, and our Arikara elder, originally from South Dakota. My twin dreamer is my Cherokee cousin born in my sun sign, Pisces. She had the counterpart to this dream.

"Hers was a dream of maps and numbers and letters that decoded the exact location in New York City of the actual event of the dream. In circle we were able to recognize and decipher the soul of the young woman in the dream, who was presently trapped in a heroin bardo as an enslaved prostitute. Although I had not recognized her in the dream, we perceived in circle that she was one of my spiritual goddaughters, a dreaming woman of our tradition. Her mother was a recluse living in the mountains of the Sonora Desert. This mother was a pure and simple spirit, a medicine woman of a most ancient Yoeme tradition, who spent her days creating sacred beadwork as a prayer form.

"The blue bead on her daughter's necklace spoke to us from the soul of her daughter through the Dream Weave. The daughter, whom we shall call Zara, had left her mother's home three months earlier, headed to New York City with a drug dealer driving a black Jaguar. Her mother had had no word, but could feel her daughter in her heart and prayed with her beading each day to be able to help her child.

"The man had turned nineteen-year-old Zara into a captive prostitute with drugs. When Zara spoke to our circle through the dream, we were able to call her mother and give her the precise location of her daughter. Her simple and beautiful mother left her seclusion, flew on a plane to New York City, took a cab to the location, and found her daughter's crumpled form at the bottom of some cement steps. She brought her home. Zara lives."

This is an amazing example of dreaming in both the third and fourth stages. You see, Zara, even at age nineteen, was a third-stage dreamer. She holds the rare privilege of being born into a lineage of master dreamers. And, as is often the case, being born at such an advanced stage is very difficult for a young woman. When she reached her teenage years, when she was supposed to be forming an ego and working on the very first levels of spiritual development, she was already thrust into some profound and sophisticated dreaming. Zara is an example of what happens when too much light comes too quickly.

Zara was in her annihilation phase. The thing that saved her was the blue bead around her neck, which was connected to the dreamer's energy. Zara's blue stone connected her to the fourth-stage dreamers who were willing to function as vessels for the light to find her and bring her home.

Heather did not incubate this dream. She did not ask to find Zara. In fact, she didn't even recognize Zara until her circle helped her decode the dream images. Had she gone looking for Zara out of her own will, she may not have been able to see as clearly. And had her cousin also incubated a dream looking for Zara, they may not have been able to assist each other.

What a portentous example of shamanic dreaming, coupled with shamanic dream circle work! Heather Valencia is a dream bodhisattva, a highly sophisticated and highly evolved dreaming woman who is dedicated to work for the healing of the greater community.

As you can see, shamanic dreaming is not for the faint of heart, and not to be entered lightly. It is real, powerful, and a dynamic aspect of our potential as we mature into fourth-stage dreamers.

phenomenal dreams

*Just as we can make Otherworld journeys,
Otherworld beings come visit us . . . to confirm the
reality of experiences in other orders of reality by
bringing a gift or a marker into this one.*

~Robert Moss[1]

PHENOMENAL DREAMS ARE PERHAPS THE HARDEST TO DEFINE BEcause they really blur the line between *what's real* and *what's a dream*. A phenomenal dream involves an action that leaves traces of itself in both realities. Shamanic dreams have aftereffects that we can see and measure in concrete reality. During a phenomenal dream, one experiences something in the dream, and when one awakens, there are indications that it actually happened simultaneously in the concrete world, or that the dreamer was taken bodily into another dimension and then sent back to the concrete world with proof. This is not telepathic or clairvoyant dreaming, because phenomenal dreams *are* local to the dreamer, and traces that something real happened are left near the dreamer. But it couldn't have happened. It was a dream! Wasn't it?

Let me give you a personal example. I was on retreat once in the mountains of Montana. I was sleeping alone in my tent, and there were probably forty other people, also in their tents, all within a hundred yards of mine. It was freezing cold, and I'm not particularly spiritual when I'm cold, nor do I sleep well. As I struggled with sleep, and cursed myself for ever having the idea to go on this retreat, I heard a bear outside my tent. It was scratching and huffing and puffing and grunting. I peeked out of the little tent window and *saw* a mediumsized brown bear. I was terrified and decided to call for help, but when I opened my mouth nothing came out. "Oh, I'm dreaming!" I thought happily. I knew I was dreaming because it was that familiar kind of dream-attempt to scream, and the scream stuck in the throat. So I calmed down and intentionally dissolved into a deeper sleep, a nap within the dream, thinking about all the medicine metaphors of a dream bear scratching at my tent, and wishing I had the ability to grow my own bear's fur to keep me warm. Where was Crystal Cave Woman and her bear rug when I needed her?

The next morning, to my astonishment, I found bear prints all around the outside of my tent, and one long scratch almost all the way through the wall of my tent. Yet there were no bear prints coming or going from my tent. The prints were only around my tent. And no one else heard the bear. You tell me, was I dreaming? Was there a bear? If so, how did he get there? If not, how did those prints get there? Did he just manifest there at my tent door and then disappear?

That's a phenomenal dream. It leaves a trace of itself in the phenomenal world.

Now, on a superficial level, this dream doesn't seem particularly spiritually elevated. It doesn't seem like a fourth-stage philanthropic dream. And perhaps it wasn't. Perhaps this particular dream was one of those sneak-preview dreams. However, it does cross the boundary between waking and sleeping realities, and it does beg the question: Where are we when we dream? Exactly where are these other dimensions into which our consciousness enters? Our waking reality is a time/space world. Where in time/space is dreaming?

It's fairly clear to me, after all these years of studying phenomenal dreams, that time/space collapses in dreamscapes, and in fact, it all overlaps. Let's look at a couple more similar dream experiences.

THE PHENOMENAL FOOTPRINT

Tamar was also camping when she had this experience:

> I seem to be awakened by many footsteps, and someone running, leaping over my sleeping bag as they pass through the campground. Soon I hear a police radio. I dream-know that this is just one incident in a big police roundup that is being featured on the national news.
>
> My mother [deceased] is watching as they describe the campground in-

cident. She knows I'm camping but thinks I'm in the Ventana so she says, "I'm glad Tamar's not there."

Then I'm sitting on a grassy hill reading and a TV reporter comes up. I realize that he's probably going to interview me and my mother will find out that I was here after all. Instead, he talks to me about Judaism and feminism.

Tamar awoke from this dream when she heard her husband getting out of his sleeping bag. Some people camping nearby were playing a radio quite loudly and he got up to go ask them to turn it down. She realized that she had been dreaming, and went back to sleep. However, the next morning when she woke up, she found fresh footprints around her sleeping bag. The footprints did not look like the shoes of anyone in her family. No one else heard anything, nor was there any reported incident in the campground that night. The footprint on Tamar's sleeping mat, just a few inches from her head, was particularly fresh and visible.

THE PHENOMENAL BICYCLE TRACKS

In case you think these dreams only happen to city girls in uncomfortable camping situations, here's a really amazing experience that happened to Peggy in her Texas bedroom.

In my dream an old woman appeared riding a bicycle. I saw her come into my room through the window beside my bed. I did not know if I was asleep or awake because I saw my room so clearly and saw the bike come through my window and land at the foot of my bed.

She was quite old. She had glasses on with a Kleenex stuffed in one side up by her left temple. Her hair was white, very curly, pulled back into a low ponytail on the nape of her neck. She was very real and I sat up in bed, leaned forward to touch her. The fabric of her dress felt like rough linen.

She looked at me and said, "I am you." I kept looking at her thinking, "No, she can't be me. I don't look like that." She continued to say, "I am you, I am you!"

She just sat on her bike and stared at me for what seemed like forever.

I began to stare back and again I thought, "She is not me." Eventually, she turned her eyes away from me, turned the bike around and flew out of the window the way she had come in.

I woke up this time. The whole dream felt so real! I crawled down to the end of the bed to look at where she had been and in my carpet were bike tread marks.

There were two interesting phenomenal indications in this dream. First, Peggy felt the fabric of the woman's dress. Of course, it's not terribly unusual in a sleeping dream to feel a texture or a fabric, so that could be dismissed as a part of the dream rather than a concrete phenomenon. But the second, the bicycle tread marks on the carpet, defies explanation. Short of "she's lying," the conclusion any red-blooded unbeliever would draw, there's no explanation other than that the two worlds collided in Peggy's bedroom.

All three of these dreams—my bear tracks, Tamar's footprints, and Peggy's bicycle tracks—fit most of the criterion for being fourth-stage dreams. In each case, the dreamer's mind wasn't creating a dream-story metaphor for some other kind of experience. The experience was real and it left real traces of itself in the concrete realm. These dreams don't really need interpretation. They are curious events, but they are not really symbolic of something else. They are experiences that crossed two dimensions. The dreamers don't think they're crazy, and they don't think perhaps the event didn't really happen.

However, on one very essential level, these dreams don't quite meet all the qualifications of being fourth-stage dreams. They do not appear to be philanthropic. They do not appear to have done something beneficial for another being. They appear to be nothing more than ordinary events. I suggest this is because these dreams were the sneak-preview type phenomenal dreams. We experience them simply to flex our muscles, to test ourselves, and to see if we would take them in stride or freak out over them. These are the workouts that lead to the later, more important dreams of this level.

A GATEWAY

Author Jamie Sams and I clicked immediately when we met. Dreamers often recognize each other on deep levels at first glance. She immediately became a supporting sister and a ruthless prod. Were it not for Jamie, I would never have published a book. I was comfortable sitting quietly in my living room with my safe little dream circle.

I'd not known Jamie long when she told me a story about herself and a dream experience she'd had that completely stunned me. In fact, it was so astonishing that I forgot about it until several years later when I started writing this book. With her permission, I share it with you now.

Jamie and I both grew up in Texas, although we did not know each other then. It's not easy to be a dreaming woman in Texas, because there's not a lot of room for alternative thinking and non–Bible belt behavior—or at least there wasn't when we were kids. After undergraduate school I did what all good Texas girls did at that time: got married, moved to Austin, and started being *normal*. The marriage lasted two whole years; the normal part only lasted about a month!

Jamie, on the other hand, went to Mexico, met some powerful medicine people, and, under their tutelage, began her deep spiritual, psychological, and emotional work. She quickly became a devoted, albeit young and stupid (her words, not mine), student of a group of teachers who belonged to a secret dreaming society. (You can read about many of her experiences in her book *Dancing the Dream*.) Because of the delicate nature of her shamanic work there, I'm not at liberty to tell the story that led up to her tragic accident. But after she'd been in Mexico about three years she fell and broke her back in three places. Miraculously, she lived, but she was eventually forced to return to the United States to convalesce.

Recovery was slow and painful, but eventually she was able to walk again. She went to Austin, started singing for a living, and did her best to become normal (like me). Although she returned to Mexico periodically, and never stopped her shamanic work, it was over ten years before Jamie mentioned her medicine training to many of her friends or family. It was seventeen years before she published her first book, and eighteen years before she published the Medicine Cards, which established her reputation as a woman of wisdom. However, during that time, she never stopped her spiritual practices. She lived in Austin, Texas, and Los Angeles, California, working in the music industry but staying highly disciplined in her spiritual training. That means she stayed sober, celibate, drug-free, participated in ceremony weekly, and practiced meditation daily—all of which was not easy in those free-flowing drug/alcohol/sex days of the late seventies.

Twenty-two years after returning from Mexico, she was living in Santa Fe, New Mexico, maintaining a relatively quiet, secluded lifestyle. Then she had met a man and decided to "break the rule" of celibacy. Her teachers had emphasized that through sexual union, and specifically through having children, you give away too much of yourself, and that diminishes the dreaming potential. Jamie, because of a hysterectomy, would not be having children, so she felt that marrying, loving, and being loved would be an acceptable decision, and certainly a personally important one for her. One afternoon during naptime (dreaming women love naptime) she had the following dream experience:

I was walking down a modern-day Mexican small city street. I caught a glimpse of myself in the window. In the mirror image, my hair was cut differently, my clothes were not the ones I had on, and my face was slightly different. I recognized the image as being the "me" that had broken her back twenty-two years earlier.

This me was apparently living in this small mountain town in Mexico, working as a healer and following to the letter the ancient protocol of my teachers. She started screaming at me. The emotion was palpable, the rage visible in her face. She screamed, "How dare you leave the path."

Clearly, she felt I should have returned to Mexico as soon as my back had healed and picked up my medicine studies. She was furious with me for contemplating marriage. To escape her rage, I moved on down the street. There she was in the next window. Each time I moved down the street, she showed up in the window. In each window I was thrust into a vignette of my personal history when I'd reached choice points in my life. She was furious with me for some of my choices. The dream was excruciating because it meant reliving so much of the painful parts of my life.

I woke up fourteen hours later lying naked on my dining room floor. I have no idea where my gown went—the one I'd put on to take my nap. I've not seen it since. In addition, I was holding a stone in my hand which had been in my medicine bundle that I used to wear when I was in Mexico. That bundle was stolen from me before I returned to the United States, and I'd not seen it since then.

This experience is an amazing example of phenomenal dreaming. The disappearance of her sleeping clothes and the appearance of one of her medicine stones are incredible cross-dimensional traces. She had no physical signs of harm. She checked for bruises or head injuries to perhaps explain why she'd been out for fourteen hours. There were no physical explanations.

The dream experience made a dramatic change in Jamie's inner life. As a result of this dream, all her fears and all her concerns about walking the path of the healer/dreamer ended. She had seen her choice points, she had seen their results, and she was able to put closure on some of the painful parts of her history. In addition, she was empowered by the dream.

This dream experience created a profound recapitulation for Jamie. She was carried (sometimes it felt like dragged) back through all her choices of the past twenty-two years. She saw the advantages and disadvantages of them. But more important, she disconnected from them, and simultaneously took full responsibility for them.

The most important result of this experience for Jamie was that she was liberated from the taboos of the old dreaming teachings. She saw that in some cases *the old rules do not apply.* She realized that every man or woman of power has to make his or her own choices and take responsibility for them. The taboo that requires celibacy in her tradition came from an old paradigm that needed to be changed. Through this dreaming experience, Jamie saw that her responsibility to that traditional lineage was to shift the paradigms that were outdated. She was here to love freely, without judgment and without limitation, to marry if she so chose, to do her heart's calling rather than to blindly obey a tradition. She certainly has not abandoned the dream teachings in any sense, but she has examined the energy behind the taboos, and broken them when they needed to be broken. Through this experience, she learned that she has the spiritual strength to do it all—to live fully, to love fully, and to be a dreamer.

In metaphysical terms, a physical object that comes to us from another dimension functions as a gateway into that dimension. Through appropriate use of such a gateway, we have the ability to move back and forth between dimensions, and thereby expand our consciousness beyond the typical barriers of human agreement. Jamie's medicine stone was restored to her during this phenomenal dreaming experience as a reminder that she is a multidimensional being. Her "work" involves not only the normal work of any Texas good girl, but also the mystical work of a dreamer. She travels freely between dimensions.

For the next two weeks after this dream, Jamie was disoriented and confused. But also, during that time, she realized that the experience had set her free. Jamie's gift to us all is the encouragement to be free. She demonstrates the new paradigm through her life. She is now the hub of a wheel that turns many more wheels. She is the inspiration of hundreds of circles of dreamers around the world.

MY MENTOR

Earlier I mentioned that fourth-stage dreamers rarely identify themselves. Such is the case with my octogenarian friend Richard. I recently had a long inspired conversation with him about his dreaming and how it has developed and transformed over the years and stages of his life. When I asked if I might use our conversation in my book, he admonished me not to reveal his real name. He modestly stated, "I've heard that one never advertises one's level of evolution."

So I won't advertise Richard's level of evolution. But I will tell you a divine story about him, and I'll reveal some marvelous dreaming stories from this remarkable man.

Remember that a legitimate fourth-stage dreamer who has a strong and authentic spiritual practice will magnetize the people who need to hear what he or she has to say. Such was the case with Richard and me.

I am a voracious reader. My husband laughingly says I'm the only person he knows who reads quantum physics for relaxation. At the time of my first meeting with Richard, I was devouring Alice Bailey's material. Alice Bailey lived in the early and middle part of the twentieth century. She had a unique intuitive relationship with a spiritual Master who simply identified himself to her as the Tibetan. He telepathically dictated to her, through her sophisticated intuitive reception, about two dozen books covering a wide range of material from the ins and outs of spiritual discipleship to esoteric astrology.

I boarded a plane one day, a last-minute decision, to make a trip to check on my house in Santa Fe, toting an Alice Bailey book and *People* magazine. It was an open-seat flight, and I was traveling alone, so I looked for a seat next to the person most likely to leave me alone with my reading. I was not interested in idle chatting that day: I was too absorbed with spiritual ideas. Then I spotted an older gentleman with a big, fabulous Santa Claus beard. He was traveling with a woman I presumed to be his wife. There was an aisle seat next to him. I nodded politely, asked if the seat were taken, fastened my seat belt, and dug out my books.

Just to be on the safe side, I hid the Alice Bailey book inside my *People* magazine so my seatmates wouldn't know I was reading an esoteric treatise on white magic. Richard sat quietly and respectfully for about twenty minutes, although in retrospect I'm sure he was laughing in his beard. Finally, he leaned toward me ever so slightly and whispered, "You know, I've been an Alice Bailey student for over forty years." Of all the seats I could have chosen, and all the flights I could have hopped, I landed next to the man who would serve as my mentor, my brother, my teacher, my friend for the next few years.

In the many years since then, Richard, who is a transpersonal therapist, has helped me mark and chart my own spiritual growth. He has taught me about service, spiritual discipleship, humility, and gratitude. Sometimes he reminds me of The Hermit in the tarot deck, waiting patiently at the top of the mountain, holding the lantern to light my way, while I scuffle and scramble around in the shrubs and rocks below.

When it came to writing about fourth-stage dreaming for this book, I called Richard first. "I'm writing beyond my own experience now. What can you say to me about dreaming at your level of evolution?" He shared several dream experiences with me, one of which I already reported in the chapter on prophetic dreams.

VISITATION

This next piece is not really a dream of Richard's. It's a waking life story. Richard sometimes appears to his clients, either in their dreams or in their waking states, without his conscious awareness of the event. These experiences occur when he is asleep, and he awakens with no memory of the visitations. Nevertheless, several times over the years clients have reported that they saw his body somewhere other than in his bed while he was asleep.

One such incident is particularly noteworthy, because two people witnessed it simultaneously! This was a couple on the verge of filing for divorce. While they both had legitimate complaints, Richard could see that they were also overreacting and quarreling inappropriately. One night he walked into their bedroom (which was in another state far away from his home), awakened them, and put his hand on both of their heads. He asked them to try to see each other's perspective, to try to switch heads, so to speak. He smiled at them, and turned and left the room. They looked at each other and, bewildered, went back to sleep.

The next morning Richard awakened fully refreshed, in his own bed, as usual, and went about his ordinary business of eating breakfast, dressing, etc. Late morning he received a phone call from the woman, who was his student. She explained what had happened and described the event. She commented on the fact that she could feel Richard's physical body, that she touched him and was touched by him. At breakfast that morning the couple had a heart-to-heart talk, ultimately deciding to work to keep their marriage together.

WHAT WAS THAT?

What happened there? How could Richard's physical body have shown up hundreds of miles away from his sleeping body? If a dream story is made up by the mind of the dreamer, how could two people have seen, heard, and felt the same thing? Were they awake or asleep?

Because of Richard's elevated spiritual development (his undisclosed level of evolution), he walks on the Dream Weave in a unique way. His physical body regenerates and restores itself, because that is the primary biological need we humans have from sleep. But his consciousness needs no regeneration, nor does his psyche need "clean up" work. As a result, he is available to serve others.

In fact, he is so unconditionally available that his personality does not even need validation or feedback. If his student hadn't called the next day, he would never have had a clue about his visitation. I'm confident that he makes hundreds of visitations in sleep about which he never knows. This is ultimate fourth-stage, philanthropic dreaming.

Richard's willingness to let Spirit, Great Dreamer, Universal Plan, whatever you want to call it, use him in whatever way It chooses stands as an example for each of us. He exemplifies the most elevated kinds of spiritual work. For Richard there is no difference in sleeping and waking, no difference in the dream and the phenomenal world. His life affects the Dream Weave by infusing it with the high frequency of his human vibration. Conversely, his dream affects waking reality profoundly by infiltrating it with the loving kindness of his spirit. Like the phenomenal dream, he leaves traces in both realms.

soul dreams

*Sleep of Clarity occurs when the body is sleeping
but the practitioner is neither lost in darkness nor in
dreams, but instead abides in pure awareness.*

~TENZIN WANGYAL RINPOCHE[1]

I CALL THIS LEVEL *SOUL DREAMS*, BECAUSE IN THE PUREST SENSE THEY
are no longer letters from the soul, nor stories one writes to remember the energetic experience in the Void. At this level, the dreamer
melts into the soul, regenerates, and then resurfaces. There is little or
no memory of the event, because the human mind dissolves itself into
soul mind. The human mind has no lexicon with which to write the
soul's story. I'll explain that further at the end of the chapter.

> **What you look forward to has
> already come, but you do not
> recognize it.**
>
> —The Gospel of Thomas 52:10

However, first, I want to give
you some examples of dream
stories that imply that the soul
level of dreaming exists. Sometimes, rarely but sometimes, we are pointed to this level of dreaming.
These are the ultimate sneak previews.

These dreams remind us that we are already what we have been
striving to become; that we already have what we think we've been
seeking. They are a sense of humor check! They tell us that while it is
necessary to go through all the stages of unfolding in order to fully
know ourselves in our own divinity, we were that all along.

THE DAVID DREAMS

I told you in the first chapter that during my "mystic's illness" I often dreamed of my first love, David. These dreams, I can now see, were my own glimpses, my own sneak previews, of the last stages of human spirituality. (I use the term *human spirituality* mindfully. There are stages of spirituality beyond human, which we'll touch on in the next chapter.)

The David Dreams were dreams of unparalleled love. They were dreams of unconditional love. They were dreams of beyond-human ecstasy. They were dreams of never-diminishing joy. In my limited understanding of the ways one could interpret dreams, I was concerned that I was hung up on days gone by, or that I had made the choice to project onto David my ideal of what true love should be. Both of those options felt wrong, but they were all I could muster at that stage of my development.

Eventually, I realized that my connection with David is a soul connection. He and I have known each other for thousands and thousands of years, and that knowing, however it is that we know each other between lives, is not going to stop now in this lifetime. Our joy in reuniting this time is the joy coming from the level of the soul! It's really not about needing to *do* anything.

And finally, I've learned to awaken from those dreams with absolute gratitude that I have a way to remember what it feels like to be loved on the soul level. It's my prayer that every being has these kinds of dreams, that every woman has her David, that every man has his Connie. If we can release our pathological fears around these "you are divinely loved" dreams, and just be loved, we can experience the love of the soul! When a dreamer awakens, feeling loved to the core of his or her being and knowing that love will never diminish and never leave, that dreamer has most certainly approached the level of soul dreaming in the Void. It's a "job well done" dream. It's a gift.

I WILL LIFT UP MY EYES

Judy has dedicated her life to being a Lover, in the Rumi-esque use of the word. When she first came to me, many years ago, she had already made significant strides on the journey to self-actualization. However, she was not happy with her dreaming life. She wanted me to teach her how to stop dreaming because her dreams scared her. They seemed dark, eerie, deathlike. I told her she'd come to the wrong place. I encouraged her to deepen her dreaming. As a result of her continued work in dream circle and her total devotion to the mystical path of Judaism, she has changed her mind. This dream is an example of how the soul will urge you toward your final destination—toward your destiny:

> I am bike riding and realize I'm not getting to my destination. I stop and look at the mountains with wonder. Suddenly, I'm transported to a busy marketplace. My teacher is there. We have a great talk; she is warm and friendly. She invites me to her apartment.
>
> I have a sack of crystals and as soon as we get into the apartment, I set them up in various locations. She doesn't seem to mind or say anything. We sit comfortably for what seems a long time talking about personal things she wanted me to know about becoming a clergywoman: information cantors should know.
>
> It is getting late and I gather up all the stones. I feel a little anxious about the long journey home by myself. I'm pleasantly surprised and moved by the spontaneity and warmth of the encounter.

Judy is riding a bicycle. We are amazed at how often we, in our circle, ride bicycles on the Dream Weave. It seems to be one of the most flexible and usable vehicles of the dream. It may be that it indicates some sort of dualistic thinking that we carry with us, or it may be that bicycles most closely represent the kind of movement we make when we're journeying on the Weave.

When she realizes she isn't reaching her destination, Judy stops and looks to the mountain. The mountain is a sacred space in almost every religious and spiritual tradition. I like the explanation I got once from an indigenous American elder. He said, "A mountain is Mother Earth's heart. Mountains look like breasts, and where there's a breast, there's a heart under there somewhere!" That made me laugh. Men!

> *I will lift up my eyes to the hills from whence cometh my help.*
>
> —Psalms 121:1

Judy's viewing the mountain contrasted perfectly with the very next statement: Suddenly I'm transported to a busy marketplace. By looking at the mountain, by looking at the heart of our Mother, by looking at the place of the sacred caves, the place of solitude and communion with nature, Judy was transported to the real workplace of the mystic: the marketplace. The true mystic and real dreamer must work, shop, sell, trade, converse in the real world. Our work now is no longer about contemplation from a mountaintop, although that may be part of our practice. Our work is to be the urban mystics. We must stop trying to "reach our destination" and be here.

Judy creates her own crystal cave, right there in her teacher's apartment. The teaching, the healing, the learning, and the communing all occur there in the busy city. Our soul's journey is not about leaving anything to go anywhere. It's about being in life, with people, living, working, loving.

All Judy's teacher did, of course, was remind her of what she already knows—"personal things." Like most of us, Judy's not fully in unity consciousness yet, so she projects "teacher" onto another person. It's hard to accept that we *know*. It's much easier to let someone else teach us. And yet Judy left the teacher's apartment knowing that the long journey home has to be taken alone.

I place this dream in this chapter to remind us of that: We are where we belong, and we are where we were going all along. A spiritual journey doesn't take us out of our home, out of our marketplace, out of society. A spiritual journey aligns us with who we are.

SKETCHING THE FACE OF CHRIST

If you remember, I used a dream of Jeanne's in the chapter on psychological dreams to illustrate the ability of a dreamer to become the observer, the witness within a dream. Then in the chapter on teaching dreams, I used another portion of the same dream to demonstrate the ability to be the scribe of dreaming. Now I want to use the end of this dream to point to the soul dreams. If you remember, we left Jeanne in a Roman city thousands of years ago. She could simultaneously see (witness) the city, and sketch (scribe) on the sepia-toned blueprint or street map of the city in front of her. She had taken pencils and drawn onto the map paper some of the residents in the city. And then she and her partner, Robert, walked into the present and onto a university campus.

I purposely omitted this one piece of the dream, which occurred just before they walked back into present time:

> Then, I see Jesus Christ. His face is so beautiful. It's almost white. He is glowing like a hologram. I take a white pencil and flesh his image out.

I use this example in this way to show that a single dream story can contain many elements of many different stages of spiritual growth and many different levels of dreaming. When one sees the face of Christ, or the face of any of the enlightened or ascended master in a dream, it is a fourth-stage soul dream. More accurately, it's a glimpse, an arrow pointing in that direction. This dream told Jeanne that her work as a dream witness and as a scribe had carried her to even higher levels of spiritual development.

Seeing the countenance of a master teacher in the dream is profound. It is, interestingly, becoming more and more common, even for people who aren't Christian in the traditional sense of the word, to see the face of Christ. Jeanne was a practicing Buddhist for more than fifteen years when she came to dream circle. Yet it was the face of Jesus Christ that blessed her in this initiation dream.

In *The Coming of the Cosmic Christ*, Matthew Fox explains this common "face of Christ" dream. He describes the Cosmic Christ as a living cosmology, a cosmic wisdom available to all, a global spiritual renaissance ready to be birthed through our acceptance of our human and yet divine nature.

Fox suggests that one of the avenues through which this renaissance will reach our lives is art. "The artist's task is awakening awe and providing vehicles of expression so that we can express our awe and wonder at existence."[2]

Fox also states that a profoundly important vehicle for the Cosmic Christ's arrival in our society is the university. Education, educing (drawing out or bringing into view) is the way that the new society based on loving kindness will emerge. He states it concisely: "True empowerment happens when we educe the divine beauty and power from one another. . . . Education can become creative again by centering its energies on educing the Cosmic Christ—by educing wisdom and creativity."[3] Jeanne's dream ends when she walks back into modern times, onto the university campus, ready to educe the Cosmic Christ by living it in her daily life with her beloved partner.

GOD IS AT THE DOOR

Theresa, our priestess of the Aqua Ashram, had another experience about six years after her induction into fourth-stage dreaming that is worth sharing. You will recall I mentioned in first-stage dreaming that as we develop into each level of spiritual growth, we often have to return to earlier stages and update ourselves. So it was with Theresa. In spite of all her personal work, in spite of the profound heart openings she experienced at the hands of her ex-husband/life teacher, in spite of her induction into the women's spiritual community in the dreamscape, and in spite of her years of waking-life spiritual practice, she was still riddled with self-doubt. She described that she always felt "clamped," never quite free from restrictions placed on her in childhood, even though she'd prayed for years to be liberated so that she could serve life in a way that reflected her authentic self. One night she had the following dream:

> I was in my living room. There was no furniture. I sensed that it was early morning because I saw light coming in under the door. A telepathic voice said, "Open the Door."
>
> When I opened the front door, God, in the form of a magnificent white light, greeted me. There was no doubt in my mind that this was God. None.
>
> God said, "Do you have a question?" I said yes and asked something about my self-worth, and God answered. I can't remember the question or the answer. What was most important to me was that God chose to show up and knock on my door! I felt blessed and humbled by this experience.

Theresa's dream, like Jeanne's, has many components. On one level it could be viewed as first-level dreaming, for it was addressing a lifelong psychological issue. On another level it was oracular, because the telepathic voice and the voice of God were clearly the primary moving energies in the dream. And yet it is also pointing Theresa toward soul dreaming. Theresa came face-to-face with God. God was at her door. She had moved beyond her psyche, beyond her mind, beyond her soul, and was standing face-to-face with the Light of God. And only the light mattered.

> God is the brightest of lights which can never be extinguished.
>
> —Hildegard of Bingen[4]

Several years later, Theresa took the Sufi promise and began a new level of her spiritual journey following the path of love. She joined in the tradition of Kabir, Rumi, and thousands of others on this mystical Sufi way. Although she is Jewish by birth, the Sufi tradition is her new spiritual home. Shortly after she took the promise, she had another dream. This dream came around the time of the Jewish High Holidays.

> I was at a friend's for a High Holiday dinner. I said to my friend, "I dreamed that God asked me to marry him."

While there wasn't much to the story of this dream, the feeling of it was totally sacred. Theresa knew that God's asking her to marry him in a dream was a new initiation, that she was now home, and that her spiritual work was to take a new depth, a new joy, a new dimension, a new name. She awoke from this dream with a sense of coming home to herself. She felt that in marrying God she was truly coming into union with her deepest essence.

All these dreams—the David Dreams, Judy's experience in the marketplace, Jeanne's seeing the face of Christ, and Theresa's love affair with God—are technically fourth-stage dreams that don't quite reach the level of soul dreams. But they are still dream stories that point the dreamer toward soul dreaming. They are extremely helpful and important in the spiritual process, because they stand as markers, as anchor points, as reminders of growth and movement. Every person who has one of these holy dreams never forgets it.

RICHARD'S DREAMING

I want to tell you another story about my mentor Richard, who I described in the last chapter. He is the only person I know who has totally reached the level of soul dreaming. About twenty years ago, at the young age of sixty-something, Richard was driving his Lincoln Continental to pick up his fiancée for an evening out, and while stopped at a red light he was rear-ended by a truck. His seat belt and the size of the car saved his life, but not his brain. He suffered a concussion, which had very interesting spiritual results. He lost short-term memory to the point that he couldn't remember the beginning or middle of his own sentence even as he spoke the last word of it. During the weeks of his recovery he felt imbued with a cosmic calm. He was immersed in a transcendental spirit. He was deeply changed.

> *If he is destroyed he will be filled with light.*
>
> —The Gospel of Thomas 61:30

This period, for Richard, was like my period of intense dreaming, except his was on a higher plain. The Spirit saw the opportunity to enter his mind, which had been rendered blank through the accident, and Richard was filled to the brim with the light of his Being. At that point, he *stopped remembering dream stories.* If you do something supramental, there is no mental story.

From the time of that magnificent spiritual transformation, his sleeping changed. Now, he puts his head on the pillow and within fifteen seconds he is not only asleep but fully dissolved into the divine blackness. He goes into sleep and any emotional, physical, or mental baggage he may have is immediately transcended. He sleeps thoroughly and without disturbance for five to six hours. Then he awakens fully refreshed and regenerated.

Approximately five times in twenty years Richard has awakened with a dream story memory. Those days are hard for him, for he doesn't awaken with the same refreshed feeling.

LIBERATION

Richard reached a level of spiritual development that resulted in liberation from himself. When he goes to sleep, his ultimate spiritual practice takes him directly to the Source. He no longer needs letters from the soul, because Richard is already free.

> *God needs nothing more than for us to offer him a quiet heart.*
>
> —Meister Eckhart[5]

Therefore, his need for sleep is simple. He needs the same period for physical regeneration that all sentient beings need, and he needs to plug in to Source.

He has no memory of his dreams because they are not his any longer. He now travels on the Dream Weave, available to assist anyone who can receive his help. Like The Hermit in the tarot deck, he carries the lantern of the blessed and beautiful light, shattering the darkness of the spiritual journey for anyone with eyes to see. Few people ever get to this level. But by the grace of God, Richard's light illumines the way for any of us willing to try.

Of course, at this level, the real questions begin. What is beyond mind? What is beyond the dream? Of what does the soul dream? What is liberation, really?

PART SIX

acting lessons

Those are good questions. What is beyond the mind? What is beyond the dream? Of what does the soul dream? What is liberation, really?

Of course, we cannot possibly know the answers. How can we? Any concept we can imagine, any scenario we can concoct, is all mindstuff. We do know, however, from Richard and a few like him, that there is apparently something beyond the dream and that the soul is at work beyond the mind. All we can really do is reach for that something, acting as if it is already with us, here and now, because in fact, on some level, it is.

In this book I've admonished you time and again not to do anything about your dreams. My dream circle sisters get frustrated with me when I tell them, "This is not about *doing*, this is about *being*."

TAKE SPIRITUAL ACTING LESSONS

Of course, our daily lives are about doing things. Things happen because we willfully make them happen. For that reason, I urge people who are on a serious spiritual path to take acting (as opposed to doing) lessons. These are not lessons you take from a coach. These are lessons you learn from yourself by changing your perspective about doing.

Acting is a way to understand the power of behavioral decisions and be fully accountable for their consequences. Acting doesn't mean pretending. Indeed, you must still attend to your daily activities in a very real and earnest way. Acting means realizing that you are role-playing. Acting means watching your decisions, your choices, your movements, your reactions, your urges, your speech as if it were all a dream. Acting means becoming a witness and scribe of your own life. Acting lessons teach you not to take *doing* so seriously.

In the first stage of dreaming, the early part of our spiritual development, doing is more reaction than anything else. We are so programmed by our upbringing that mostly what we do early in our spiritual development is simply re-create the past by reacting to the present through our programming. This is clearly a stage of life when it's best to do (use your personal will) as little as possible in order to let the past go. This is the ripest time to learn acting.

The second stage of dreaming, a slightly more mature leg of the spiritual journey, makes us less reactive but horribly self-important. This is the stage in which we "speak our truth," and thereby create a "truth competition." If your truth and my truth clash, then one of us must be right and that makes you wrong. Right? Unfortunately, in second-stage work, we are still measuring "truth" by external scales. We look to the outside world for proof of our rightness. This is definitely a time to commit deeply to acting lessons, because at this stage if we *do* from personal will, we run the risk of overpowering our spiritual growth.

> *The outward work will never be puny*
> *If the inward work is great.*
>
> —Meister Eckhart[1]

In the third stage of dreaming, we are more spiritually sophisticated, so we take deeper levels of responsibility for our doing-ness. However, it's still a little treacherous to do much. Remember that the third stage is usually when our personal egos are going through profound transformation, and our lives are shattering. During these times it is easy to fall into victim mentality, and if we become willful, we may do just that. How many times did I willfully demand to be healed, to be fixed, to be validated during my shattering? If we can remember to watch ourselves during this stage, to witness and scribe our acting, we will learn deeper lessons of truth.

Finally, at the fourth stage of development, we are ready to stop "acting." Now we can take action. Why? Because our spiritual work has resulted in aligning our personal will with Great Dreamer, with the Creator. Prior to this we tried to write our own script. Now we see the Sacred Script, and we are honored to be cast in a role. In other words, we are humble, compassionate, and free of attachment. Our doing-ness becomes perfectly clear to us, because it is no longer separate from our being-ness. Now we can dream the new dream.

IF YOU CAN'T ACT, ACT AS IF

Of course, few of us fully achieve fourth-stage dreaming and that elevated stage of spiritual development. However, all is not lost. We can act *as if*. Acting as if is a Buddhist teaching. Disciples of Buddhism are encouraged to act as if they were enlightened, actualized, realized even if they know they're not. It is a tool for helping the disciple establish habits of right action. Similarly, we can act as if we are the fourth-stage dreamers we are destined to become.

In the last chapter of this book, I'd like to look at some of the actions a dreamer does take in the world and the ways he or she arrives at the decisions for action.

living the dream

Merlin said, "I saw a dragonfly and wanted to look at it more closely. It flew across my path like a fluttering dream, but after a moment I forgot whether I was dreaming of this dragonfly or whether it was dreaming of me."

~DEEPAK CHOPRA[1]

DEEPAK CHOPRA AND I HAVE ONE VERY SPECIAL THING IN COMMON. We both believe in Merlin. In his book *The Way of the Wizard*, Chopra explains his reasons: "A wizard can turn fear into joy, frustration to fulfillment. A wizard can turn the time-bound into the timeless. A wizard can carry you beyond limitations into the boundless."[2] I suggest you replace the word *wizard* with *dreamer* and put those sentences on your refrigerator door.

Chopra makes another statement about wizards that I simply love. He says, "A wizard does not believe himself to be a local event dreaming of a larger world. A wizard is a world dreaming of local events."[3] Again, change wizard to dreamer and you have a definition of yourself after you've gone through the final firing and become the purified vessel. One way to imagine yourself is as a small self, a false self, an individuation of the One. See yourself sending your dream fibers out to interact with the larger perspective. Another, more accurate way, is to see yourself as one who dreams the world into being.

I compare Merlin to a master dreamer, because both wizards of fantasy literature and master dreamers come to the present out of the future. They bring perspective that is reversed from our linear concept of time.

THE EARTH'S DREAM

Father Thomas Berry is widely known as one of the most provocative and influential ecotheologians of our time. A deeply spiritual man, he has immense passion for the Earth, for every species, and for every human being. He maintains that the Earth dreams, and that we humans participate in that dream in profound ways. Further, he maintains that the universe, Creation itself, is a dream. In his book *The Great Work* he elaborates:

> The universe seems to be the fulfillment of something so highly imaginative and so overwhelming that it must have been dreamed into existence.
>
> But if the dream is creative, we must also recognize that few things are so destructive as a dream or entrancement that has lost the integrity of its meaning and entered an exaggerated and destructive manifestation.[4]

This is what I saw that night many years ago when I watched the nine o'clock news and realized that it is time for us to dream a new dream. Our collective dream has lost its integrity. Our participation with Earth's dream has become an entrancement that is out of alignment with Creation. Too many of us are in first- and second-stage dreaming, myopically and narcissistically speaking "my" truth, and forgetting to be awed, forgetting to be in wonderment, forgetting to live the greater dream and be dreamed by it.

It is our imperative as dreamers to complete the spiritual journey as quickly and as thoroughly as we can, because it is time to dream a new dream. We must get to it now. We must dream the creative dream now.

FREEDOM TO LIVE THE DREAM

This spiritual journey is a movement toward freedom. Each stage of the journey liberates us from old patterns and gives us freedom to live the dream. My dream teachers assisted me through the third stage of dreaming, my annihilation period. In addition, each of them planted a seed in me that, when it sprouted, would free me to live the dream.

FREEDOM TO EXPLORE THE CHAOS

Star Woman took me into the Void. I experienced through her the ability to dissolve my ego without losing my being-ness. I see now that she planted the seed that gave me the freedom to explore chaos, to go "to the edge," to melt into the not-yet, as a creative act. Those dreams prepared me for a new kind of doing-ness. When one is familiar with the Void, one ceases to be afraid of chaos. A pivotal responsibility dreamers have in concrete reality is to live in it fully informed, yet fearlessly. When I watch the eleven o'clock news and read the newspapers, as I mentioned before, I see our modern-day cave walls with our dreams painted dramatically on them. I see that our world, our dream, is filled with random, chaotic, violent, desperate acts, which are cries for help from our brothers and sisters. I also see that sensationalist and fear-based news reporting is the trend of the day.

One of the most important things you can do as a spiritual disciple is read the newspaper and watch television. I know people who brag about the fact that they don't read the newspapers or watch television. They actually demonize "the media" as the evil forces that are destroying our society. I'm amazed that people actually say that out loud. I wonder what contribution these people think they're making? We must be informed. We must know what's going on in our world. Equally important, we must be polished, wise, astute, intuitive, and practiced, so that we can identify and separate the lies, fear, and propaganda of sensationalist journalism from the true cries for help. If you withdraw from knowing, hide from civic responsibility, vote irresponsibly (or not at all), and tunnel vision away from society's mirrors, then you are the problem, not the solution. You're lost in the dream of enchantment.

To dream the new dream, we must first know thoroughly and purify completely the dream we've already manifested. As Thomas Berry points out, we have become enchanted by a dream of violence, destruction, species annihilation, pollution, irresponsible use of polluting products, technology, and progress. We must become lucid within this enchantment and dream a new dream.

FREEDOM TO BE AMAZED

Grandmother Teacup took me to new landscapes, new venues, new dimensions, and taught me to find the power spots there. I searched for the right placement for the teacup at every tea party. She wanted me to find the source of the belief system in each of those places. These dreams planted the seed of amazement, reminding me to be present to and in awe of the *is-ness* of a situation.

Our job as radical mystical activists is to be amazed. Our sense of wonder and awe must never falter, even in the face of tragedy, destruction, violence, emergency. Behind every circumstance of life, no matter how horrible, no matter how mundane, there is a mighty power, an invisible force, a sourcing that is awesome. If we forget that for one instant, we mentally put the teacup (the origin of our origin, the root of our roots) in the wrong place, and we lose our deepest connection to life. If we lose the ability to see the unseen forces behind any moment, we are no longer servants to life.

Have you ever been part of an organization that was founded on one person's vision: a school, a church, a spiritual community? If so, you know that they usually work pretty well as long as the visionary is central to the organization, and as long as he or she stays true to the original vision. When the person holding the vision either leaves the organization or becomes owned by the corporate nature of the organization, the whole thing falls apart. It's sad to watch, but it always happens. Someone must hold the vision in its purity, never losing sight of the awesome potential of the fundamental dream.

As an awakened dreamer, part of your imperative is to hold the vision. See the unseen forces behind a manifestation, see the blueprint, the intent, the archetypal structure, the Greater Plan, and hold that in wonderment, amazement, and awe. Bring to your community the beauty of the vision. Hold fiercely to the divinity of the dream. This is what keeps you and the community from becoming depressed and lured into the destructive enchantment.

The Hero's Journey of Joseph Campbell

of course, Hitler had a vision, too.

FREEDOM TO DANCE

Outward Bound Man showed me the tricks of moving freely on the Dream Weave. These dreams were in many ways the most magical work I did during that period, because they were totally transfiguring. By making me work out in the dream, Outward Bound Man proved to me that physical manifestation (my physical body) is sourced in the unseen realms. Physicality is affected, changed, and transformed by the work we do in the dream.

> *To be human is to be born into a dance, a sacred dance in which every animate or inanimate, visible or invisible being is also participating.*
>
> —Andrew Harvey[5]

Outward Bound Man planted the seeds that allow us to dance the dance of life with grace, with ease, and with the confidence that we can create positive change. These dreams planted the seeds of movement. We must be daring, courageous, outrageous, interested, and interesting. We must not be complacent, comfortable, inert, bored, or boring. Our job as master dreamers is to interfere, infiltrate, expose, shake the web. We must ask the unasked questions of our politicians, our religious leaders, our governmental structures, our corporations, our universities, our societal icons.

If we look back at the late 1960s, we perceive that for a moment in time, most people under thirty became mystical activists. By the end of Watergate in the mid-1970s, there was not a question left unasked in any arena of our society. Unfortunately, too many were left unanswered, and most of us who had stirred up the whole thing were too discouraged to pursue the answers. And besides, too many of us were over thirty by then. According to our own liturgy, we couldn't be trusted.

That was a very powerful era in the United States and, by ripple effect, in the rest of the world. The activists, however, were simply too young. We were first-stage dreamers. We were too narcissistic to see the truth and hold the vision. Now we must reawaken that passion for questioning, that ardor for justice, that enthusiasm for beauty, that desire for peace, and that dedication to love. We must do all this acting *as if* the age of peace is upon us, *as if* justice is possible, *as if* we've dreamed the new dream!

FREEDOM TO SEE CLEARLY

Grandfather Jack taught me to chase rabbits in the dream! I can still feel the sensations of those dreams in my cells. I can still see the differences in the light of the rabbits and the light of the sage plants and the light of the stone beings along the path! Grandfather Jack taught me to *see*.

Grandfather Jack planted the seeds of seeing clearly, no matter what the situation. Those dreams seemed so nonspiritual. I mean, really, how spiritual is it to chase rabbits in the desert? On the other hand, can't every action be taken in absolute awe of the doing-ness? Isn't Grandfather Jack simply saying that everything one does is a holy act, because life itself is holy?

I wonder if Grandfather Jack knew Meister Eckhart. He apparently knew Al Capone, so why not a thirteenth-century mystic? A Grandfather Jack–style lesson appears in one of Meister Eckhart's sermons in which he turned a familiar New Testament story upside down. Traditionally, the story is told that Jesus went to visit two sisters, Mary and Martha. Mary accompanied Jesus into the living room and sat at his feet absorbing his every word. Martha went into the kitchen and prepared lunch. Martha complained to Jesus that Mary wasn't helping with the woman's work, and Jesus responded by saying that Mary was right to sit and listen to the teachings. Patriarchal clergymen have used this story to diminish "woman's work" as less than spiritual.

Meister Eckhart says, "No! That's not what Jesus meant at all." Eckhart says, Jesus was telling Martha that Mary was not evolved enough to listen and work at the same time. Mary was doing what was right for her according to where she was on the spiritual path. Mary was a first-stage dreamer (my words) and she needed to give all her attention to learning, to expanding her mind, to transforming her belief system. Mary was a virgin (Eckhart's words). Martha, on the other hand, was multidimensional. She could simultaneously do her chores *and* listen deeply, making both sacred activities. She had become her doing-ness. Martha was a fourth-stage dreamer (my words). Martha could experience the awe and wonder of the mundane world. Martha was a wife (Eckhart's words).[6]

The Grandfather Jack dream stories teach us to see the sacred in the profane; they teach us to be a wife. They remind us that we are multidimensional, and challenge us to act as if we know that in every waking moment. He instructs us to see the original primordial light, the root of our roots, in every form, even while we perform the most ordinary of tasks.

FREEDOM TO REMEMBER

Whenever the Mermaid came, we went deep into the water and spoke about the most profound topics: philosophy, theology, love. Ultimately, she reminded me that life as we know it came from the waters. She taught me that Earth's evolution and ours are inextricably connected. She planted the seeds of remembering.

The Mermaid came to remind me that my Mother's health and mine, my Mother's well-being and mine, my Mother's spiritual welfare and mine are inextricable. Every choice I make affects my Mother Earth. Every product I buy comes from her and returns to her in some form. In fact, I come from her and return to her. This simple shift in thinking demands a radical shift in consumerism, userism, and disposalism.

If we think back to the Dreamer's Creation Story, the overall message there was that we live in a universe, and more specifically on a planet, in which everything is interconnected. Every form is primordial energy expressing itself in unique and temporary configurations, and every form relies on every other form for a period of time. For a new form to appear, new energy doesn't emerge; rather, old energy gets recycled and reconfigured. Everything that manifests in concrete reality is actually a visible exchange of energy.

> *A direct relationship with the Mother could create nothing less than a worldwide mystical and practical revolution, because it would empower every being with his or her own divine truth.*
>
> —Andrew Harvey[7]

From that perspective, how I expend my energy profoundly and inextricably affects everything else in the universe. In our modern capitalistic societies, money has become our metaphoric form of energy exchange. I give you money, you give me products, services, etc. That makes every purchase a holy activity, a divine exchange of energy. I play God when I buy something. I make powerful choices about how primordial energy is to be recycled!

The mystical activist is magnetized to products, services, lifestyles, and communities that are healthy. The mystical activist purchases nothing, consumes nothing, endorses nothing without realizing the global impact of that one little action. The mystical activist is a radical consumer who demands quality, wholeness, honesty, and humility for his or her money.

FREEDOM TO RETREAT

Crystal Cave Woman took me time and again to the crystalline cave so that I could receive the most profound of the dream teachings. She taught me that we cocreate this world through our own dreaming. She showed me the sacred prayer form called Dream Circle. She instructed me in the art of being a scribe in the dream, reminding me to access the ancient records so that I remember the full spectrum of human potential. She reminded me to lay myself down in the dream, to connect to the moon, and to allow myself to be dreamed.

In *The Way of the Wizard*, Chopra suggests that Merlin's crystal cave is actually a sacred spot in the heart of every human being. "It is the refuge of safety where a wise voice knows no fear, where the turmoil of the outside world cannot enter. In the crystal cave there has always been a wizard and always will be—you only have to enter and listen."[8]

Crystal Cave Woman plants the seeds of sacred retreat. She reminds us to go to the crystal cave within our hearts. She reminds us to pray. She reminds us to participate in the sacred group forms: dream circles, spiritual councils, holy relationship. She implores us to dream the new dream and to walk our dreams consciously.

Unless we attend to our spiritual practice on a daily basis, unless we pray constantly, unless we turn our every step into a leap of faith, unless we go regularly to our crystal cave, we cannot know that our doing-ness is well-grounded. Through our dedication and discipline to an ever-deepening spiritual life, we can become more and more efficient, effective, empowered. Without that key piece, we're willfully stomping our feet and demanding to get our way.

FREEDOM TO BE LOVE

And finally, there were the David Dreams. What seed did they plant?

The David Dreams remind us that we are loved, that we are lovable, and therefore that we can be Love. The safety and security of being held in the arms of Love allows us to act in loving ways. What is to fear if we are truly loved? Why do we need to be defensive, offensive, aggressive, or combative if we are truly loved?

The David Dreams point us to the end of dreaming as we know it. They point us to the level of the soul, where we are so divinely loved that there are no images to tell the story. As my mentor Richard has learned, there is something beyond the images of the dreamtime, but that something is without vocabulary, without visual interpretation, and without need to be spoken. That something comes when we become infused with divine spirit.

> *When I come to the point when I no longer project myself into any image and fancy no images in myself, and toss away everything within me, then I can be transported into God's naked being, and this is the pure essence of the Spirit.*
>
> —Meister Eckhart[9]

The David Dreams planted the seeds of Love. The lover makes no move that isn't Love. The lover takes no action that isn't Love. The lover dreams no dream that isn't Love. The lover dissolves into Love.

EPILOGUE

I STARTED THIS BOOK BY TELLING YOU IT WAS A LETTER CONVEYING A love story, and indeed I hope it has been. It is designed to bring you closer to the truth of Love. Our stories are the way we connect with one another, the way we teach one another, and the way we encourage.

I have one more story to tell you. This is the story of Freya. Freya was the most beautiful, real, eccentric, wild, insane, and sane person I'd ever met. She was beyond the beyond. Freya was the one I called when I needed a total makeover, when it was time to redecorate, when it was time to play dress up, when it was time to laugh or cry. Freya always had a new perspective. She always knew the hippest place to be whether we were in Los Angeles or the French Riviera. She was a step ahead of Madonna in the lingerie-as-clothes fad (she's reported to have shown up at her twenty-fifth high school reunion in Toledo, Ohio, in 1978 wearing a merry widow bra and a big full taffeta skirt and cowboy boots). She went to the American Music Awards wearing high heels and socks before Cindi Lauper ever thought of it. Freya lived life backwards: She came to the present directly out of the future.

Freya was my best friend, my nearest and dearest, and I was hers. I knew that definitely, beyond a shadow of a doubt. Freya told me everything, I kept her secrets, I counseled her, I giggled with her, I supported her fantasies, I shopped with her. I knew I was her best friend because she didn't have time to have another friend like me.

Freya died unexpectedly in January of 1997. At her memorial service we passed the microphone, like a talking stick, simulating a dream circle, so that everyone there could share their fondest memories. Guess what? I found out that day that there were at least a hundred other people who also considered Freya their best friend. These people were from widely different backgrounds, totally different parts of the country, ranging in age from eleven to eighty, all with completely different lifestyles and interests. What an amazing woman, my Freya. How could one person make dozens and dozens of people feel loved so uniquely, so thoroughly, so absolutely? The answer, of course, is obvious. Freya was magical. She could be in many places at once, loving many people at once, giving warm cuddles to lots of people at once.

I loved Freya, and I trusted her unconditionally. Even after she died, I trusted the dreams I had when she appeared. Almost a year after her death I had the following dream:

> I was giving myself a big birthday party. We were meeting at my house and then going to a Chinese restaurant. I invited lots of Freya's "best friends." We were all dressed up as if we'd all just stepped out of her closet.
>
> Several of us got into my van. On the outside it looked like a regular van, but on the inside it looked like a bordello. Red velvet, lots of fringe and beads. Carole, Peggy, and Barbara were with me.
>
> I started driving down the street, following several other cars full of "best friends." I saw Freya sprawled across the back seat of my van, looking very sexy, with an eerie grin on her face. I gasped. All the other girls squealed and giggled and screeched and twittered.
>
> I said, "Okay, Frey, you have to tell me what it's like to be dead."
>
> She said, "Well, you still dream!"
>
> I asked, "Wait a minute—you dream when you're dead?"
>
> She answered, "Yep. I'm dreaming you right now!"
>
> Peggy and Carole and Barbara were still cooing and preening and fussing. Peggy said, "Frey, where did you get that dress? Do you shop when you're dead?"
>
> Freya said, "No. You just think it together. Some things are the same, some are different." Then she looked at me and winked.

Freya came that night to tell us that we are being dreamed from the level of soul. She is our ancestor now. She dreams us. Who are the teachers who show up in our dreams? They are the beings who dream us. They are the beings who reside at the level of soul and choreograph the energy for us. They are the beings who dwell within the invisible fields of the Dream Weave.

This has been about the journey that every person takes in life, knowingly or unknowingly, consciously or unconsciously. This journey involves achieving ever-higher levels of integrity between the unseen spiritual source of our world, and the manifestations in our world. As humans, we have the ability, the physiological and mental structures, and the propensity to peer into Source, so that we can more fully understand, as Rudolf Steiner puts it, earthly truth.

> With his waking consciousness a human being sees only the outer side of minerals, plants and animals. But he is in the company of the spiritual element indwelling these creatures of the natural world when he is asleep. . . . It is man's relation to sleep which gives him his awareness of earthly truth.
>
> —Rudolf Steiner[1]

Dreaming is one of the primary avenues we have into those unseen realms. Through sleeping and dreaming, we make regular visits into the realm that I call the dimension of Truth. There, in the dreamtime, we receive direct transmissions of truth from the level that connects us to the all and the everything, the level of soul.

Our dreams are letters from the soul. They tell us continuously and consistently who we are, why we're here, what's coming, how we're interconnected with each other, and what we need to accomplish together and individually to create more fulfilled lives, not only for ourselves and our families, but for all beings on the planet.

What is beyond the mind? What is beyond the dream? Truth. Truth is not a provable fact, but rather a reference point beyond the mind, beyond the dream. Our teachers, our ancestors, the designers of our dream ceremonies, those who are dreaming us, live in Truth and are constantly calling us to listen to its vibrations in the dream.

This journey, this dream, never ends. We never finish perfecting the vessel, expanding the dreaming potential, pushing "the edge." According to Freya, even when we die, we start to dream anew from the perspective of the soul!

The destination of this journey is not a place or a state of being. It is the realization that we are all the same. Even in our differentiation, we are the One expressing in many forms. If each of us lived from the core of ourselves, we would manifest a new dream. It would be a dream of actualization for each being, mineral, plant, animal, and human. All the kindoms would thrive in this new dream.

I believe that there is little we can do in this world that is more important than honoring our dreams, understanding them as messages to be integrated into our lives, and remembering that they are not separating us but uniting us because they come from a unified field.

> *May the inhabitants of earth become one in their hearts,*
> *Unite their plans and designs with the dwellers in heaven!*
> *All separation and polytheism and duality will vanish*
> *For there's only unity in real existence!*
> *When my spirit recognizes your spirit fully,*
> *Then the two of us remember being one before.*
>
> ~RUMI[2]

NOTES

PART ONE: A LOVE STORY

1. Daniel Ladinsky, trans., "I Follow Barefoot." In *The Subject Tonight Is Love: 60 Wild and Sweet Poems of Hafiz* (Myrtle Beach, S.C.: Pumpkin House Press, 1996), 57.

2. Matthew Fox, *Breakthrough: Meister Eckhart's Creation Spirituality in New Translation* (New York: Image Books, Doubleday, 1980), 116.

CHAPTER ONE: TEACHERS OF THE DREAM

1. Sri Aurobindo, *Letters on Yoga, III* (Pondicherry, India: Sri Aurobindo Ashram, 1970), 1488.

2. Andrew Harvey, *Light upon Light: Inspirations from Rumi* (Berkeley, Calif.: North Atlantic Books, 1996), 83.

3. Russell Salamon (Unpublished poetry. Used by permission of author).

CHAPTER TWO: THE DREAMER'S CREATION STORY

1. Serinity Young, *Dreaming in the Lotus: Buddhist Dream Narrative, Imagery, and Practice* (Boston: Wisdom Publications, 1999), 32.

2. Andrew Harvey, *Light upon Light: Inspirations from Rumi* (Berkeley, Calif.: North Atlantic Books, 1996), 81.

3. Brian Swimme and Thomas Berry, *The Universe Story* (San Francisco: Harper San Francisco, 1992), 17.

4. Ibid., 29.

5. Russell Salamon (Unpublished poetry. Used by permission of author).

CHAPTER THREE: REDEFINING DREAMING

1. Matthew Fox and Rupert Sheldrake, *Natural Grace* (New York: Image Books, Doubleday, 1997), 198.

2. Sri Aurobindo, *Letters on Yoga, III* (Pondicherry, India: Sri Aurobindo Ashram, 1970), 1487.

3. Matthew Fox, *Breakthrough: Meister Eckhart's Creation Spirituality in New Translation* (New York: Doubleday, 1980), 139.

4. Florinda Donner, *Being in Dreaming* (San Francisco: Harper San Francisco, 1992), 123.

5. Ibid., 126.

6. Fox, *Breakthrough*, 297.

7. Tamar Frankiel and Judy Greenfeld, *Entering the Temple of Dreams: Jewish Prayers, Movements, and Meditations for the End of the Day* (Woodstock, Vt.: Jewish Lights, 2000), 126.

8. Edmond Bordeaux Szekely, ed., *The Essene Gospel of Peace* (International Biogenic Society, 1981), 45.

9. Ibid.

CHAPTER FOUR: MUNDANE DREAMS

1. This quotation is anecdotal—not published and perhaps not really anything Sigmund Freud ever said. However, it's used so often as to become a part of the vernacular.

2. Matthew Fox, *Breakthrough: Meister Eckhart's Creation Spirituality in New Translation* (New York: Doubleday, 1980), 41.

3. Andrew Harvey, *Light upon Light: Inspirations from Rumi* (Berkeley, Calif.: North Atlantic Books, 1996), 21.

4. Sri Aurobindo. *Letters on Yoga, III* (Pondicherry, India: Sri Aurobindo Ashram, 1970), 1492.

CHAPTER FIVE: PSYCHOLOGICAL DREAMS

1. Llewelyn Vaughn-Lee, *Catching the Thread: Sufism, Dreamwork, and Jungian Psychology* (Inverness, Calif.: Golden Sufi Center, 1998), 19.

2. Andrew Harvey, "The Wine and the Cup." *In Teachings of Rumi* (Boston: Shambhala, 1999), 3.

3. M. C. Richards, *Centering in Pottery, Poetry, and in the Person* (Middletown, Conn.: Wesleyan University Press, 1989), 130.

4. Matthew Fox, ed., *Hildegard of Bingen's Book of Divine Works* (Santa Fe, N. Mex.: Bear and Company, 1987), 255.

5. Andrew Harvey and Eryk Hanut, *Perfume of the Desert: Inspirations from Sufi Wisdom* (Wheaton, Ill.: Quest Books, Theosophical Publishing House, 1999), 48.

6. e. e. cummings, "i sing of Olaf glad and big." In *The New Oxford Book of American Verse*, ed. Richard Ellmann (New York: Oxford University Press, 1976), 636–37.

7. Matthew Fox, *Breakthrough: Meister Eckhart's Creation Spirituality in New Translation* (New York: Doubleday, 1980), 253.

8. Personal journal entry, August 1989, Kalachakra Initiation teachings by His Holiness the Dalai Lama at the Santa Monica Civic Center in Santa Monica, California.

9. Vaughan-Lee, *Catching the Thread*, xiv.

CHAPTER SIX: LUCID DREAMS

1. Serinity Young, *Dreaming in the Lotus: Buddhist Dream Narrative* (Boston: Wisdom Publications, 1999), 25.

2. Henry David Thoreau, "A Week on the Concord and Merrimack Rivers." In *Walden* (New York: Library of America, 1985), 242.

3. Tenzin Wangyal Rinpoche, *The Tibetan Yogas of Dream and Sleep* (Ithaca, N.Y.: Snow Lion Productions, 1998), 33.

4. Sri Aurobindo, *Letters on Yoga, III* (Pondicherry, India: Sri Aurobindo Ashram, 1970), 1481.

5. Ibid., 1482.

PART THREE: COLLECTIVE DREAMING: THE SECOND STAGE

1. Rupert Sheldrake, *The Presence of the Past: Morphic Resonance and the Habits of Nature* (Rochester, Vt.: Park Street Press, 1988), xviii.

2. Sri Aurobindo, *Letters on Yoga, III* (Pondicherry, India: Sri Aurobindo Ashram, 1970), 1487.

3. Ibid., 1486.

CHAPTER SEVEN: TELEPATHIC DREAMS

1. Andrew Harvey, *The Return of the Mother* (Berkeley, Calif.: Frog, Ltd., 1988), 101.

2. Sri Aurobindo, *Letters on Yoga, III* (Pondicherry, India: Sri Aurobindo Ashram, 1970), 1500.

3. Matthew Fox, ed., *Hildegard of Bingen's Book of Divine Works* (Santa Fe, N. Mex.: Bear and Company, 1987), 117.

CHAPTER EIGHT: CLAIRVOYANT DREAMS

1. Russell Salamon (Unpublished poetry. Used by permission of author).

2. Andrew Harvey, *The Return of the Mother* (Berkeley, Calif.: Frog, Ltd., 1988), 160.

3. Ibid.

4. Ibid.

5. Matthew Fox, *Meditations with Meister Eckhart* (Santa Fe, N.Mex.: Bear and Company, 1983), 34.

CHAPTER NINE: PROPHETIC DREAMS

1. Tenzin Wangyal Rinpoche, *The Tibetan Yogas of Dream and Sleep* (Ithaca, N.Y.: Snow Lion Publications, 1998), 69.

2. Brian Swimme and Thomas Berry, *The Universe Story* (San Francisco: Harper San Francisco, 1992), 53.

3. Andrew Harvey, *Light upon Light: Inspirations from Rumi* (Berkeley, Calif.: North Atlantic Books, 1996), 160.

4. Tamar Frankiel and Judy Greenfeld, *Entering the Temple of Dreams: Jewish Prayers, Movements, and Meditations for the End of the Day* (Woodstock, Vt.: Jewish Lights, 2000), 129.

5. Ibid.

6. Matthew Fox, *Sins of the Spirit, Blessings of the Flesh: Lessons for Transforming Evil in Soul and Society* (New York: Harmony Books, 1999), 108.

7. Matthew Fox, *Meditations with Meister Eckhart* (Santa Fe, N.Mex.: Bear and Company, 1983), 87.

8. Fox, *Sins of the Spirit*, 108.

PART FOUR: TRANSFORMATIVE DREAMING: THE THIRD STAGE

1. Llewellyn Vaughan-Lee, *Catching the Thread: Sufism, Dreamwork, and Jungian Psychology* (Inverness, Calif.: Golden Sufi Center, 1998), 225.

CHAPTER TEN: HEALING DREAMS

1. Andrew Harvey, "On Gratitude." In *Light upon Light: Inspirations from Rumi* (Berkeley, Calif.: North Atlantic Books, 1996), 149.

2. Andrew Harvey, *The Return of the Mother* (Berkeley, Calif.: Frog, Ltd., 1988), 131.

3. Andrew Harvey, *Light upon Light*, 63.

CHAPTER ELEVEN: TEACHING DREAMS

1. Andrew Harvey, *The Way of Passion: A Celebration of Rumi* (Berkeley, Calif.: Frog, Ltd., 1994), 88.

2. Andrew Harvey, "The Housewife and the Chickpea." In *Teachings of Rumi* (Boston: Shambhala, 1999), 115.

3. Tenzin Wangyal Rinpoche, *The Tibetan Yogas of Dream and Sleep* (Ithaca, N.Y.: Snow Lion Publications, 1998), 70–71.

4. Ibid., 100.

CHAPTER TWELVE: ORACULAR DREAMS

1. Joseph Rael with Mary Elizabeth Marlow, *Being and Vibration* (Tulsa, Okla.: Council Oaks Books, 1993), 46.

2. Robert Bly, ed., "Time Before Death." In *The Soul Is Here for Its Own Joy: Sacred Poems from Many Cultures* (Hopewell, N.J.: Ecco Press, 1995), 81.

3. Andrew Harvey, "Keep Your Heart Awake." In *Teachings of Rumi* (Boston: Shambhala, 1999), 36.

4. Russell Salamon (Unpublished poetry. Used by permission of author).

5. Andrew Harvey, *The Direct Path* (New York: Broadway Books, 2000), 13.

PART FIVE: PHILANTHROPIC DREAMING: THE FOURTH STAGE

1. Matthew Fox, *Breakthrough: Meister Eckhart's Creation Spirituality in New Translation* (New York: Doubleday, 1980), 381.

CHAPTER THIRTEEN. CEREMONIAL DREAMS

1. Malidoma Patrice Some, *The Healing Wisdom of Africa* (New York: Tarcher/Putnam, 1998), 23.

2. Rudolf Steiner, *Colour* (Sussex: Rudolf Steiner Press, 1982), 39.

3. Some, *Healing Wisdom of Africa*, 21.

CHAPTER FOURTEEN: SHAMANIC DREAMS

1. Tenzin Wangyal Rinpoche, *The Tibetan Yogas of Dream and Sleep* (Ithaca, N.Y.: Snow Lion Publishing, 1998), 103.

CHAPTER FIFTEEN: PHENOMENAL DREAMS

1. Robert Moss, *Dreamgates* (New York: Three Rivers Press, 1998), 107.

CHAPTER SIXTEEN: SOUL DREAMS

1. Tenzin Wangyal Rinpoche, *The Tibetan Yogas of Dream and Sleep* (Ithaca, N.Y.: Snow Lion Publications, 1998), 146.

2. Matthew Fox, *The Coming of the Cosmic Christ* (San Francisco: Harper San Francisco, 1988), 199.

3. Ibid., 209.

4. Matthew Fox, ed., *Hildegard of Bingen's Book of Divine Works* (Santa Fe, N. Mex.: Bear and Company, 1987), 239.

5. Matthew Fox, *Breakthrough: Meister Eckhart's Creation Spirituality in New Translation* (New York: Image Books, Doubleday, 1980), 381.

PART SIX: ACTING LESSONS

1. Matthew Fox, *Meditations with Meister Eckhart* (Santa Fe, N. Mex.: Bear and Company, 1983), 99.

CHAPTER SEVENTEEN: LIVING THE DREAM

1. Deepak Chopra, *The Way of the Wizard* (New York: Harmony Books, 1995), 29.

2. Ibid., 3.

3. Chopra, *Way of the Wizard*, 35.

4. Thomas Berry, *The Great Work* (New York: Bell Tower, 1999), 165.

5. Andrew Harvey, *The Return of the Mother* (Berkeley, Calif.: Frog Ltd., 1995), 161.

6. Matthew Fox, Sermon Twenty: "How Letting Go and Letting Be Are to Bear Fruit." In *Breakthrough: Meister Eckhart's Creation Spirituality in New Translation* (New York: Doubleday, 1980), 273.

7. Harvey, *Return of the Mother*, 143.

8. Chopra, *Way of the Wizard*, 4.

9. Fox, *Breakthrough*, 328.

EPILOGUE

1. Rudolf Steiner, *Colour* (Sussex: Rudolf Steiner Press, 1992), 156.

2. Andrew Harvey, *Teachings of Rumi* (Boston: Shambhala, 1999), 169.

READING LIST AND REFERENCES

Traditions of Dreaming

Donner, Florinda. *Being in Dreaming*. San Francisco: Harper San Francisco, 1992.

Frankiel, Tamar, and Judy Greenfeld. *Entering the Temple of Dreams: Jewish Prayers, Movements, and Meditations for the End of the Day*. Woodstock, Vt.: Jewish Lights, 2000.x

Guiley, Rosemary Ellen. *Dreamwork for the Soul: A Spiritual Guide to Dream Interpretation*. New York: Berkeley Books, 1998.

Kaplan, Connie. *The Woman's Book of Dreams: Dreaming as a Spiritual Practice*. Portland, Oregon: Beyond Words Publishing, 1999.

Mansell, Marueen E. *By the Power of Their Dreams: Songs, Prayers, and Sacred Shields of the Plains Indians*. San Francisco: Chronicle Books, 1994.

Moss, Robert. *Dreamgates*. New York: Three Rivers Press, 1998.

Norbu, Mankhai. *Dream Yoga and the Practice of Natural Light*. Ithaca, N.Y.: Snow Lion Publications, 1992.

Rael, Joseph, with Mary Elizabeth Marlow. *Being and Vibration*. Tulsa, Okla.: Council Oaks Books, 1993.

Sams, Jamie. *Dancing the Dream: The Seven Sacred Paths of Human Transformaion*. San Francisco: Harper San Francisco, 1998.

Some, Malidoma Patrice. *The Healing Wisdom of Africa: Finding Life Purpose Through Nature, Ritual, and Community*. New York: Tarcher/Putnam, 1998.

Valencia, Heather. *Queen of Dreams: The Story of a Yaqui Dreaming Woman*. New York: Simon and Schuster, 1993.

Vaughan-Lee, Llewellyn. *Catching the Thread: Sufism, Dreamwork, and Jungian Psychology*. Inverness, Calif.: Golden Sufi Center, 1998.

———. *In the Company of Friends*. Inverness, Calif.: Golden Sufi Center, 1994.

Wangyal Rinpoche, Tenzin. *The Tibetan Yogas of Dream and Sleep*. Ithaca, N.Y.: Snow Lion Publications, 1998.

Young, Serinity. *Dreaming in the Lotus: Buddhist Dream Narrative, Imagery, and Practice*. Boston: Wisdom Publications, 1999.

Creativity

Harman, Willis, Ph.D., and Howard Rheingold. *Higher Creativity: Liberting the Unconscious for Breakthrough Insights.* Los Angeles: Jeremy P. Tarcher, Inc., 1984.

Creation Spirituality

Fox, Matthew. *The Coming of the Cosmic Christ.* San Francisco: Harper San Francisco, 1988.

———. *Original Blessing.* Santa Fe, N.Mex.: Bear and Company, 1983.

———. *Sins of the Spirit, Blessings of the Flesh: Lessons for Transforming Evil in Soul and Society.* New York: Harmony Books, 1999.

Fox, Matthew, and Rupert Sheldrake. *Natural Grace.* New York: Image Books Doubleday, 1997.

Ancient Literature and Gospels

The Nag Hammadi Library. San Francisco: Harper, 1978.

The Essene Gospel of Peace. United States: International Biogenic Society, 1981.

The Upanishads.

The Bhagavad Gita.

The Bible

Mystical Poetry

Barks, Coleman, with John Moyne, trans. *The Essential Rumi.* San Francisco: Harper San Francisco, 1995.

Bly, Robert. *The Soul Is Here for Its Own Joy: Sacred Poems from Many Cultures.* Hopewell, N.J.: Ecco Press, 1995.

Harvey, Andrew. *Light upon Light: Inspirations from Rumi.* Berkeley, Calif.: North Atlantic Books, 1996.

———. *Love's Glory.* Berkeley, Calif.: North Atlantic Books, 1996.

———. *Teachings of Rumi.* Boston: Shambhala, 1999.

Harvey, Andrew, and Eryk Hanut. *Perfume of the Desert: Inspirations from Sufi Wisdom.* Wheaton, Ill.: Quest Books, Theosophical Publishing House, 1999.

Ladinsky, Daniel, comp. and trans. *The Subject Tonight Is Love: 60 Wild and Sweet Poems of Hafiz.* North Myrtle Beach, S.C.: Pumpkin House Press, 1996.

Whyte, David. *The House of Belonging*. Langsley, Wash.: Many Rivers Press, 1996.

The Mystics

Fox, Matthew. *Breakthrough: Meister Eckhart's Creation Spirituality in New Translation*. New York: Doubleday, 1980.

———. *Meditations with Meister Eckhart*. Santa Fe, N.Mex.: Bear and Company, 1983.

———, ed. *Hildegard of Bingen's Book of Divine Works*. Santa Fe, N.Mex.: Bear and Company, 1987.

Harvey, Andrew. *The Return of the Mother*. Berkeley, Calif.: Frog, Ltd., 1995.

———. *The Way of Passion: A Celebration of Rumi*. Berkeley, Calif.: Frog, Ltd., 1994.

Sri Aurobindo. *Letters on Yoga (I, II, III)*. Pondicherry, India: Sri Aurobindo Ashram, 1970.

———. *The Mother*. Twin Lakes, Wis.: Lotus Light Publications, 1994.

Oracle

Gadon, Elinor W. *The Once and Future Goddess*. San Francisco: Harper & Row, 1989.

Stone, Merlin. *When God Was a Woman*. New York: Harcourt Brace Jovanovich, 1976.

———. *Ancient Mirrors of Womanhood*. Boston: Beacon Press, 1979.

Science

Sheldrake, Rupert. *The Presence of the Past: Morphic Resonance and the Habits of Nature*. Rochester, Vt.: Park Street Press, 1988.

Sheldrake, Rupert, and Matthew Fox. *The Physics of Angels: Exploring the Realm Where Science and Spirit Meet*. San Francisco: Harper San Francisco, 1996.

Swimme, Brian, and Thomas Berry. *The Universe Story*. San Francisco: Harper San Francisco, 1992.

Others

Berry, Thomas. *The Great Work*. New York: Bell Tower, 1999.

———. *The Dream of the Earth*. San Francisco: Sierra Club Books, 1988.

Braden, Gregg. *The Isaiah Effect: Decoding the Lost Science of Prayer and Prophecy.* New York: Harmony Books, 2000.

Chopra, Deepak. *The Way of the Wizard.* New York: Harmony Books, 1995.

Frankiel, Tamar. *The Gift of Kabbalah: Discovering the Secrets of Heaven, Renewing Your Life on Earth.* Woodstock, Vt.: Jewish Lights, 2001.

Harvey, Andrew. *The Direct Path.* New York: Broadway Books, 2000.

Richards, M. C. *Centering in Pottery, Poetry, and the Person.* Middletown, Conn.: Wesleyan University Press, 1989.

Sams, Jamie. *Animal Medicine: A Guide to Claiming Your Spirit Allies* (audio tape series). Boulder, Colo.: Sounds True, 1997.

Steiner, Rudolf. *Colour.* Sussex: Rudolf Steiner Press, 1982.

Thoreau, Henry David. "A Week on the Concord and Merrimack Rivers." In *Walden.* New York: Library of America, 1985.

ABOUT THE AUTHOR

CONNIE KAPLAN holds master's degrees in communication and psychology and was awarded a doctorate from the University of Creation Spirituality in Oakland, California, in Spring 2002. You may experience her work by connecting with the many dreamers who participate in an online circle at her website, www.turtledreamers.com. Kaplan also teaches courses on the website.

She lives in Santa Monica, California, with her husband and two children, where she holds dream circles, leads seminars, and has a private practice in spiritual counseling.